The Book of Change®

by

Richard H. Carson

❀ Carson & Associates ❀ Portland, Oregon ❀

Printed in the United States of America
Library of Congress Cataloging-in-Publication Data
Library of Congress Control Number: 2021917432

Carson, Richard H.
Book of Change®

Trademark Reg. No. 6,444,590
Copyright TXu002104249/2018-06-27

A comprehensive guide to strategic management that includes models, bibliography, glossary, and quotes.

Hardcover ISBN: 979-8-218-24933-5

1. Organizational change management. 2. Organizational psychology. 3. Strategic management. 4. Continuous improvement. 5. Performance measurement. 6. Business process reengineering. 7. Total quality management

Contents

PREFACE

The *Book of Change®* website and blog was launched in January 2018 and in my essay titled "The Nature of Change" I identified 14 types of global change events. The first of those was "Human diseases (Pandemic – AIDS, Ebola, Zika, H1N1, SARS)." I started the essay by asking, "What is the 'Next Big Thing?' What causes it? How can you anticipate it?" And I explained that "Your very survival depends on you anticipating change." And I was right.

I created this online publication to help you be prepared for the "Next Big Thing." I will tell right now that COVID-19 is just the beginning of what I call the "cultural pandemics." The world as you and I know it is going to change so dramatically that it will make the days of World War II and the 1960's pale in comparison! My admonishment to you is simple. *Either you manage change or change manages you!* So, if you are smart enough and brave enough, then join me on the adventure. I will take a phrase from Shakespeare's *Macbeth*,

I throw my warlike shield. Lay on Macduff,
And damn'd be him that first cries, 'Hold enough!'

The change we face is as exponential, as it is existential. How many predicted the Twin Towers attack on 9/11, the Great Recession, the Presidency of Donald Trump, the European Brexit, or the COVID-19 pandemic? Not since the tumultuous years of World War II rationing has the world been in such turmoil and forced change. Today's changes are nothing short of a cultural pandemic. In medical terms, a pandemic is an epidemic of infectious disease that spreads across a large region, multiple continents, or even worldwide. But a disease is curable. Either you cure it, or it kills you. Humanity has faced these many times from the Black Death to the COVID-19. But a cultural pandemic is not curable. A cultural pandemic is immutable. In other words, it changes you, you don't change it. I use the word immutable for a very good reason. What we are facing is nothing short of **immutable change**. Immutable means unchanging over time or unable to be changed. Ponder that. It is exactly what Heraclitus of Ephesus told us 2,500 years ago, *"The only thing that is constant is change."* There is the oxymoron for you - immutable change.

The *Book of Change®* is both meta-analysis model and a resource publication where you, the reader, can learn about the change management process. You can learn about the history, terminology, institutions and current thinking regarding the topic. But much of the publication is built on the thinking of others who have been or are contributing to the field.

I must advise you beyond the academic analysis and conclusions presented here, I also occasionally debunk and criticize what I consider either misinformation or self-serving infomercials. The field of organizational change management can, at times, be a mine field of information created to sell books that are really vanity press pieces doled out to potential clients in order to sell consultant services or loss leaders for very expensive training programs at destination resorts. Mine are neither. All I am selling is an academically researched step-by-step approach to organizational change management.

> A cultural pandemic is not curable. A cultural pandemic is immutable. In other words, it changes you, you don't change it.

Author's notes: I have tried to attribute the work of others where appropriate in the text and in the bibliography. Let me know if there needs to be any corrections in terms of attribution so I can fix this in future print editions. As I note in the Introduction, Sir Isaac Newton said that his work was not simply because of his genius. It was simply a matter of "seeing farther by standing on the shoulders of giants."

I have tried to keep my personal views on our current and future political and economic problems out of this publication. My aim is not to recommend organizational policy, but to provide the tools to achieve organizational policy. However, I have posted numerous essays covering a variety of topics on the *Book of Change®* website (https://www.bookofchange.com).

One of my aims in writing the *Book of Change®* is to present organizational change management from as many perspectives as possible in order to give you as wholistic an understanding as possible. So, the book's narrative at time may take a Rubik's Cube approach in its presentation. Having said that, I wanted to provide you with a change management anecdote. I hired a computer technician to fix my computer after contracting a virus. On the computer desk was my daughter's Rubik's Cube. The technician bragged to me that he could solve it in under a minute. Some 10 minutes later he stopped in frustration and examined the Cube carefully. "Shit, someone has taken off the color patches and moved them!" What I had failed to mention to him was that my 8-year-old daughter had found a simple way to solve the mystery of the Rubik Cube. She simply pulled off the color patches and put them back in the correct order. I am not recommending this as a universal organizational change management solution, but it is worth keeping in mind.

DEDICATED TO

My Loving Wife Emma Louise Carson

CHAPTER 1

INTRODUCTION

Change is not made without inconvenience,

*even from worse to better. – **Samuel Johnson***

L et's start with a quick primer on what organizational change management is and why it is important. Every organization undergoes constant changes, big and small, that may or may not impact the trajectory of the business. Sometimes it is hard to tell just how big or small the impact is. Organizational change management or OCM refers to the actions when the company alters a major component of its organizational culture (such as new leadership), new technology, changes in organizational structure, or changes to internal processes (such as a new business model). The organizational change management process has three distinct phases: *preparation, implementation,* and *follow-through.*

The types of organizational change are either *adaptive* changes which are small, incremental changes, or *transformational* which are larger scale changes (Sobierski, 2020). One of the major problems in managing organizational change is misinterpreting which is which. For example, a change in the use of technology is often underestimated in terms of its impact both internally and externally. This could also be underestimating both the cost of the change, or the impact on employee morale, vendor interactions, or customer service to end users.

The success in addressing organizational change is directly related to the organization's ability to understand and address it. For example, a large organization will probably have a person designated to address *risk management* problems. These are people who specialize in resolving organizational impacts after the impact occurs or identifying impacts that may occur and are therefore *reactive.* However, most organizations don't have a person designated to address *change management* problems. These are people trained to deal with organizational changes in real time, as they occur. They are also trained to create a change management program to identify and manage internal and external changes over time that is *proactive*.

The underlying premise of the *Book of Change*® is to help your organization create a change management program to deal with changes big and small.

> The Book of Change® is a step-by-step guide for business leaders who want to manage organizational change in their workplace.

So, what is so interesting about this book and why should you read it?

Literature Review. To begin with, my book is the first and only doctorate level, systematic literature review, and meta-analysis of the seven decades of both the historical and the contemporary change management models. I focused my review on 22 different organizational change management (OCM) processes published since Kurt Lewin created the field in 1951.

As an academic, I spent my doctoral research reading every publication, periodical, and research paper on this subject so that you, the reader, don't have to. And I will tell you that some of what I read wasn't worth reading. I can't stress the importance of my doing a doctorate level, literature review and meta-analysis. I did this in three stages. Stage 1 was a review of 153 publications that I called the *Polymatheia Project*. That study was built on the original work of Dr. Peter Vaill of George Washington University (Vaill, 2001). In the end I narrowed my focus down to three dozen publications. This was a literature scan of publications purported to be about organizational change management or organizational development. Stage 2 was a review of some three-dozen selected books for what I call relevancy. In the final Stage 3, I identified 22 productive models to work with. I cannot stress the importance of this foundational work. The product of my academic literature review was the creation of People Sustained Organizational Change Management (PSOCM®). This model presents the first complete life-cycle series of steps that can be utilized in total, in phases or as discrete actions.

> PSOCM® is a 3-Phase, 10-Step, 39-Action comprehensive,
> life-cycle series, change management model based on
> a systematic literature review and meta-analysis of the
> top 22 change management processes.

Literature Terminology. One of the more annoying aspects of my research was the dealing with the constant creation of new terminology by authors who hope that people will start using their terms in the technology field and that will in turn create consulting work and training sessions. Consider the recent creation of words like *scrum master, agile,* and *servant leader.* A *scrum master* is simply a *project manager* or *team leader.* Consider that *scrum* is actually a Rugby term. Do you know anything about the game of Rugby? Let me give you Oscar Wilde's view of the game, *"Rugby is a good occasion for keeping thirty bullies far from the centre of the city."* I don't know about you, but this is not how I want my team described.

The real money in the field of change management is not just selling books, it is in selling consultant services and program training. One of the top change management programs charges $4,400 for their three-day seminar at a destination resort. That is a pittance compared to the $18.95 they sell their book for. Spoiler alert. My book comes with no expensive training at some expensive destination resort hotel complex. I will also strive to not introduce new terms into the field for personal gain.

Comprehensiveness. One of my main criticisms of the existing literature is that most of the literature is theoretical at best. Some of them read like metaphysical self-help books. Even the best of them has step-by-step actions that are extremely vague. My People Sustained Organizational Change Management (PSCOM®) model is both comprehensive and detailed. Therefore, one criticism of my methodology is that it is too complex. I would only reply that I have constructed the model so that it can be used in discrete sets of actions. The comprehensive model is meant to be used over the lifetime of the organization. However, discrete components can be used to address specific organizational events as they occur. For example, the heart of the model is contained in Step 5.0 Diagnosis, 6.0 Design Interventions, and 7.0 Implement Change. These steps can be used as a standalone approach to addressing a needed change.

The advisability of doing just this depends on the situational analysis where the urgency outweighs the advisability.

The Butterfly of Change

The choice of the butterfly on the cover is a metaphor for both the biology and physics of change.

Biologically the butterfly begins life as an egg, emerges as a caterpillar, and undergoes a complete metamorphosis in body form during development. The caterpillar then enters the pupal stage, when it doesn't feed or move. From the outside it appears as a chrysalis that is resting. In reality, though, the larval tissues completely break down and reorganize within the pupal skin. What emerges from the chrysalis is a fully formed butterfly (American Museum of Natural History, 2023).

In physics, the Chaos Theory says that a tiny, insignificant event can have an enormous influence in shaping the way a large, complex system evolves in the future. This is called the *butterfly effect*. In the early 1970s, meteorologist and mathematician Edward Norton Lorenz articulated the *butterfly effect* in science and launched the field of chaos theory. The effect says that initial conditions strongly influence the evolution of highly complex systems. In Lorenz's metaphor, the flapping of a butterfly's wings in Brazil could ultimately lead a tornado in Texas that wouldn't have happened otherwise (Sinitsyn, 2020).

The clash of cultural values occurring in America and Europe has far reaching societal impacts into the 21st Century. The Brexit election in the United Kingdom and the Red States v. Blue States election battles in United States are key indicators of the struggle between the economic and cultural forces of capitalism and socialism. In America there is a backlash against corporations promoting sustainability and the ESG or "environment, social, and governance" (CFI, 2023) agenda. The World Economic Forum has come under attack for similar reasons. The concerns about "Global Warming" have shifted to "Climate Change" because of these cultural challenges. I am old enough to remember the "Global Cooling" scare of the 1970s and the "Population Bomb" overpopulation and starvation theory of Dr. Paul Ehrlich. I am not going to be so bold as to project a Rapture of the cultural outcomes.

I merely want to point out that this battle for the hearts and minds of humanity will continue well into the future. The answer, in part, will depend on who controls the levers of technology and what their political versus profitability agenda is. Are we headed for the corporate socialism of the People's Republic of China? We have seen the massive failures of state-controlled economies in the past. Their weakness is that an economic or cultural misjudgment is magnified to a much greater extent as it ripples through society. The Butterfly Effect is much more pronounced than in a decentralized capitalist economy. The reverse can be argued in a decentralized capitalist society where it tends toward a more "anything goes" mentality. Corporate profitability can sacrifice social welfare in extreme examples. So, which is better or worse?

The problem here is that these questions are not answered in an objective, rational, and scientific manner. We cannot always "trust the science" because science has its own political agenda and massive egos as noted by the earlier examples. History is riddled with examples of science gone bad or perverted. Galileo was persecuted for having the audacity to say the Sun did not revolve around the Earth. At the end of the 19th Century, Ignaz Semmelweis was ridiculed for his belief that washing hands before surgery would save lives. Alfred Wegener's theory on continental drift was rejected at the turn of the century (TechnologyNetworks, 2016).

The Nature of Change

The western mindset of change is based on "Judeo-Christian, Greco-Roman, and European Enlightenment (e.g., Descartes and Newton) beliefs, assumptions, and concepts." This western view of change is linear and destination oriented. On the other hand, the eastern view of change is cyclical and journey oriented (Van Enyde, 1997). My take on model and outcomes is based on the former. I subscribe to Albert Einstein's view that "God does not play dice with the universe." This clarified his argument that quantum particles must adhere to certain rules that don't change randomly, and that the quantum world required better explanations for particle behavior. I agree with Einstein, in that change is predicable. **This is the most important premise of my book.**

I categorize the realm of predictable changes to be *internal* (e.g., physical layout/assets, organizational culture, rules/procedures/ processes, technology and tools, employee resources, financial resources) and *external* (e.g., socio-cultural, technology, economic, political, pandemic, and environment).

I describe the *nature of change* in terms of quantitative impacts and qualitative events. The *change impacts* allow us to categorize and then measure the *quantitative* impact of change. In doing so we can then understand the cost-benefit of doing various alternatives versus doing nothing. We can also start to evaluate the performance efficiency of taking action to manage change. The *change events* allow us to categorize and evaluate the *qualitative* nature of the event of change.

There are two general types of *change impacts* on the individual, the organization and on the socio-cultural. The Internal Change Impacts affect the individual and the organization. The External Change Impacts affect the individual, the organization and all of the socio-cultural. These are distinct from what I call *change events*.

Internal Change Impacts. There are six types of internal change impacts on the individual and the organization. They are the physical layout/assets, organizational culture, rules/procedures/processes, technology and tools, employee impacts, and financial impacts. I have created the acronym PORTEF for them.

+ **P**hysical layout/assets (buildings, offices spaces, parking, satellite offices)
+ **O**rganizational Culture
+ **R**ules/Procedures/Processes
+ **T**echnologies and tools
+ **E**mployee impact
+ Financial impacts

External Change Impacts. There are six types of external change impacts on the individual, the organization, and on humanity. They are socio-cultural, technology, economic, political, pandemic, and environment. I have created the acronym STEPPE for them.

+ Socio-cultural (gender, race, nationality)
+ Technological (artificial intelligence, technological advances, pharmaceutical, medical)
+ Economic (recession, depression, trade wars, monetary devaluations, economic systems)
+ Political (elections, coup d'état, regulatory/legislative)
+ Pandemic (global diseases such as COVID-19, AIDS, Ebola, Zika, H1N1, SARS)
+ Environmental (volcanic, tsunami, weather, flooding, earthquakes, climate change)

Change events. There are three kinds of *change events* for you to manage. I like to call them The Good, The Bad, and The Ugly. These names are taken from the 1966 cult favorite spaghetti Western starring Clint Eastwood. These rather colorful euphemisms stand for what I more mundanely call the Predicted, the Predictable and the Unpredictable. I came across these three concepts after reading two very different authors, as part of my doctorate research, who independently came to the same conclusion. One is Nassim Nicholas Taleb, the author of *The Black Swan*, who gained fame by prophesizing and capitalizing from the financial Crisis of 2007. The other was Donald H. Rumsfeld, who was the Secretary of State to both President Ford and President Bush. With the latter he played a central role in the invasion of Afghanistan (2001) and Iraq (2003).

What fascinated me was that two men, from such different backgrounds, came to the similar conclusions about the nature of change. Taleb would call them The White Swan, The Grey Swan and The Black Swan. Rumsfeld would call them the Known-Known, the Known-Unknown, and the Unknown-Unknown. I hasten to add that while Taleb was lauded as a financial genius for uttering such phrases, Rumsfeld was derided as a political eccentric for saying the same thing. The difference being that one man made a lot of money in the process and the other lost public confidence in the process. As a doctorate researcher searching for some answers, I was amazed that they both agreed on the nature of change. What was even more amazing was they had similar ideas on how to manage it.

Nassim Taleb	Donald Rumsfeld	Book of Change
White Swan	Known/Known	The Good
• Certainty	• No knowledge gaps	• Predicted
Grey Swan	Known/Unknown	The Bad
• Predictable	• Knowledge gaps exist	• Predictable
Black Swan	Unknown/Unknown	The Ugly
• Unpredictable	• No knowledge	• Unpredictable

Table 1.1

Causality. In physics and philosophy, there is the almost metaphysical concept of "causality" or what is known as "cause-effect." So, one important aspect to keep in mind is that the type of change requires a specific organizational change management process. It is not only the outcome that matters. By this I mean that the order is: *change → process → outcome*. It is a little like product development. The analogy is you have an idea for a product at the same time as a competitor. You develop a manufacturing process to deliver the product. So, it's: *idea → manufacturing process → product*. You both get to market at the same time with a similar product. The difference is cost which was determined by the process. You win or lose in the marketplace based on process cost.

It is the same with change management. How you manage change will determine how successful you are in the final outcome. The recent COVID-19 is a good example. The disease occurred in several American cities at the same time. However, the outcome or death rate varied greatly depending on the type of containment/testing/mask process put in place by each municipality (i.e., city, county, state).

As you will see in the following chapters, there are numerous change management processes that have been developed in the post-World War II years. Many have been modeled after the basic Lewin process of 1951. Others have taken different paths. So, there is a lot of competition out there in the marketplace of ideas on how to handle your specific change problem.

Change Is Driven By Three Swan Events

Unpredictable Existential "Black Swan" Events (No Knowledge/ Highly Improbable/Massive Impact):

- Human diseases (Pandemic – COVID-19*, AIDS, Ebola, Zika, H1N1, SARS)

- Human events (assassinations, trade wars, inventions, surprise attacks)

- On earth (volcanoes, weather, earthquakes)

- Off earth (meteorites, solar flares, , electron magnetic resonance)

Predicted "White Swan" Events (No Knowledge Gaps/High Certainty/Impact easily estimated):

- Political elections (cyclical)

- Economic recessions (cyclical)

- Social/cultural changes (1960s)

- Technological

- Wars

Predictable "Grey Swan" Events (Knowledge Gaps Exist/High Probability/Impact can easily cascade):

- Inflation/Deflation

- Climate Change

- Rising National Debt

- Rise of Populism

The Who Predict Such Events:

- ◆ Science fiction writers
- ◆ Futurists
- ◆ Philosophers
- ◆ Theorists
- ◆ Economists
- ◆ Religious leaders
- ◆ Prophets (real and fake)

[*Editorial note: This was an essay on the online version of the *Book of Change* published January 2018 and was a precursor to the "Pandemic" of COVID-19. If this essay had been taken seriously, then the U.S. Federal Emergency Management Agency (FEMA), as well as any other global emergency management group, could have been ready for COVID-19.]

Exponential Change Theory

It is a bit trite to think that the moment we live in is really so important to the entirety of humanity and civilization. Magazine articles scream that we are at an incredible "crossroads" or that we are approaching dangerous "turning point." But if we step back from our moment in time, we will see that we are just a dot on the curve of **exponential change.** If it seems that events are happening faster, then it's because they are.

There are a number of theories that explain this. There is Moore's Law, Kurzweil's Accelerating Returns, and Vinge's Singularity. All of them lead to a rather bleak possibility – human extinction. There is some unknown tipping point where technological growth becomes uncontrollable and irreversible in terms of the fate of humanity. Quite simply we create our own extinction. This extinction foretold by futurists like Stephen Hawking and Elon Musk need not be the pure technology of artificial intelligence run amok (Sparks, 2020).

One of the ideas that I will posit and explore here will be the change has two modalities. There is the naturally occurring organic change and there is the artificially induced change. Thus, the observation of "Either you manage change or change manages you." But more on that later.

As we have seen more of in recent years, change may not be technological. It could also be biological. We could unleash a pandemic so virulent and fast that humanity could be sent back to the Stone Age in a matter of days. Either of these scenarios, technology or biological requires and emergency plan of epic proportions. For example, if there is an outbreak of a truly deadly virus, then we would we have the foresight to ground all air travel. Would the world leaders in North America, Europe and Asia have the *hutzpah* to pull up the drawbridge and stop the air travel disease carriers? Social distancing is greater than six feet because pandemics are intercontinental.

There are three predominant change theories to consider.

Moore's Law. Gordon Moore, the co-founder of Intel, predicted the doubling every year in the number of components per integrated circuits. This became the accepted norm or "law" and was the driving force of technological and social change, productivity and economic growth in the later 20th Century (Takahishi, 2005).

Kurzweil Law of Accelerating Returns. Ray Kurzweil's prediction of technological evolution was quite dire. He foresaw, "technological change so rapid and profound it represents a rupture in the fabric of human history" and that a technological singularity will be over by 2045. The result will be the "merger of biological and nonbiological intelligence, immortal software-based humans, and ultra-high levels of intelligence that expand outward in the universe at the speed of light" (Kurzwiel, 2001).

Vinge Theory of Technological Singularity. Many of the great thinkers of our day are projecting the end of humanity at the hands (or bits) of artificial intelligence (AI). The term for this is "singularity." It was coined by John von Neuman and popularized by Vernor Vinge in his 1993 essay *The Coming Technological Singularity* (Vinge, 1993). In his writings he envisioned it happening by 2030. Both Stephen Hawking and Elon Musk believed that AI could overtake humans and result in human extinction (Sparkes, 2020). I think that the end of humanity via technology is overblown.

I think that we should be able to manage technology unless some morons unleash it in a Wuhan Laboratory. I am more concerned that the combination of AI and robotics will cause widespread unemployment. Humanity has transitioned from working 24/7 to Sundays off for Church to a 5-day work week. Many companies in Europe are starting to move to a 4-day work week. The coronavirus has made teleworking the "new normal." I think that what may happen is an entirely new economy built on leisure time.

Carson's Theory of the Half Life of Technology. I will peg the starting point of the growth in human technology to Gutenberg's Bible and the use of movable type. However, my graph is the inverse of the accelerating growth (see Figure 1.1). I am worried that we are dealing with an *exponential deceleration* where the speed of bio/technological change reaches a terminus for humanity as we know it.

I use the metaphor of the half-life of radioactive decay. Radioactive decay is the time it takes to exponentially terminate the radioactivity. For example, the half-life of uranium is 4.5 billion years. Carbon is 5,730 years and Plutonium[243] is 5 hours. It is worth noting that radiocarbon dating is how we determine the age of inanimate objects.

Am I projecting the extinction of the human race? Without a doubt. Quite frankly, we could end up a moving beyond the Borg of Star Trek, who are half human and half machine, and download our thoughts into a computer brain. The idea of the humanoid robot can be dated back to Leonardo da Vinci's Automaton knight of 1495 (Figure 1.2). The first Gutenberg Bible is dated to 1454. And the New World is dated to 1492. Carson's Theory puts us in year 566 (2020-1454) on deceleration curve. We already are on the trajectory in terms of artificial limbs and organs. So, when does humanity as an evolutionary organic being end? I don't know because I am not that smart. The variables of gene splicing, nano technology, DNA manipulation, and artificial intelligence are all on the timeline. Ecocide (ecological), ecophagy (nanotechnology), micro-blackhole (molecular), and eschatology (theology) all have their predictions.

However, Kurzwiel says that "I set the date for the Singularity—

representing a profound and disruptive transformation in human capability—as 2045" (Rébé, 2021). If I take Kurzwiel seriously, and after the coronavirus pandemic I do, then we are 96 percent of the way to the tipping point. Note that I say, "tipping point" and not "end point." Because Carson's Theory does not project the end of humanity – just its *transmogrification* or to "change in appearance or form, especially strangely or grotesquely."

There is an alternative future. It is one where technology is limited to serving humanity. In that future, humans will no longer work for a living. Indeed, work will be optional and minimal. For example, elected officials will still exist at the federal, state, and local level. Their existence will continue to either hire service managers or direct their robotic replacements. In this new world humans will spend their leisure time in recreational pursuits. As a young reader I read everything by science fiction writers like Asimov, Bradbury, and Heinlein. So, there is no point in predicting how we will end up. However, whatever our future, it will come fast and furious.

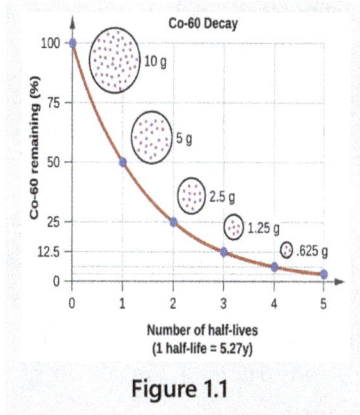

Figure 1.1

Misinterpreting the Nature of Change

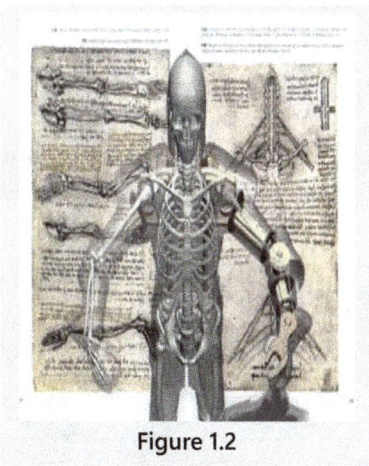

Figure 1.2

Much of today's "new age" millennialist change management literature is full of ideas meant to liberate employees in the belief that they will innovate and that will promote positive change. One publication noted that "Innovation is constrained by deep-rooted beliefs such as micromanaging people to increase performance and production." So, I found it amazing to read the same publication turn around and lament that "trained business transformation consultants are often stumped when they work with companies that employ seemingly irrational behavior." They see the challenge as a need for "mastering organizational social patterns" (Buler, 2018). I would suggest that the latter is called good old fashioned "management." Instead of unleashing the human potential to do nothing or even meaningless activities like underwater basket weaving, we should train people to think better.

There is a ubiquitous cartoon that has a light bulb going on over the character's head. It is "Eureka" or the "Aha Moment." When I see that cartoon, I always think about the man who created the light bulb. Thomas Edison had an idea. But then he did the painful hard work to try it and failed 1,000 times. That takes an enormous amount of discipline and belief in an idea.

There is always a problem when the theorist pendulum swings so far from center that it almost tips over. I would argue that the best way to address exponential change is not to pour gas on it. Indeed, it might be more rational to put the fire out before it burns the house down. "Burn baby burn" is a great Antifa chant, but it is not a productive business mantra.

I wrote this book, in part, out of my own personal and professional frustration with change management books. I spent 30 years as a manager/practitioner in organizations. I developed a profound interest in the subject of organizational change management (OCM). I spent another 10 years working for a company whose mission was performance auditing. I also started my academic doctoral quest to build on that consulting experience and came to realize that the key to improved performance was the need to make organizational changes. This should not be an amazing realization. But when I talked to the owner of the consulting company about the need to help companies with organizational change management, I could not convince him of its importance. Luckily, that led me to branch out on my own and create Carson & Associates.

I had a similar problem with my doctorate research into the subject. If you Google the words "change management" it says, "About 4,610,000,000 results (0.53 seconds)." A search on Amazon narrows it down to 10,000. My academic literature review narrowed that down further, but the results were disheartening. I only came up with 22 of the approximately 153 that I studied. As a practicing consultant, I found little of this was really useful information. Most of the literature was theoretical at best. Some of them read like metaphysical self-help books. The work of organizational change management is not a metaphysical exercise where one needs to channel the spirit of Kurt Lewin with a chakra stone.

My doctorate focus was organizational psychology where OCM models treated the organization the same as a very neurotic, dysfunctional person. It is not productive to put the organization on the couch and ask, "Well, what do you think?" Organizations, like people, come seeking answers and direction, and not internal revelatory questions.

These metaphysical, self-help, psychologist approaches to change management may help account for the fact that 70 percent of planned organizational change initiatives fail (Harvard Business Review Press, 2011). This includes reengineering and total quality management change management programs that fail (Cameron, 1999). I find it interesting that 70 percent of small business owners fail by their 10th year in business (U.S. Bureau of Labor Statistics, 2016). There is a correlation here. Small businesses are a change management exercise in real time.

As a consultant, I am always called in when it had become painfully obvious that the organization, or one of its units, was dysfunctional. And since organizations consist of people, it was the people who were primarily the problem. It is rare when a dysfunctional organization's problems can be blamed on bad software. Truth is that it was probably a dysfunctional person who created or bought the wrong software solution.

My interest is in organizational psychology and not the psychology of the individual. I can tell you that as a practicing consultant, I come across two types of organizational problems. One is when an organization needs to change to become more productive or competitive. Organizations can always improve and be more productive, more creative, or more cost-efficient. However, the other type is an organizational problem which is rooted in one dysfunctional person, group, or process. And the answer might be to eliminate that person or persons from the organization. Some would argue that it would be possible to retrain such people. But it is my experience that you can change a process, but you cannot change a person's underlying psychology.

Organizations

I have created a Glossary section to help the reader understand the unique lexicon of organizational change management (OCM). However, there are a few terms that are fundamental to understanding the change management process. First and foremost is understanding the word *organization*. Before we can change something, we must understand what that something is. A common conceptualization is that *organizations are social structures created by individuals to support the collaborative pursuit of specified goals* (Handel, 2003).

The leading theorist in the field is W. Richard Scott who gives us three perspectives.

These are of the Rational System, Natural System, and the Open System.

- Rational System. *Organizations are collectives oriented to the pursuit of relatively specific goals and exhibiting relatively highly formalized social structures.*

- Natural System. *Organizations are collectives whose participants share a common interest in the survival of the system and who engage in collective activities, informally structured, to secure this end.*

- Open System. *Organizations are systems of interdependent activities linking shifting conditions of participants: the systems are embedded in—dependent on continuing exchanges with and constituted by – the environments in which they operate.*

- Three levels of analysis are identified:

- The *social psychological*, which emphasizes the interaction of individuals and groups with organizations and examines the impacts of organizational characteristics on processes.

- The *structural*, which attempts to examine and account for variations in the patterned structural features of organizations.

- The *ecological* which views the organization as an actor or a component in some more comprehensive system of relationships (Scott, 1992).

However, there are various ways to describe the form and function of organizations. In the fields of psychology, sociology and political science, there are thousands of books, essays and dissertations written about the distinctions between the individual and collectives of individuals called organizations. There is no more fundamental aspect of our humanity than what we do together when we form an organization to do something. I am not being flippant when I say that an *organization is a bunch of people doing something together*.

Organizational Psychology

My doctorate studies were in organizational psychology. The fundamental building block of the organization is the individual. As noted in Handel's description, an organization is a social structure created by and for individuals. From the beginning of humanity's origins, people worked together to meet the basic physiological and safety requirements of Maslow's Hierarchy. They worked together to hunt for food, shelter against the environment, and defend the tribe against existential threats.

To understand human behavior and his or her needs, we turn to Abraham Maslow who in 1943 published "A Theory of Human Motivation" in *Psychological Review* (Figures 1.4 and 1.5). Once organizations consist of groups of individuals, it makes sense the organizations also progress through similar stages. There is an entire sub-field called organizational behavior that I will touch on throughout our OCM journey. "Organizational behavior (OB) is a field of study devoted to understanding, explaining, and ultimately improving the attitudes and behaviors of individuals and groups in organizations" (Colquitt, 1992).

The individual as organization is more than a metaphor. When we get to **Step 5.0 Diagnosis**, you will see that the diagnosis of an organization mirrors that of the individuals. Indeed, one of the fundamental issues within organizations is the need for couples' therapy. For example, in the private sector it might be the Chair of the Board of Directors being in conflict with the CEO/President or in the public-sector it might be the City Mayor with the City Manager.

Maslow's Hierarchy of Needs is used to study human behavioral motivation. Maslow used the terms "physiological", "safety", "belonging and love", "social needs," "esteem", and "self-actualization" to describe the patterns through which human motivations generally move. This means that in order for motivation to arise at the next stage, each stage must be satisfied within the individual themselves. Additionally, this theory is a main base in knowing how effort and motivation are correlated when discussing human behavior. Each of these individual levels contains a certain amount of internal sensation that must be met in order for an individual to complete their hierarchy. The goal in Maslow's theory is to attain the fifth level or stage: self-actualization.

Figure 1.4

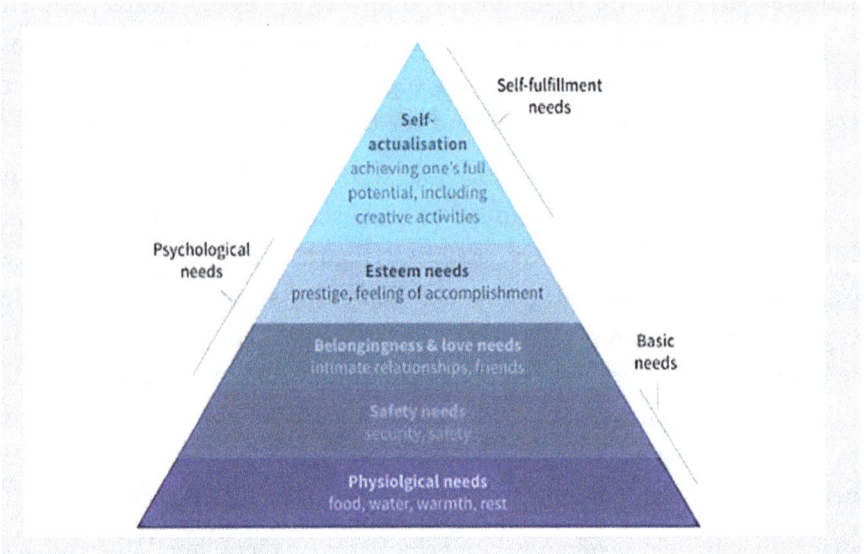

Figure 1.5 – Maslow's Hierarchy of Needs

CHAPTER 2

HISTORY OF ORGANIZATIONAL CHANGE MANAGEMENT

Not everything that is faced can be changed.
But nothing can be changed until it is faced.
– James Baldwin.

Organizational change management or OCM, as we know it, has its birth and practical application in the post-war years of the 1950s. However, its historical antecedents are in the pre-Socratic age some 2,500 years earlier. Its philosophical foundations began with two Greeks. Heraclitus of Ephesus (500-480 B.C.) and Parmenides of Elea (515-450 B.C.) were philosophical protagonists who held opposite views on the nature of change. One could say they present the Yin and Yang of OCM in that their views are contrary forces that may actually be complementary, interconnected, and interdependent in the human world.

Heraclitus believed that change was constant. He said, "The only thing that is constant is change." Heraclitus puzzled over this principle of creation and destruction two thousand years before the birth of the modern biological sciences and drew the ultimate lesson for the human condition. As material beings, we live in a world of flux and thus we *are* flux. As physical bodies, we are growing and dying all the time, consuming light and resources to replicate our structure, while shedding matter continuously. So, his observation of the human condition was that change, and death are ubiquitous features of the natural world.

Unlike Heraclitus, Parmenides denied that everything is change and motion. He believed that while anything which can be spoken of meaningfully may not exist, it must still subsist and therefore have being. In other words, Parmenides took the view that nothing changes in reality; only our senses convey the appearance of change. He denied the existence of time, plurality, and motion. The said the past and future are illusions, the universe is timeless and unchanging. According to Parmenides, everything that exists is permanent, ungenerated, indestructible, and unchanging. Parmenides point-of-view is difficult to come to terms with. If you accept the fact that all matter exists at a cellular level, then his ideas make some sense. Of course, Parmenides did not have a microscope or any understanding of cellular science (NNDB, 2022).

Pre-Lewin: The Philosophers of Change

The field of organizational change management came into being as an academic field and professional practice in the post-war years after World War II. To be more specific, it was the 1957 ideas of Curt Lewin. Although many men and women have historically commented on the nature of change, only a few seriously considered it as a force of nature worth studying, either scientifically or philosophically. Here are four such takes on change management in terms of evolution, existentialism, metaphysics, and quantum physics.

Charles Darwin (1809-1882) and Evolution.

Charles Darwin, the British naturalist is believed to have said that "It is not the strongest of the species that survives, nor the most intelligent; it is the one most adaptable to change" (Laidlaw, 2022). I say "believed" because it is noted that a professor at Louisiana State University said this about Darwin's theory of evolution. Darwin theorized that if the environment changes rapidly, some species may not be able to adapt fast enough through natural selection. Through studying the fossil record, we know that many of the organisms that once lived on Earth are now extinct. Dinosaurs are one example. An invasive species, a disease organism, a catastrophic environmental change, or a highly successful predator can all contribute to the extinction of species. With the epic *epidemiological* event of COVID-19, we humans can now appreciate just how frail we are to such change. The only exception I would take with Darwin is that with humans it takes "intelligence" to be able to identify and act in order to be "adaptable to change."

Darwin understood there was no such thing as change for change's sake. As Edward Abbey famously said, "Growth for the sake of growth is the ideology of the cancer cell." I will discuss this elsewhere, but the change manager must be mindful of the almost pathological need some managers have to constantly make changes in the pursuit of some goal of profit or performance. Sadly, some managers use such a pointless strategy in order to prove they are the boss. Constant change is indeed a mindless ideology that impedes performance because it is an organizational distraction.

Friedrich Wilhelm Nietzsche (1844-1900) and Existentialism.

This German philosopher was a totally uncompromising and fiercely independent thinker who questioned everything and accepted nothing. The following *Twilight of the Idols* quote summarizes his outlook on possible change:

> "With the unknown, one is confronted with danger, discomfort, and care; the first instinct is to abolish these painful states. First principle: any explanation is better than none. Because it is fundamentally just our desire to be rid of an unpleasant uncertainty, we are not very particular about how we get rid of it: the first interpretation that explains the unknown in familiar terms feels so good that one "accepts it as true".... The 'why' shall, if at all possible, result not in identifying the cause for its own sake, but in identifying a cause that is comforting, liberating, and relieving" (Nietzsche, 1889).

This desire to find a simple and explainable answer to change is called "confirmation bias." Confirmation bias is the tendency to search for, interpret, favor, and recall information in a way that confirms or supports one's prior beliefs or values. People display this bias when they select information that supports their views, ignoring contrary information, or when they interpret ambiguous evidence as supporting their existing attitudes. The effect is strongest for desired outcomes, for emotionally charged issues, and for deeply entrenched beliefs. That said, confirmation bias cannot be eliminated, but it can be managed, for example, by education and training in critical thinking skills.

Alfred North Whitehead (1861-1947) and Metaphysics.

Alfred North Whitehead was a British mathematician and philosopher best known for his work in mathematical logic and the philosophy of science. He was instrumental in pioneering the approach to metaphysics now known as Process Philosophy. He summarized this as "The Art of Progress is the Preserve Order amid Change and Preserve Change amid Order." The implication in this quote is the balance required maintaining some measure of order in business organizations and plans while at the same time identify and execute change strategies in order to achieve real progress. My experience suggests many businesses are doing one aspect of this process well but struggling to do the other and/or both to full effectiveness. For Whitehead, change is fundamental and inescapable. He emphasizes that all things "flow" and that everything changes from moment to moment.

Whitehead influenced the philosophy of business admin-istration and organizational theory. This has led in part to a focus on identifying and investigating the effect of temporal events (as opposed to static ones) within organizations through an organizational studies discourse that accommodates a variety of 'weak' and 'strong' process perspectives from numerous philosophers. (RPC, 2022).

Albert Einstein (1879-1955) and Quantum Physics.

Einstein had a lot to say about change. For example, he said that:

+ "The Definition of Insanity is doing the same thing over and over and expecting a different result."

+ "We cannot solve our problems with the same thinking we used when we created them."

+ "When you change the way you look at things, the things you look at change" (Parade, 2022).

Einstein's curiosity about physics included how everything came into being. However, he believed there was a theoretical explanation for everything – including change. That means that change can be managed because change can be both predicted and adapted to. The problem with predicting change is that sometimes the people with the power to effect change don't listen. The COVID-19 pandemic is a good example of science mismanaged from inception to reception to action. All hindsight is 20/20, but we can always find the warning signs of any change event, be it big or small. The problem is how to make our knowledge operational. It takes a different way of thinking as spelled out in *The Universal Traveler* by Don Koberg and Jim Bagnall (1974). Einstein was a proponent of 'combinatory play' — taking seemingly unrelated things outside the realms of science (art, ideas, music, thoughts), and blending them together to come up with new ideas.

The Birth of OCM

The field of organizational change management or OCM starts with the work of Kurt Lewin whose seminal model was developed and published posthumously in 1951. I discuss his work and others in Chapter 3. OCM is the child of the post-war years, but organizational change management, in the current milieu, was the rebellious youth of the infamous 1960s cultural revolution. It was the same years that gave us civil rights, feminist equal rights, the end of the Vietnam War, birth control, and of course "Sex & Drugs & Rock & Roll" (Ian Dury, 1977).

The question, of course, is why then? Why not in the Industrial Revolution of the early 1800s or a century later during the Roaring 20s? The answer is not about "how" we did things, as much as it "why" we did things. The Industrial Revolution gave us mass production and process standardization. The 1960s was a change in our cultural mind set. The phrase "question authority" captures this quite nicely. The essence of managing change is to understand the nature of change. And change is not about being predictably mass produced or standardized.

The answer was that the old way of doing things stopped working. The American dominance as the world's premiere industrialist was failing. It was no longer enough to mass produce a product. People started to want quality. One of the great ironies of World War II was that the very countries that we defeated on the battlefields of war, Japan and Germany, were now defeating us on the battlefield of industry. We had bombed their industrial capacity into oblivion. So, the irony was that they built new factories. Factories that were newer and more advanced than ours.

In the post-war year of 1945-1960, America ruled the industrial world when it came to mass production. The factories that had geared up to build tanks and planes, now mass-produced automobiles and televisions. But with this hard-won preeminence came complacency. We rested on our laurels. And the Americans were producing an acceptably shoddy product. The Japanese and the Germans started to outsell the American automobile industry in the 1960s. In 1966 the Japanese introduced the best-selling car of all time. It was the Toyota Corolla. Their quest for industrial excellence led to the Japanese to out producing the United States in the 1980s and 1990s, as the production leader with up to 13 million cars per year manufactured. This global competition was over more than cars. Japan also became the leader in electronics such music and television. The Sony Walkman was introduced in 1979 and revolutionized the music industry.

This brutal and embarrassing loss of prestige forced American industry to rethink its approach to manufacturing. The book *In Search of Excellence* was published in 1982 and was a turning point in American industrial thinking. Change management had finally found its niche. A decade later, the public-sector followed suit with the publication of *Reinventing Government* in 1992.

The paradigm shift from reactively managing change to proactively managing change was well underway by the time the high technology boom began. Microsoft was born in 1975 and Apple in 1976. Both quickly out designed and out manufactured the 800-pound gorilla of IBM. By the 1990s, Microsoft had 90% of the world personal computer market share.

Once the need for managing change became apparent, then the history is really about the evolution of both the types of need and the various models that were created over time to meet the perceived needs of an era.

Conclusion

There was a need to address the *technological* changes in the workplace brought about first by the evolving technology that came with the birth of

Microsoft (1964) and Apple (1965), Internet *economic* changes Amazon (1994) and Google (1998), *cultural* changes created by Facebook (2004) and Twitter (2006).

The year 2020 saw yet another shift from the need to manage the *economic* change created by a global *technological* and the perceived need to address the *environmental* impacts of global climate change, to the *biological* changes created by a global pandemic.

In the global society of today's world, we must be ready to manage any change that occurs that impacts humanity. The change may be *sociocultural, technological, economic, political, biological,* or *environmental.* But we must be ready to manage it. Because,

Either you manage change, or change manages you.

The truly frightening prospect of global change is that it exponentially threatens humanity. There are endless science fiction scenarios where humanity teeters on the brink of extinction. These are not merely the stuff of scary movies. As we have seen over and over, Oscar Wilde's proposition that "life imitates art" was correct. The *China Syndrome* foretold Chernobyl and Fukushima. The movies *Pandemic* and *Contagion* foretold AIDS, Ebola, SARS and COVID-19. The movie *2001: A Space Odyssey* came out in 1968. In it, the onboard computer HAL decides it knows better than the humans what to do. It foreshadowed the rise of artificial intelligence (AI), as did Star Trek's cybernetic organisms the "Borg."

The human race has one common trait (Table 2.1). We are constantly at a "crossroads" that threatens our very existence. Change management is proactive. Emergency management is reactive. There may come a day when the emergency management fails us. It's called "doomsday." The last crossroad. Let us hope that organizational change management wins the day.

Global Change Events		
Event	Type	Dates
Hindu Religion	Cultural	1500 BC
Christian	Cultural	4 BC - 33 AD
Muslim	Cultural	600 AD
Roman Empire	Cultural	27BC-1453AD
Gutenberg Bible	Technological	1450
Renaissance	Cultural	1300-1600
Black Death	Biological(75-200m dead)	1346-1353
Reformation	Cultural	1517-1648
Enlightenment	Cultural	1715-1789
American Revolution	Cultural	1775-1783
French Revolution	Cultural	1789-1799
Industrial Revolution	Economic	1760-1840
Asiatic Flu Pandemic	Biological (1m dead)	1889-1890
World War I	Cultural (40m dead)	1914-1918
Russian Revolution	Cultural	1917-1923
Spanish Flu Pandemic	Biological (17-50m dead)	1918-1920
Great Depression	Economic	1929-1939
World War II	Cultural (85m dead)	1939-1945
Post-War Expansion	Economic	1945-1973
1960s	Cultural	1960-1969
Recession	Economic	1973-1975
Microsoft/Apple	Technological	1975-1976
AIDS/HIV Pandemic	Biological (770k dead)	1981-2005
Chernobyl Disaster	Environmental	1986
Amazon/Google	Technological	1994-1998
SARS Pandemic	Biological (774 dead)	2002-2004
Facebook/Twitter	Technological	2004-2006
H1N1 Swine Flu	Biological (34k dead)	2009-2010
Fukushima Disaster	Environmental	2011
CONVID-19	Biological (644k est dead)	2019-2020

Table 2.1

CHAPTER 3

ORGANIZATIONAL CHANGE MANAGEMENT AND OCM STRATEGIES

It is not the strongest of the species that survive, not the most intelligent, but the one most responsive to change. – **Charles Darwin**

Organizational Change Management

Effective change management balances strategic organizational focus, processes and people. Organizational change management (OCM) begins with a systematic diagnosis of the current situation in order to determine both the need for change and the capability to change. The objectives, content, and process of change should all be specified as part of a change management plan.

Companies today are racing to analyze data for new insights and tapping into employees and customers for innovative ideas to stay ahead of competitors – all resulting in changes that require implementation.

This process and the rapid evolution of customer requirements, governmental regulation, and the competitive business environment requires organizations to adapt quickly and constantly to making organizational change. The most common change drivers include technological evolution, process reviews, organizational crisis, consumer habit changes, pressure from new business entrants, acquisitions, mergers, and organizational restructuring.

It includes methods that redirect or redefine the use of resources, business process, budget allocations, or other modes of operation that significantly change an organization. Organizational change management considers the full organization and what needs to change. Change management may be used solely to refer to how people and teams are affected by such organizational transition. It deals with many different disciplines, from behavioral and social sciences to information technology and business solutions.

In a project-management context, the term "change management" may be used as an alternative to change control processes where changes to the scope of a project are formally introduced and approved.

> Organizational change management (OCM) is the process, tools and techniques used to manage the people side of change to achieve a required organizational outcome.

OCM Strategies

#1. "If it ain't broke don't fix it." There are two ways to deal with change. Ignore it or fix it. I used to work for a conservative, Republican governor whose favorite saying was, "If it ain't broke don't fix it." The opportunity or dilemma facing you at the moment may be best left unsolved because it will resolve itself. This is the "No news is good news" approach. In the world of organizational change management, the corollary is "We have always done it this way." So, let me begin my book by saying that this concept has some merit – but left unresolved may be fatal.

#2. Beware the Tech Salesperson Bearing Gifts. On the other hand, change for the sake of change is not good. The very first quote in my Quotes section is "Growth for the sake of growth is the ideology of the cancer cell" by Edward Abbey (writer, essayist, novelist 1927-1989). There are folks who love change. One of my in-laws was a gadget collector. There wasn't a gadget made by Ronco that he didn't buy. Ronco sold gadgets on television with the suffix of "-O-Matic" up until 2018. In today's organizational environment beware of the "Tech-O-Matic" salesperson. Some of the greatest organizational change disasters have been because someone bought what I like to call Tech-O-Matic software. The 20th and 21st Century landscape are littered with Tech-O-Matic casualties of almost Biblical proportions (Figure 3.1).

For you, it might be that your homemade software program built for your specific needs that has outlived its usefulness and is now failing a lot. So, what to do? You send your technology person(s) forth to find a solution. WRONG!!! Techies are great at running software, but terrible when buying it. They are too easily sold crap by glamorous, sexy, or savvy tech talking salespeople. I know that sounds a bit unfair. But look, it's kind of like the difference between driving a car and buying one. We have to study for and then take a test to drive one. But when it comes to buying one, we are clueless. Car salespeople are trained to sell cars and they have you sized up, through some Dale Carnegie-like class, within the first few minutes of meeting them.

Software salespeople are no different. They took a lot of Tech-O-Matic sales classes on how to sell you their product. And their product is only the best because that's who they work for. Think about it. They didn't spend hundreds of hours researching the most effective software in the universe to represent. They spent a few hours researching who paid the most in salary and benefits. In the land of salespeople that means commissions and perks. Duh! So, what is the answer? Spend a few extra bucks and hire someone who knows the software business and can provide unbiased third-party answers to be your representative. And when it comes to organizational change management? Yes, get a change management specialist to help you navigate the change management swamp.

#3. Don't Try This at Home Kids! I hope you see where I am going with this. When you are thinking about making any kind of consequential change, then hire a change manager.

Hang on to my book because there is another saying. It's called "Shit happens."

The oft used cultural meme of "Don't try this at home kids" also has its basis in the world of change management. One of the most often used statistics is that 70 percent of planned organizational change initiatives failed (Harvard Business Review Press, 2011).

Software Disasters. They have featured occurred in most every conceivable organizational setting. But the Top 10 software disasters were in the spacecraft program, federal government, and in the automobile and finance industry.

Top 10 Software Disasters

Year	Event	Cost
1987	Wall St. "Black Monday"	$500 billion
1998	NASA Mars Orbiter	$327 million
2000	Y2K Millennium Bug	$500 billion
2003	NOAA-19 Satellite	$135 million
2004	EDS Child Support (UK)	$ 8 billion
2005	FBI Virtual Case Files	$105 million
2006	Internal Revenue Service	$300 million
2011	Mt. Gox BitCoins Hacked	$500 million
2013	Nissan Takata Airbags	990,000 autos
2015	Volkswagen Dieselgate	500,000 autos

Table 3.1

This includes business process reengineering (BPR) and total quality management (TQM) change management programs that fail (Cameron, 1999). I find it interesting that 70 percent of small business owners fail by their 10th year in business (U.S. Bureau of Labor Statistics, 2016). There is a correlation here. Starting a small business and undertaking a serious change in the way an existing organization performs is all about doing something new where the risk/reward odds are not in your favor. The failure rate of managing change is terribly daunting. You can get better odds in Las Vegas. My father liked playing Blackjack, also known as "21." He liked it because it had the highest odds of his winning. In Vegas the house only wins at least 51 percent of the time. So, what can you do to put you in the winner's circle? Hire a subject matter expert (SME).

#4. Choices, Choices, Choices: Proactive, Inactive, Reactive.
When I was in my 20s, I had a great poster with the caption, "Choices, Choices, Choices." It pictured a red Ferrari, a vintage bottle of wine, and a back view of a curvaceous female. Remember that I was only 19 and male. Your life and the life of your organization means you will be making choices when faced with events, large and small, that may impact you and your organization. Such choices are either *proactive, inactive,* or *reactive* depending on the circumstances. Any change in your life can be imperceptibly small or incredibly huge. It is your choice when and how to deal with any change. So, the first step in the change management process is to contemplate and evaluate a potential change event for its impact.

Proactive. Being proactive has its drawbacks. If you spend all of your time looking for potential changes, then you may end up not doing your real job. Proactive micro-managers are also time wasters. Some people need to always be looking for something to do in order to feel needed.

In one of my past lives, I secured a federal grant to create an interactive GIS map of seismic areas in the Portland, Oregon metro area. This region is not as susceptible as Southern California to earthquakes. However, it is due to have a subduction zone earthquake that can reach a magnitude 8-9. Long story made short; this kind of emergency preparedness will save thousands of lives and millions of property damage dollars. Needless to say, that on a change management scale of 1-10, this was a 10.

Inactive. I find it odd that in my literature review work, I didn't come across anyone talking about the virtues of doing nothing or what I refer to as the *inactive*. To be quite honest, I think it's because there is no money in a change management consultant selling it.

There is a lot to be said for the inactive approach. That being making no choice at all and hoping if goes away. Many potential change events will not materialize if you do nothing.

There are lots of quaint sayings about this. As I mentioned before, *No news is good news* and *If it ain't broke, then don't fix it* come to mind.

I have done this on numerous occasions. In my lifetime, I have raised children. I can tell you from experience that what is a major event in the life of a teenager was not to me as a middle-age father. And I found that the best course of action was to often ignore such events and teenagers.

The problem is that ignoring a potentially life-threatening event to you or your organization can be fatal. So, the first step in the change management process is to evaluate a potential change event for its impact.

Reactive. I recently watched a video about the volcanic eruption of Mt. Vesuvius (79 A.D.) and the following destruction of the city of Pompeii and the death of some of the region's 20,000 residents. Before people died from the pyroclastic surges and ashfall, one person died differently. A gladiator, in the streets of Pompeii, died when hit by a small piece of pumice shot a mile into the air that came back to earth at 122 miles per hour. So, what's my point? Shit happens and you can't plan for it!

Somewhere in most large organizations there is a person and/or office with the title Risk Management. It is this person's job to contemplate potential financial risks and what to do about it. Unfortunately, this person is primarily concerned with potential risks that may hinder the finances of the organization, but not more than that. There is probably not a similar person in your organization with the title of Change Management whose job is to be proactive, inactive, and reactive. I am glad to say that this is changing. Not all impacts are immediately financial. They may be more about impacting performance efficiency than cost-effectiveness.

Conclusion

Your organization faces changes, big and small, every day. When I started writing this book the SARS (2002), Swine Flu (2009), West African Ebola (2014), and Zika Virus (2015) were all pandemics of the past that surely would never happen again. But then COVID-19 happened, and we weren't ready. We didn't learn our change management lesson. What about you? What have you not learned from your work-life experiences?

Let me close with another life story. It is about the short life story of a turkey. In Nassim Nicholas Taleb's book, *The Black Swan*, he tells the tale of such a bird. It's the 1,001 days in the life of a turkey from egg birth to Thanksgiving Day in America. The turkey's entire life is pretty good. There are no predators. So, fear is not a problem. It gets fed every day. So, food is not a problem. At night it has comfortable quarters shared with birds of a feather. The turkey's perspective is that "It is fed every day by friendly members of the human race 'looking out for its best interests.'" That is until on the 1,001st day when, "It will incur a revision of belief" (Taleb, 2007).

The point of this book is to make sure that you will not be a turkey.

CHAPTER 4

ORGANIZATIONAL CHANGE MANAGEMENT MODELS AND META-ANALYSIS

Intelligence is the ability to adapt to change.
– Stephen Hawking

There are seven decades of organizational change management models that were researched in this longitudinal, meta-analysis of 22 different approaches (Table 4.1). It starts with the work of Kurt Lewin whose seminal model was developed and published posthumously in 1951. Lewin's framework of *unfreeze, movement,* and *refreeze* is reflected in my model of *initiate, change,* and *maintain.* The main differences are twofold. There is the level of detailed actions that my model adds value to thanks to the intervening researchers. Yes, the devil is in the details. Most of the models basically following Lewin's structure. What I have done is to move beyond the theory and generalities of many of Lewin's followers.

Organizational Change Management Processes	
1951	Lewin's Change Management Model
1958	Lippitt Phases of Change Theory
1964	Satir Change Management Model
1965	Stages Group Development
1967	Reason Action and Planned Behavior
1969	Kübler-Ross Change Curve
1977	Beckhard-Harris Change Management
1980	Deming Management Method
1982	McKinsey 7-S Model
1983	Prochaska/DiClemente's Change Theory
1985	Accelerated Implementation Methodology
1986	Social Cognitive Theory
1991	Bridges' Transition Model
1991	Koberg-Bagnall Model
1992	Burke-Litwin Model
1993	Sigma Six
1995	Kotter's 8-Step Process for Leading Change
1996	Prosci ADKAR
2001	Five-Stage Change Curve
2008	Nudge Theory
2014	DICE Framework
2016	Change Path Model

Table 4.1

Literature Search and Meta-Analysis

Before I could undertake the comparative analysis of the types of organizational change management (OCM) models currently in existence, I needed to come up with an analytical framework and a common understanding of what I was talking about. One of the first things I realized, when I looked at the three-dozen organizational change management type models that I found during the literature review, was that I was dealing with apples and oranges. This was after the initial literature review of 153 publications.

My mission in developing an OCM model was to develop a process model that would provide the practitioner, consultant, or academic researcher with a rational, sequential methodology that could be utilized and replicated in order to manage and produce organizational change. However, the various OCM models that I found were developed and presented for differing purposes.

What I will be presenting are the results of a meta-analysis of all of the mainstream organizational change management models in a form you can easily understand and apply. If you are familiar with the world of political polling, then I am talking about the equivalent of RealClearPolitics which was the first political poll aggregator. What I have been building, based on my doctoral research at Washington State University, is a comprehensive, life-cycle organizational change management model. I have trademark it as **PSOCM®** or **People Sustained Organizational Change Management.**

What's a Model?

To begin with there is the basic question of what is a model? In general, all models have an information input, an information processor, and an output of expected results. The *Business Dictionary* says that a model is used to: "(1) to facilitate understanding by eliminating unnecessary components, (2) to aid in decision making by simulating ‹what if› scenarios, (3) to explain, control, and predict events on the basis of past observations." Models can be either scientifically quantitative or conceptually qualitative. The models used in organizational change management are generally either concept, categorical or process models.

A *concept model* is a generalized representation of a system, made of the composition of concepts which are used to help people know, understand, or simulate a subject the model represents. So, it is used to explain what something is about and why it functions. For example, the Bridges' Transition Model consists of three phases: ending, losing, and letting go. Lewin's Model of Change is similar and is freeze, movement, and refreeze.

A *categorical model* describes components of a model in contrast to the process itself. The latter is really what happens and are descriptive, prescriptive, and explanatory. The McKinsey 7-S Model is an example of this with categories such as strategy, structure, systems, shared values, style, staff and skills. Another example is the Prosci (ADKAR) categories of awareness, desire, knowledge, ability and reinforcement.

A *process model* is what I was seeking. It is a further refinement of the first two. One aspect of this is the business process model (BPM). In business process management and systems engineering this is the activity of representing processes of an enterprise, so that the current process may be analyzed and improved. So, the *process model* is used to describe how something functions and not why.

As a consultant, I provide my clients with a systematic set of steps that are actionable, programmable, accountable and measurable. In other words, I tell them what needs to be done, by who, when it should be accomplished and how they can be sure it was successful.

One of the more valuable aspects of the process model is that of process mapping. Process mapping is a before and after exercise. The before part is when you sit down with the client and ask their staff to map out what they do from beginning to end. You can't fix something until you can explain what that something is. The first thing that becomes evident is that the staff won't agree on what the current process is. The discussion always results in a comment like "That isn't the way I do it!" Red flag number one is that there isn't consistency in the process. The after part is to create a process map of the new program that everyone agrees to! Again, you want consistency in the process actions. The process map also allows for documentation of the process. You can't expect consistency unless you document what is to be done. But more on this later.

Change Management Models

Here are 22 types of change management process models identified and researched as part of my literature review:

1. (1951) Lewin's Change Management Model

2. (1958) Lippitt Phases of Change Theory

3. (1964) Satir Change Management Model

4. (1965) Stages Group Development

5. (1967) Reason Action and Planned Behavior

6. (1969) Kübler-Ross Change Curve

7. (1977) Beckhard-Harris Change Management Process

8. (1980) Deming Management Method

9. (1982) McKinsey 7-S Model

10. (1983) Prochaska and DiClemente's Change Theory

11. (1985) Accelerated Implementation Methodology

12. (1986) Social Cognitive Theory

13. (1991) Bridges' Transition Model

14. (1991) Koberg-Bagnall Model

15. (1992) Burke-Litwin Model

16. (1993) Sigma Six

17. (1995) Kotter's 8-Step Process for Leading Change

18. (1996) Prosci ADKAR

19. (2001) 5-Stage Change Curve

20. (2008) Nudge Theory

21. (2014) DICE Framework

22. (2016) Change Path Model

Lewin's Change Management Model (1951)

"Kurt Lewin (1951) three-step change model is both foundational and seminal. This social scientist viewed behavior as a dynamic balance of forces working in opposing directions. Driving forces facilitate change because they push employees in the desired direction. Restraining forces hinder change because they push employees in the opposite direction. Therefore, these forces must be analyzed, and Lewin's three-step model can help shift the balance in the direction of the planned change.

"According to Lewin, the first step in the process of changing behavior is to unfreeze the existing situation or status quo. The status quo is considered the equilibrium state. Unfreezing is necessary to overcome the strains of individual resistance and group conformity. Unfreezing can be achieved by the use of three methods. First, increase the driving forces that direct behavior away from the existing situation or status quo. Second, decrease the restraining forces that negatively affect the movement from the existing equilibrium. Third, find a combination of the two methods listed above. Some activities that can assist in the unfreezing step include: motivate participants by preparing them for change, build trust and recognition for the need to change, and actively participate in recognizing problems and brainstorming solutions within a group.

"Lewin's second step in the process of changing behavior is movement. In this step, it is necessary to move the target system to a new level of equilibrium. Three actions that can assist in the movement step include: persuading employees to agree that the status quo is not beneficial to them and encouraging them to view the problem from a fresh perspective, work together on a quest for new, relevant information, and connect the views of the group to well-respected, powerful leaders that also support the change.

"The third step of Lewin's three-step change model is refreezing. This step needs to take place after the change has been implemented in order for it to be sustained or "stick" over time. It is highly likely that the change will be short-lived, and the employees will revert to their old equilibrium (behaviors) if this step is not taken. It is the actual integration of the new values into the community values and traditions. The purpose of refreezing is to stabilize the new equilibrium resulting from the change by balancing both the driving and restraining forces. One action that can be used to implement Lewin's third step is to reinforce new patterns and institutionalize them through formal and informal mechanisms including policies and procedures.

"Therefore, Lewin's model illustrates the effects of forces that either promote or inhibit change. Specifically, driving forces promote change while restraining forces oppose change. Hence, change will occur when the combined strength of one force is greater than the combined strength of the opposing set of forces" (Kritsonis, 2004).

- *Unfreeze* your process and perceptions
  - o Increase driving forces directing behavior away from existing situation/status quo
  - o Decrease restraining forces that negatively affect situation/status quo
  - o Find a combination of the two methods.
  - o Motivate participants by preparing them for change, build trust and recognition for the need to change, actively participate in recognizing problems and brainstorming solutions with group

- *Movement.* Make your changes in behavior
  - o Persuade employees to agree that status quo is not beneficial and encourage them to view problem from fresh perspective
  - o Work together for change of new, relevant information
  - o Connect views of the group of well-respected, leader that support change

- *Refreeze* the new status quo. Stabilize new equilibrium of change by balancing both the driving and restraining forces.

Lippit Phases of Change Theory (1958)

"Lippitt, Watson, and Westley (1958) improved Lewin's Three-Step Change Theory. Lippitt, Watson, and Westley created a seven-step theory that focuses more on the role and responsibility of the change agent than on the evolution of the change itself. Information is continuously exchanged throughout the process. The seven steps are:

1. Diagnose the problem.

2. Assess the motivation and capacity for change.

3. Assess the resources and motivation of the change agent. This includes the change agent's commitment to change, power, and stamina.

4. Choose progressive change objects. In this step, action plans are developed, and strategies are established.

5. The role of the change agents should be selected and clearly understood by all parties so that expectations are clear. Examples of roles are: cheerleader, facilitator, and expert.

6. Maintain the change. Communication, feedback, and group coordination are essential elements in this step of the change process.

7. Gradually terminate from the helping relationship. The change agent should gradually withdraw from their role over time. This will occur when the change becomes part of the organizational culture.

"Lippitt, Watson, and Westley point out that changes are more likely to be stable if they spread to neighboring systems or to subparts of the system immediately affected. Changes are better rooted. Two examples are: the individual meets other problems in a similar way, several businesses adopt the same innovation, or the problem spreads to other departments of the same business. The more widespread imitation becomes, the more the behavior is regarded as normal" (Kritsonis, 2004).

Satir Change Management Model (1964)

"The Satir Change Model is a model developed by family therapist Virginia Satir. Her foundational idea was that improvement is always possible: she, therefore, created a transformation system She developed a transformation system that helps improve people lives by transforming the way they see and express themselves.

"An element of the Satir System is a five-stage change model that describes the effects each stage has on feelings, thinking, performance, and physiology. There is definitely a resemblance to the Kübler-Ross Change Curve, although there is also some difference, especially for the part that allows predicting the effect of changes on performance. Which is also the main reason why this model is often abused. You find it basically in every Agile presentation these days. Most people depart from the misconception that this model guarantees a *positive performance* at the end. Which is wrong. Although Virginia Satir core concept is that there can always be a positive improvement out of a change process, this model is only a portion of her theory, which BTW is normally applicable through a Family setting. I still find the model truly useful, with the caveat just mentioned.

"Here the five stages of the Satir Change Model:

1. Late Status Quo

2. Resistance

3. Chaos

4. Integration

5. New Status Quo

"Also, before diving into the final change management model, note that the Satir model focuses on tracking rather than affecting performance. Without using a supporting model to tackle these negative effects you're left with little more than a way to measure the effect of your change" (Caredda, 2020).

Stages Group Development (1965)

The *forming–storming–norming–performing* model of group development was first proposed by Bruce Tuckman in 1965, who said that these phases are all necessary and inevitable in order for a team to grow, face up to challenges, tackle problems, find solutions, plan work, and deliver results.

"These stages are commonly known as: Forming, Storming, Norming, Performing, and Adjourning. Tuckman's model explains that as the team develops maturity and ability, relationships establish, and leadership style changes to more collaborative or shared leadership.

"Tuckman's original work simply described the way he had observed groups evolve, whether they were conscious of it or not. In CORAL, the real value is in recognizing where a team is in the developmental stage process and assisting the team to enter a stage consistent with the collaborative work put forth. In the real world, teams are often forming and changing, and each time that happens, they can move to a different Tuckman Stage. A group might be happily Norming or Performing, but a new member might force them back into Storming, or a team member may miss meetings causing the team to fall back into Storming. Project guides will be ready for this, and will help the team get back to Performing as quickly as possible (Westchester, 2021)."

1. Forming

2. Storming

3. Norming

4. Performing

5. Adjourning

Reasoned Action and Planned Behavior (1967)

The theory of reasoned action states that individual performance of a given behavior is primarily determined by a person's intention to perform that behavior. There are two major factors that shape the individual's attention. First, the individual's attitude towards the desired behavior must be positive for change to occur. Second, the influence of the person's social environment or subjective norm is another factor that shapes the individual's attention. This includes the beliefs of their peers and what they believe the individual should do as well as the individual's motivation to comply with the opinions of their peers.

The theory of planned behavior includes the concept of perceived control over the opportunities, resources, and skills necessary to perform the desired behavior. The concept of perceived behavioral control is similar to the concept of self-efficacy. A vital aspect of the behavioral change process is perceived behavioral control over opportunities, resources, and skills necessary to perform a behavior. (Kritsonis, 2004).

1. Individual performance of a given behavior is primarily determined by a person's intention to perform that behavior.

2. An individual's attitude towards a desired behavior must be positive for change to occur.

3. The individual's social environment influences the change in behavior (i.e., belief of peers about what the individual should do and the individual's motivation to comply with that).

4. Perceived control over opportunities, resources and skills needed to make the change in behavior.

Kubler-Ross' Change Curve (1969)

The Kübler-Ross model, or the Five Stages of Grief, postulates a series of emotions experienced by terminally ill patients prior to death, or people who have lost a loved one, wherein the five stages are: denial, anger, bargaining, depression, and acceptance. Although commonly referenced in popular media, the existence of these stages has not been empirically demonstrated and the model is not considered helpful in explaining the grieving process. It is considered to be of historical value but outdated in scientific terms and in clinical practice.

"The model was first introduced by Swiss-American psychiatrist Elisabeth Kübler-Ross in her 1969 book *On Death and Dying*, and was inspired by her work with terminally ill patients. Motivated by the lack of instruction in medical schools on the subject of death and dying, Kübler-Ross examined death and those faced with it at the University of Chicago's medical school. Kübler-Ross's project evolved into a series of seminars which, along with patient interviews and previous research, became the foundation for her book. Although Kübler-Ross is commonly credited with creating stage models, earlier bereavement theorists and clinicians such as Erich Lindemann, Collin Murray Parkes, and John Bowlby used similar models of stages of phases as early as the 1940s.

"Later in her life, Kübler-Ross noted that the stages are not a linear and predictable progression and that she regretted writing them in a way that was misunderstood. 'Kübler-Ross originally saw these stages as reflecting how people cope with illness and dying,' observed grief researcher Kenneth J. Doka, 'not as reflections of how people grieve'" (Doka, 2016).

- Denial

- Anger

- Bargaining

- Depression

- Acceptance

Beckhard and Harris Change Management Process (1977)

The Beckhard & Harris Change Process involves the following five sequential steps:

1. Internal Organizational Analysis – the first step of this process is to determine the overall attitude toward change in the organization. More specifically, change makers must identify those employees who might be resistant to change. In addition, change makers must identify any external forces that might impede the change process.

2. Identifying the need for change – in order to create the impetus for change to occur, key change agents must all agree that the change is necessary for the success and longevity of the organization. This requires that change agents be able to articulate where they want the organization to go and why, the reasons implementing the change would help bring the organization closer to the desired state and the disadvantages associated with lack of change.

3. Conducting a gap analysis – before any change can actually be implemented, change makers must first determine what discrepancies exist between where the organization is currently

and where the organization should be. Identifying these deviations is important for being able to articulate the vision for the organization's future.

4. Action planning stage – in this stage of the process, the plan for change is implemented. More specifically, change makers must pinpoint the key players in the change process (i.e., who will be implementing the changes and who will be most affected by the changes). For those who will be executing the change, the responsibilities of each change maker are identified.

5. Managing the Transition – once the change has been carried out, change makers are also responsible for continuously monitoring the progress of change and making adjustments as they see fit. (Upboard).

Deming Management Method (1980)

W. Edward Deming's management method is similar to the scientific method but is designed to help people make better business decisions. The Deming cycle, also known as the Plan, Do, Check, Act (PDCA) cycle, focuses on continuous improvement of a manufacturing process instead of worrying about cutting costs. If the process is performed correctly, costs should drop as a result of improving the quality of the output. Deming traveled to Japan to teach his method after World War II, increasing the country's productivity and contributing to its economic rise. It is worth noting that American companies did not initially adapt Deming's methods and suffered for it.

1. Create constancy of purpose for improvement of product and service.

2. Adopt the new philosophy

3. Cease dependence on mass inspection

4. End the practice of awarding business on price tag alone

5. Improve constantly and forever the system of production and service

6. Institute training and retraining

7. Institute leadership

8. Drive out fear

9. Break down barriers between staff areas

10. Eliminate slogans, exhortations, and targets for the workforce

11. Eliminate numerical quotas

12. Remove barriers to pride of workmanship

13. Institute a vigorous program of education and retraining

14. Take action to accomplish transformation (Walton, 1986).

McKinsey 7-S Model (1982)

McKinsey 7s model was developed in 1980s by McKinsey consultants Tom Peters, Robert Waterman and Julien Philips with some help from Richard Pascale and Anthony G. Athos. Since the introduction, the model has been widely used by academics and practitioners and remains one of the most popular strategic planning tools. It sought to present an emphasis on human resources (Soft S), rather than the traditional mass production tangibles of capital, infrastructure and equipment, as a key to higher organizational performance. The goal of the model was to show how 7 elements of the company: Structure, Strategy, Skills, Staff, Style, Systems, and Shared values, can be aligned together to achieve effectiveness in a company. The key point of the model is that all the seven areas are interconnected and a change in one area requires change in the rest of a firm for it to function effectively.

- ◆ Strategy

- ◆ Structure

- ◆ Systems

- ◆ Shared values

- ◆ Style

+ Staff

+ Skills

Prochaska and DiClemente's Transtheoretical Theory (1983)

The transtheoretical model of behavior change is an integrative theory of therapy that assesses an individual›s readiness to act on a new healthier behavior, and provides strategies, or processes of change to guide the individual. The model is composed of constructs such as: stages of change, processes of change, levels of change, self-efficacy, and decisional balance. The transtheoretical model is also known by the abbreviation "TTM" and sometimes by the term "stages of change", although this latter term is a synecdoche since the stages of change are only one part of the model along with processes of change, levels of change, etc.

1. Precontemplation - unaware or fails to acknowledge problem

2. Contemplation - consciousness of issue

3. Preparation - ready for change behavior and plans

4. Action - increased coping behavior, engage in change activities

5. Maintenance - actions taken to reinforce change and establish new behavioral change to lifestyle and norms (Norcross, 1993).

AIM-Accelerated Implementation Methodology (1985)

The *Accelerating Implementation Methodology (AIM)* is a flexible, but business-disciplined framework for managing organizational changes, including transformational change, through to full Return on Investment. **It's an integrated system of operationalized principles, strategies, tactics, measurement analytics and tools,** supported by certification and learning programs (IMA, 2021).

+ Define the implementation

+ Generate sponsorship

+ Build change agent capability

- Develop target readiness
- Communication
- Develop reinforcement strategy

Social Cognitive Theory (1986)

Social cognitive theory (SCT), used in psychology, education, and communication, holds that portions of an individual's knowledge acquisition can be directly related to observing others within the context of social interactions, experiences, and outside media influences. This theory was advanced by Albert Bandura as an extension of his social learning theory. The theory states that when people observe a model performing a behavior and the consequences of that behavior, they remember the sequence of events and use this information to guide subsequent behaviors. Observing a model can also prompt the viewer to engage in behavior they already learned. In other words, people do not learn new behaviors solely by trying them and either succeeding or failing, but rather, the survival of humanity is dependent upon the replication of the actions of others. Depending on whether people are rewarded or punished for their behavior and the outcome of the behavior, the observer may choose to replicate behavior modeled. Media provides models for a vast array of people in many different environmental settings.

- People learn from direct experience, human dialogue and interaction, and observation.

- Behavior change is from environmental influences, personal factors, and attributes of behavior itself.

- Behavior is a result of consequences. People react to how they perceive consequences of their behavior (positive outweigh negative).

- Three methods to increase self-efficacy: provide clear instruction, provide opportunity for skill development/training, and model ideal behavior they can relate to (neat, attractive, compelling, attention grabbing, something they care about).

- Four processes to increase likelihood of employee training success: attentional, retention, motor reproduction, and reinforcement.

- Changed behaviors get greater attention, better rewards, and performed more often (Bandura, 1986).

Bridges' Transition Model (1991)

The Bridges Transition Model is a model that helps a business or person with organizational change. The strength of this model is that it focuses on the transition to change. It's this transition that's often uncomfortable for people, leading to resistance. We know why people are resistant to change and with that knowledge, and this model, we can remove that resistance. Change is often implemented to make things more efficient, safe, or easy. Although these reasons are meant to benefit the organization and performance, employees often turn out to be the biggest obstacle.

According to the Bridges Transition Model, they don't have to be. In this model of change, Bridges helps to clarify the personal aspect of change management, showing employees as supporters rather than obstacles. In short, Bridges' Transition Model identifies three stages people go through as they gradually enter and accept the new organizational landscape. The model mainly focuses on psychological change during the transitions between each stage. The model was developed and published by William Bridges (1933 – 2013). He was an American author, organizational consultant, and public speaker (Toolshero).

- Ending
- Losing
- Letting go

Koberg-Bagnall Model (1991)

According to PRINT, "The Universal Traveler happily demystifies the creative process by describing short, compact tasks that anyone can pursue along the non-linear path to confronting problems. Dozens of exercises unfold within the book's overall trajectory, which begins by accepting and defining a problem and ends with implementing decisions and evaluating results. Diagramming a big spiral that ends close to where it begins, the authors describe this iterative journey as a 'round trip' (feel free to conjure multiple meanings for the word 'trip')" (Lupton, 2009). The process outline is:

+ Accepting

+ Analyzing

+ Defining

+ Idea-Finding

+ Selecting

+ Implementing

+ Evaluating

As a former architecture student at the University of Oregon, I recommend this particular process because of its "out-of-the-box" methodology. It is similar to my Rubic Cube approach to OCM. The best solution to implementing positive change is not always the obvious one (Occam's Razor). I seriously considered dedicating an entire chapter to explaining this process, but decided it would be better if you just bought the book (The Universal Traveler, 1974).

Burke-Litwin Model (1992)

Burke Litwin model helps to assess what are the effects of internal and external factors on the performance of the organization. It provides a framework on environmental and organizational success and the impact of such framework on the performance of company. The model describes a relationship between what can be achieved in real-life scenario and what has been achieved thorough research and theory (S. Thakur, 2013). Undertaking organizational phenomena may cause many complications and this model classifies important organizational dimensions that help to detect the problem (T. Chawane, L. Van Vuuren, G. Roodt, 2003).

1. External environment

2. Mission and strategy

3. Leadership

4. Organization culture

5. Structures

6. Systems

7. Management practices

8. Work unit climate

9. Task requirement/Individual skills

10. Individual needs

11. Motivation

12. Individual and organizational performance

Sigma Six (1993)

Six Sigma (6σ) is a set of techniques and tools for process improvement. It was introduced by American engineer Bill Smith while working at Motorola in 1986. Jack Welch made it central to his business strategy at General Electric in 1995. A six-sigma process is one in which 99.99966% of all opportunities to produce some features of a part are statistically expected to be free of defects. Six Sigma strategies seek to improve the quality of the output of a process by identifying and removing the causes of defects and minimizing impact variability in manufacturing and business processes. It uses a set of quality management methods, mainly empirical, statistical methods, and creates a special infrastructure of people within the organization who are experts in these methods. Each Six Sigma project carried out within an organization follows a defined sequence of steps and has specific value targets, for example: reduce process cycle time, reduce pollution, reduce costs, increase customer satisfaction, and increase profits (Eckes, 2003).

+ Define

+ Measure

+ Analysis

+ Improve

+ Control

Kotter's 8-Step Process (1995)

John Kotter, leadership and change management professor at Harvard Business School, introduced his ground-breaking 8-Step Change Model in his 1995 book, "Leading Change". Built on the work of Kurt Lewin, the model sets out the 8 key steps of the changes process, arguing that neglecting any of the steps can be enough for the whole initiative to fail.

Prosci ADKAR (1996)

The Prosci ADKAR® Model is a goal-oriented change management

Accelerate	Leading Change
1. Create a Sense of Urgency	1. Establishing a sense of urgency
2. Build a Guiding Coalition	2. Creating the guiding coalition
3. Form a Strategic Vision and Initiatives	3. Developing a vision and strategy
4. Enlist a Volunteer Army	4. Communicating the change vision
5. Enable Action by Removing Barriers	5. Empowering broad-based action
6. Generate Short-Term Wins	6. Generating short-term wins
7. Sustain Acceleration	7. Consolidating gains and producing more
8. Institute Change	8. Anchoring new approaches in the culture

model that guides individual and organizational change. Created by Prosci founder Jeff Hiatt, ADKAR is an acronym that represents the five tangible and concrete outcomes that people need to achieve for lasting change: *awareness, desire, knowledge, ability* and *reinforcement* (Prosci, 2021).

- ✦ Awareness

- ✦ Desire

- ✦ Knowledge

- ✦ Ability

- ✦ Reinforcement

5-Stage Change Curve Model (2001)

"Organizational Change evolves in a fairly predictable and manageable series of phases that she [Jeanie Daniel Duck] calls the Change Curve." It is a "'simplification and an approximation' of complex, ambiguous, and volatile human emotions that accompany all types of organizational change, from externally driven mergers and acquisitions to internally planned and managed new programs." (Cawsey, 2016).

+ Stagnation

+ Preparation

+ Implementation

+ Determination

+ Fruition

Nudge Theory (2008)

Nudge is a concept in behavioral economics, political theory, and behavioral sciences which proposes positive reinforcement and indirect suggestions as ways to influence the behavior and decision making of groups or individuals. Nudging contrasts with other ways to achieve compliance, such as education, legislation or enforcement. The nudge concept was popularized in 2008 book *Nudge: Improving Decisions About Health, Wealth, and Happiness*, by two American scholars at the University of Chicago: behavioral economist Richard Thaler and legal scholar Cass Sunstein. It has influenced British and American politicians. Several nudge units exist around the world at the national level (UK, Germany, Japan and others) as well as at the international level (e.g. World Bank, UN, and the European Commission). It is disputed whether "nudge theory" is a recent novel development in behavioral economics or merely a new term for one of many methods for influencing behavior, investigated in the sciences of behavior analysis.

+ Clearly define your changes

+ Consider changes from your employees' point of view

- Use evidence to show the best option

- Present the change as a choice

- Listen to feedback

- Limit obstacles

- Keep momentum up with short-term wins

DICE Framework (2014)

A DICE score is a leading indicator of the likely success of a project based on objective measures. The DICE framework allows for consistency in evaluating various projects (even though the inputs are subjective) and the framework can be used to track projects, manage portfolios of projects, and force the right conversations. The power in the DICE framework is that it initiates a real two-way conversation at multiple levels of an organization. With enormous pressure on employees' time, this simple tool provides an efficient way to target potential issues before they cause a project to go off-course. Using this framework, leaders can predict and manipulate project outcomes and allocate resources strategically to maximize delivery of an overall program or portfolio of initiatives. Ultimately, DICE is an extremely powerful tool for an organization's leadership to manage change programs and the implementation of strategic initiatives. (Sirkin, 2005/ Tahir, 2020).

The four-factors are Duration, Integrity, Commitment, and Effort (DICE).

Duration. This is the change review interval.

Integrity. Review team leader's skills and credibility, and the staff's motivation and focus.

Commitment. C_1 Do senior executives communicate the need for change, and C_2 do employees most affected understand the need for change and believe it's worthwhile.

Effort. What is the level of increased effort that employees must make to implement the change effort?

Overall DICE Score = $D + (2 \times I) + (2 \times C_1) + C_2 + E$

Scores between 7 and 14: The project is likely to succeed (Win Zone).

Scores higher than 14 and lower than 17: Project's success rising (Worry Zone).

Scores over 17: Project is extremely risky, over 19 is unlikely to succeed (Woe Zone).

Change Path Model (2016)

Change Path Model combines process and prescription, it provides more detail and direction compared to both Lewin and Kotter's theories. This theory critically analyzes the environment and assesses the factors both internal and external that are in favor and those that are against the change.

The theory involves a lot of analysis and stakeholders are involved in the change process. The insights, I gained from this assignment are (1) The significant difference between the Change Path Model on one side and Lewin and Kotter's theory on the hand is that the Change Path Model uniquely combines personal, organizational and environmental experience in dealing with change whiles the other two doesn't; (2) The lack of consideration of human feeling and experience could be a problem for both Lewin and Kotter's theory (Cawsey, Deszca & Ingols, 2016).

+ Awakening
+ Mobilization
+ Acceleration
+ Institutionalization

A Legal Framework

One of the aspects all of the other models overlooked is a minor issue called the law. Yes, there is actually a legalistic aspect to this to consider. In some cases, the federal government requires that government related organizations follow the widely regarded "Yellow Book" standards. This is the common name for the *Generally Accepted Government Audit Standards* (2018 Edition). This is a publication of the United States Government

Accountability Office (GAO). You are probably wondering why I am concerned about financial audits. I am not. The Yellow Book has seven chapters, two of which address Performance Audits. The "significance" of the performance audit is that "quantitative and qualitative factors" are "measured" by the "magnitude," "relevance," and "impact of the matter to the audited program or activity" (USGAO, 2018). As noted earlier, my model is about *performance-efficiency* and *cost-effectiveness*. Even if you are not involved in a federal government audit, it is worth understanding this as another very important theoretical aspect of change management.

For example, the GAO introduces two concepts widely overlooked in many of the mainstream OCM process models. These are "validity" and "reliability." These are actually important academic research concepts. It has to do with the question of being able to replicate the process and the output. The GAO "Recommendations" section (7.29) is especially relevant as it notes that "recommended actions are specific, practical, cost effective, and measurable."

In general, performance audits are required by government related organizations such as federal agencies, tribal governments, state departments, academic institutions, local governments (i.e., cities, counties, special-purpose districts), and charities, associations, foundations, cultural institutions, and other not-for-profit organizations. The performance audit generally follows a six-step process which includes perform a risk assessment, develop audit plan, conduct fact finding, analyze performance, prepare findings and recommendations, provide draft and final report.

I mention the GAO Performance Audit process for two reasons. First, I personally have participated in or conducted several performance audits and this experience greatly influenced by interest in creating a better organizational change management process. Second, I have drawn on the "validity" and "reliability" criteria to inform the **PSOCM**® or **People Sustained Organizational Change Management model process.**

CHAPTER 5

PEOPLE SUSTAINED ORGANIZATIONAL CHANGE MANAGEMENT (PSOCM®)

Different change models have been introduced in the literature, but since organizational change is a piecemeal process, there has not been one coherent model for managing organizational change.

– Iris A. Billy, PhD (2014)

Sir Isaac Newton said that his work was not because of his genius. It was simply a matter of "seeing farther by standing on the shoulders of giants." So, it is with *People Sustained Organizational Change Management* or PSOCM®. For many of the individual steps outlined here, I have quoted sources that have already explored them. There is no point in my reinventing what has been created. Keep in mind that it is the comprehensive nature of PSOCM® that makes it unique. It is the most well-developed model created to date.

One important distinction to keep in mind when considering using PSOCM® is that it is free. In the high-tech world there are numerous open-source software programs from which the original source code is made freely available and maybe redistributed and can be modified. That is the beauty of PSOCM®. You can use it or modify it to fit your specific organizational needs. Indeed, when you find improvements, then please contact me about your experience – positive or negative. Over time I will be adding information about such experience here on my website (https:// www.bookofchange.com).

The model was developed as part of my doctorate research at Washington State University's Interdisciplinary Doctorate Program. The model is the most comprehensive change management models available today. It presents the first complete life-cycle series of steps that can be utilized in total, in phases or as discrete actions (Figure 5.1).

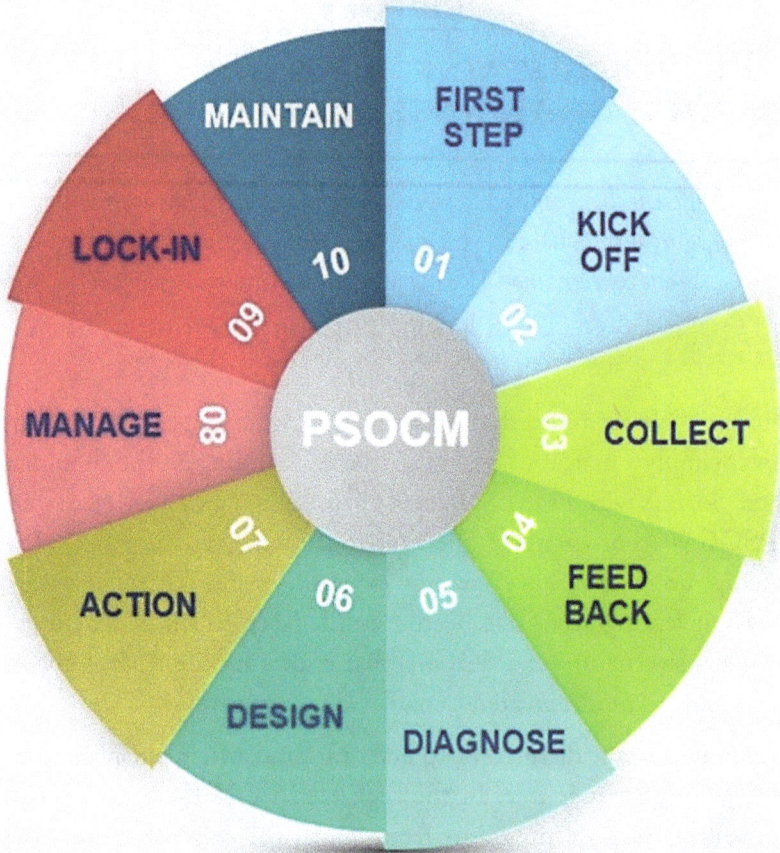

Figure 5.1

PSOCM® is a 3-Phase, 10-Step, 39-Actions comprehensive, life-cycle series, change management model based on a systematic literature review and meta-analysis of the top 22 change management processes.

There are various change management theories and models that have been presented over the years since the 1950s. Many have taken a piece meal approach to organizational change management (OCM). Phrases such as total quality management (TQM), strategic planning, performance measurement, benchmarking, balanced scorecard, planning-programming-budgeting-systems (PPBS), strength-weakness-opportunities-threats (SWOT), and continuous improvement provide answers to the organizational change management problem. Approaches and methodologies such as Prosci (ADKAR), Sigma Six, etc. also provide more detailed step-by-step methods. The PSOCM® model incorporates much of what these earlier methods provide but develops a much more seamless and integrated process that is unique to the needs of today's organizations.

The PSOCM® process is driven by defined actions, with statistical metrics that produce measurable results. The underlying premise is **"performance efficiency and cost-effectiveness"** that can be measured for success. All of these produce quantifiable, statistical metrics that can be used later in the process to monitor real success.

The PSOCM® process from is very different from its predecessors because it looks at the basic issue of the nature of change differently from Lewin et al. His view and many of his predecessors was based in social psychology, whereas mine is modeled after Taleb and Rumsfeld which is based on statistical probability tempered with behavioral psychology.

I then looked at the change management process through a rigorous academic meta-analysis process to come up with a much more comprehensive, systematic, and quantitative approach. Instead of giving you a three to five phase program with a lot psychological, qualitative narrative about how to handle a particular phase, I became very specific. **PSOCM® is a 3-Phase, 10-Step, 39-Actions, comprehensive, life-cycle series, change management model.** It presents the first complete life-cycle series of steps that can be utilized in total, in phases, or as discrete actions.

Each of these actions is the result of my professional experience as a consultant with clients who needed actions with directions that produced results. For example, Step 4.0 Feedback from Stakeholders is broken down into four well established Actions of Participant Observation (4.1), Structured interviews (4.2), Focus groups (4.3), Open Houses (4.4), and Surveys (4.5). I have used all of these, and they produce quantifiable, statistical metrics that can be used later in the process. In short, the PSOCM® process is driven by defined actions, with statistical metrics that produce measurable results. The underlying goal of PSOCM® is to achieve **"performance efficiency and cost-effectiveness"** that can be measured for success.

Summary

PSOCM® is first and foremost a three-phase model. This is important because all of the models that followed Lewin's model are basically the same formula. My model follows his with its *Initiate, Implement, Maintain* phases. The difference with my model and from all the others is the level of 39 Actions that it generates. You are not left to wonder what to do now! In the past, you needed to hire a consultant to bridge the gap. Now you can use your own internal change management specialist to accomplish this on a routine basis. Every large organization has a risk management specialist. His or her job is to keep you from making costly mistakes. This is essentially a reactive function. The change management function is proactive. It works like having an organizational radar to anticipate change and in some cases initiate change.

I want to note that this model is more than a theory. In the latter part of my 30-year management experience, I implemented various organizational change management projects. I followed this with another 10 years as an organizational change management consultant. I did this first with a national company and then through my own company Carson & Associates. So, I learned the hard way what works and what does not.

Finally, the model is titled "People Sustained" for a very good reason. Organizations only exist because of the people who make them function. The three phases of my model are driven by the precepts of behavioral psychology. The process is initiated, implemented and maintained by humans. At the center of the process is a cultural assessment. People create the organizational problems and are the key to solving them.

This is important because many of the problems inherent in organizations stem from the corporate culture. Every great organization has – from Amazon to Apple to Nike, the imprint of the founders. One of the changes that you may be dealing with is the need to transcend such founders. Time has a way of making some organizational missions irrelevant. Witness the demise of such turn of the century models as J.C. Penny (1902), Montgomery Wards (1872), and Sears (1892). As noted earlier, the American automobile industry suffered serious setbacks at the hands of their Japanese competitors in the 1980s.

The most recent example of this phenomenon is the transformation Amazon made in the retail industry beginning in 1994. Amazon has been referred to as "one of the most influential economic and cultural forces in the world" (Kantar, 2020). The retail giant; when combined with the trend setting technological changes of Apple, Facebook, and Google; changed the global culture of the early 21st Century. However, the cultural tsunamis were created by people. The brand names only exist because of people with names like Bezos, Gates, Jobs, and Zuckerberg.

Global change is defined by its impact on humans. It doesn't matter if it is in a pandemic disease, economic depression, or a world war. It is how people, and their organizations adjust to that change that matters. Organizations are initiated, implemented, and maintained by people.

On final note of the use of the PSOCM® process. The process is designed so that the user can take the process in its entirety or use only specific parts of it. If you have the time, resources, and due diligence to take the process in its entirety that will give you the best result. However, if you need to use parts of it to address specific issues, then can be done.

Phase I - Initiate the Organizational Assessment

Day one of the change management process is the most daunting. It's like the first day on the new job! You have to ask yourself, "What the hell have I got myself into?" But never fear, that's why you and I are here. I will share my 40 plus years of experience as a practitioner/manager, consultant/advisor, and academic/researcher with you.

As a **practitioner,** I have the management experience – which includes my share of mistakes. Learning from your mistakes and the mistakes of others is an important way to identify a pending change and how to solve the problem.

As a **consultant,** I was usually called in to help an organization that has a problem. And that problem was that someone had not seen change coming. My advice to you, which will greatly reduce my consulting practice, is to anticipate change and to *manage change before it manages you.* One of the casualties of an unanticipated problem is the person who didn't see it coming. Fair or not, I have seen this occur over and over. And it is usually a high-level manager who didn't manage the change. When a costly mistake, be it financial or cultural, is made then the overseers like to blame someone other than themselves. In business the overseers are a board of directors and in government they are a body of elected officials like a city council or county commission.

As an **academic**, I have gained access to some of the great thought leaders in the field of change management. One of them, Nassim Nicholas Taleb, has given one of the more profound treatises regarding change in his book *The Black Swan: The Impact of the Highly Improbable* (2007). It is the "improbable" that we need to anticipate. I will weave his ideas and others into the narrative of my book. O.K. let's get with the program.

You have identified a problem. So, let's get things started with "Step 1.0 First Steps." You are one person, an individual, in an organization and you believe there is a problem that threatens the organization's mission. Bottom line is you believe that something needs to change in order for the organization to survive and thrive. What are you going to do?

You have turned to me, your mentor. The Chinese phrase for me would be: "Lǎoshī dǎoshī péngyǒu (老师导师朋友)" or "teacher, mentor, friend." I make such a reference because I am married to a Chinese woman, I have a Chinese stepson and two adopted Chinese daughters. And as your older and wiser mentor, I ask,

"So, what's your problem?"

Introduction

*Change is the law of life. And those who look only to the past or the
present are certain to miss the future.*
– John F. Kennedy

In the beginning there was a problem, and it became yours. Lucky you.
This problem could be internal or external. It could have been identified
by the management team (i.e., CEO, COO, CFO, CIO). Maybe it came
to you via the board of directors or, in a perfect world, the Change
Management Manager. How it got here or where it came from really
doesn't matter – yet. Because you now own it, or it now owns you. You
may actually feel it's the latter. Which of course is why you are reading this.

But you made a good decision on the road to solving the problem
and in managing the change by coming here. Because I not only theorize
change management academically, but I also had to implement it as a
practitioner, and later advise on it as a consultant.

In this initial phase there is:

Action 1.1 **Problem Identification.** Identify what the problem is and
how big a problem it is.

Action 1.2 **Starts at the Top.** Create ownership of change management
process by the key players.

Action 1.3 **PSOCM Schedule.** Create a working schedule of events
based on the 6 "w's"

Action 1.4 **Human Dynamic.** Understand the human dynamic

Action 1.5 **Communication Plan.** Communicate the problem and
process to all of the players.

At the completion of Step 1.0, you will have the information you
require to move into the next phase – Step 2.0 - Kick Off Program.

1.1 Problem Identification

So, what's your problem? A "problem," by definition, is a condition or situation in need of change or repair. "Problem-solving" is a sequence of unique actions leading to the realization of some aim or intention (Koberg, 1974). The change management process starts with the recognition that either (a) something has changed that impacts the organization negatively and needs to be fixed, or that (b) something needs to change to prevent something bad from happening later. For your sake, let's hope it the latter. If you have a robust OCM program, then you go looking for trouble before it finds you. Because if you don't find trouble and trouble finds you, then your job just got harder.

Let's start with the basics. Change management is proactive. Emergency management is reactive. If you are doing damage control, then you have two problems. First, you need to fix the damage, and second you need to make sure it doesn't happen again. With change management you work to the prevent the problem one time for all time.

Problem Identification. So how do we go about getting the right problem identified? I found two very good answers. The suggestions use the "what, why, who, how, when, and where" question process.
First, there is the Centers for Disease Control (CDC).

+ What is problem identification?

    o Clearly identify the cause of the problem.

    o Develop a detailed problem statement that includes the problem's effect on the organization.

+ Why is problem identification important? Make sure you are identifying the true, underlying cause of the organizational problem because it's not always obvious.

+ Who should you involve in problem identification?

o Many stakeholders may be involved.

o Talking to them will help identify the true, underlying problem, and frame the problem accurately.

+ How do you identify the problem?

o Identify the root cause of the problem by collecting information and talking to the stakeholders and be specific.

o Develop your problem statement. Describe how the problem occurs, how big the problem is, its impacts. Make sure you include the following: who is affected, how big is the problem, what contributes to the problem, when and where the problems seem to occur.

+ Finally, how do you know if you have successfully identified the problem? Review your problem statement with the previous mentioned stakeholders (Center for Disease Control, 2021).

Second, there is a Harvard Business Review (HBR) webinar was titled "Are You Solving the Right Problem?" Good question. What if you are off on some pointless exercise because you were solving the wrong problem? The introduction to the webinar noted that, "most companies aren't sufficiently rigorous in defining the problems they're attempting to solve and articulating why those issues are important" (Harvard Business Review, 2005). Their approach is threefold.

+ First, establish the need for a solution.

o What is the basic problem?

o What is the desired outcome?

o Who stands to benefit and why?

o How does it align with the organization's mission?

o What are the desired benefits for the organization?

+ Second, conceptualize the problem.

- o What have others tried?
- o What are the internal and external constraints on implementing a solution?

+ Third, write the problem statement.

- o Is it one problem or a bundle of them?
- o What requirements must be met?
- o Which problem solver people/groups need to be engaged?
- o What information should the problem statement include?
- o What do solvers need to submit?
- o How will the solutions be evaluated or measured?

The Problem Statement. There are obviously a lot of similarities between the two examples that I selected. However, the problems that I had with these, and others was finding source material on how to write a straightforward problem statement with illustrative sample problems statements. You would think that this would be a major area of interest to places like Harvard or MIT. What I found was that there was a lot of talk and little substance on this specific issue. It was the same problem I faced regarding organizational change management (OCM) as a consultant. As a consultant I wanted to advise my clients on how to address the need for change management. But there was no model that specifically detailed a process. It all started with Kurt Lewin's model of *unfreeze, movement, refreeze.* All of the models discussed here are basically following that very generic phasing. But the *devil is in the details.* Or in this case, the lack of them.

The 5W2H (what, when, where, why, who, how, how much) method of SixSigma is relatively straightforward (Morgan, 2020). Ask the right questions in the right order and let the answers lead you to a great problem statement.

Question 1: What is the problem that needs to be solved?

Question 2: Why is it a problem? (highlight the pain)

Question 3: Where is the problem observed? (location, products)

Question 4: Who is impacted? (customers, businesses, departments)

Question 5: When was the problem first observed?

Question 6: How is the problem observed? (symptoms)

Question 7: How often is the problem observed? (error rate, magnitude, trend)

Sample Problem Statements.

+ Measured over the last 6 months, year on year, the defective rate of products (TV sets) from the factory has increased by 50% resulting in a loss of $10,000 for 6 months cumulative (Simplilearn).

+ In the last 3 months, 12% of our customers are late by over 45 days in paying their bills. This represents 20% of our outstanding receivables & negatively affects our operating cash flow (Six Sigma Institute).

+ For the western region fulfillment center, an average of 1749 shipments per day miss the 12- and 20-hour deadline for premium shipments. This equates to over 500,000 shipments per year – over 1/2 million customers that will receive their package later than promised (Shmula.com).

+ In the southwestern call center, we received an average of 323 contacts about missing instructions for product Y in the last 27 days. Annually, this amounts to 4380 contacts at an average cost per contact of $6.75; these unnecessary contacts will cost the company almost $30,000 – money the company does not have to spend (Shmula.com).

Conclusion

A public-sector process like this is a great deal more predictable and has more controllable process elements that a private-sector process where a consumer product is involved. On the other hand, there is no representative citizen involvement in the private-sector product development process. However, the consumer may or may not buy the end product. So, the great leveler here is Adam Smith's invisible hand.

So, now you have identified the problem and created a *preliminary problem statement* to explain it to others in and out of the organization. But you, the change agent, need to sell it to the people who matter. And those are the people who ultimately decide that change is needed – or not. Unfortunately, a great deal of the people in charge subscribe to the "If it ain't broke, don't fix" philosophy. These are the same people who hope that a problem, if ignored, will resolve itself and just go away. That approach works when it comes to certain minor issues. However, it is not a good idea when faced with a cancerous problem. Problems like this are best addressed early on. The Chinese General Sun Tzu (544-496 A.D.) said that "Do the difficult things while they are easy and do the great things while they are small."

1.2 STARTS AT THE TOP

Every article and book on the topic of change management tells you that it is imperative that the change must be totally embraced by top management. It is not necessary that the CEO is the brainchild behind the change initiative. He or she needs to be intelligent enough to accept and understand the need for it. Or at least the change management agent needs to convince them that they should. The bottom line is that the organization's management team has to be 100 percent behind the initiative. That means they must communicate that fact to every person in the organization that the change is necessary, urgent and has all of the resources needed to accomplish it. The management team includes the top manager (i.e., CEO, president, boss), the first-tier managers (e.g., COO, CIO, CFO, division heads) and any governing body (e.g., board of directors, family).

The Critical Role of Leadership Development During Organizational Change.

"Most business leaders today would agree on two things: (1) organizational change is constant, and (2) leading change is one of the most difficult burdens of a leader's command. In last week's article I focused on the seven mindsets necessary for successful leadership development. In this article, I want to take it a step further and look at the role leadership development should play in organizational change.

"This topic arose quickly during a major transformation a company I previously owned was undergoing. We had been doubling in size (revenue and headcount) each year since our inception but began to suffer from the inevitable growing pains all organizations face. We were outgrowing legacy systems and processes, needed a culture upgrade, new talent acquisition strategies, new divisions, new software programs and a new approach to sales and marketing. The list goes on.

"And while we knew that research points to the fact that the majority of major organizational change efforts fall short of meeting their intended objectives, we remained vigilant. But some of the major hurdles most companies face during transformations include resources being stretched thin, competing priorities, new systems to learn, fear, fatigue and managers facing issues they've never dealt with.

"So, when I proposed that we pile on leadership development programs and emotional intelligence training to better equip ourselves to successfully lead through change the eyes really started rolling!

"Do you really think that is a priority right now?' one senior executive asked.

"Budgets are super tight right now with the increase in headcount and investment in the new software program – not to mention the training everyone needs for these new systems,' a board member exclaimed.

"In my opinion we can't afford not to invest in these programs. If we don't improve our ability to lead in dynamic situations, we will fail," I said.

"As a former Navy SEAL, I knew that without sound leadership at all levels during chaotic times, the mission goes south. Fast. So, I pushed back to support my case by reminding everyone of several key leadership challenges that could force us to become a sad statistic of failed organizational change:

+ Leadership alignment (or misalignment) on exactly how to execute our change mission
+ Clearly articulating the changes needed across the organization
+ Emotionally connecting the team to our renewed mission narrative
+ Underdeveloped middle managers (and some senior leaders!)
+ Managing fear, fatigue and conflict as unforeseen issues arise
+ Leading teams through various specific changes related to the larger transition
+ Maintaining trust and accountability
+ Handling all aspects related to maintaining (or improving) culture during the transformation

"My point was that this was the best possible time to invest in leadership development programs starting with custom 360-degree feedback and overall sentiment analysis. By using that data, we could create actionable programs designed to meet specific needs. As accountable leaders we were going to have to mature and evolve in order to handle the unique obstacles that come with leading organizational change. Eventually, everyone got on board. And not only did the feedback and programs improve our leaders across the organization, it built trust with the entire company. Why? Because everyone knew we were truly investing in our ability to lead them. And therefore, in a way, we were investing in each of them too.

"For any organization facing change (which is all of us), I recommend the following approach when considering leadership development programs:

+ Think outside the box and make the experience both highly valuable and fun

+ Ensure that the participants have enough bandwidth to be fully engaged and take advantage of the opportunity

+ Make sure that those participating have the seven mindsets necessary for successful leadership development

+ When appropriate and applicable, articulate to the participants the potential incentives for improving as a leader such as more responsibility, upward mobility or increased compensation

+ Ensure that the content and curriculum of the program have practical on-the-job applications (i.e. if the company is experiencing widespread change, make sure change leadership is part of the program!)

+ Be transparent with the entire organization (not just participants) about WHY the investment is being made and what the positive outcomes are to be expected

+ Begin with data collection and analysis with custom 360-degree surveys (or something similar), leadership assessments and even organization-level assessments – use that data to design programs that not only address specific challenges (at the team and individual level) but also fit the timing of the changes the company is facing TODAY.

"Leading organizational change always starts with a bit of mindset transformation because we usually have to pull time, budget and resources from one important area to invest in another. Leading change is hard. You can't afford not to invest in leadership improvement.

"Doing so dramatically improves the chances of transformation success!" (Gleason, 2018).

"The Role of Leadership in Change Management

"Leaders aren't immune to the pressure of people's expectations. After all, employees look to their leaders for a lot—clarity, connection, and accountability—particularly in the midst of change.

"A September 2013 Forbes article revealed some surprising insights about change management and leadership. For example, although 55% of leaders felt the changes met initial goals, change management initiatives over the long term were successful only 25% of the time. More than 87% of leaders said they trained their managers to oversee the process of change management, but the changes, once implemented, didn't last. In fact, training was effective among just 22% of those surveyed. A third of those understood the reasons for organizational change, but that important message never fully trickled down to middle managers or front-line supervisors.

"So, what does this tell us about the role of leadership in change management?

"Having and practicing a change management mentality are two different things. Lots of leaders want change, but only a select few actually help make it happen.

"Adopting the Change Management Mentality

"The reasons for not adopting the right mindset vary, and most are understandable. Some leaders allocate time and resources from the perspective of revenue—versus change initiatives. Others have difficulty gaining support in a consensus-driven culture. A few might even be unwilling to share their "intellectual capital" (the resources that contribute to the enterprise's value and ability to compete) for the good of the change initiative. Some might even want to avoid the career risk a failure might incur. Many leaders learn through trial and error how to lead effectively during change. Unfortunately, their learning curve can be at the expense of the organization.

"For example, I worked with a corporate CEO who had already made several significant changes within his organization prior to engaging me. He reached out for help because he was having difficulty getting his management team to adopt the changes he'd implemented and couldn't understand why this was.

"As we diagnosed and learned about the situation, it was clear that what he thought he was doing effectively and what was being received by his team members were two different things. Moreover, he had failed to clarify how the changes would reshape their roles, how they'd be equipped to fulfill those new roles, and how they'd be held accountable. As a result, people questioned the change—and ultimately his role as the team leader.

"The above scenario underscores the importance of adopting a change management mentality and the necessary skills to communicate and execute it properly. Those who fail to do so will have a difficult time enacting profound and lasting change."

"Manage the Change or It Will Manage You

"Anytime leaders fall short on fulfilling expectations, their teams become disillusioned, confused and unmotivated. The business suffers. Leaders must manage the change, or it will manage them. When leaders fulfill the change management role, changes are made efficiently and sustainably, and the expectations of their staff, partners, stakeholders and clients are met.

"AlignOrg Solutions has developed specific strategies to help leaders' step into the change management role. To highlight a few of the principles that leaders should embrace when leading through change, consider the following:

+ Clarify the vision and communicate it effectively. The role of leadership in change management requires that you help people buy into your vision for the organization. This type of communication needs to occur consistently, no matter if it's the mundane, day-to-day issues or more serious change programs. Your message needs to be clear and consistent. Leverage your audience's preferred communication methods to ensure receptiveness. That means making the most of social media. According to a November 2015 Harvard Business Review article, we spend an average of 3 hours each day on various social media platforms, with over 50% of employers using such platforms for internal communications. The same article noted that just 17% of employees rated their leader highly when it came to recent change-related communications.

+ Stay connected with your employees. Without this awareness, you'll have a difficult time explaining your vision and enlisting support. Your employees look to you to be direct and transparent. They also want you to be approachable. The Harvard Business Review piece cited another study in which nearly three-quarters of employees said their CEO's preferred social media platform allowed them to communicate more directly with the CEO. Similar numbers of CEOs believed such interactions helped them get a quick idea of what employees were thinking/feeling, which is important when aligning your change management initiatives with the capabilities of your people.

+ Be accountable and transparent. During times of change, leaders must be accountable for what is working and what isn't working. Being accountable fosters a desire and commitment to fix problems to yield the best results. To be truly accountable means you are willing to let others see behind the curtain to candidly assess how things are going. As you do this, your team will embrace a similar, no-blame openness to performance. Accountable leaders look at all aspects of the organization—culture, processes, management, and employees—to ensure all are functioning optimally. If they are not, a good change management leader must be willing to admit the gaps or misalignments and take actions to address shortcomings.

"Remember, perceptions of leaders are often shaped during times of transition and change. The principles outlined above help leaders conquer the change management challenge. Don't let people question your leadership and the mission of the organization. Such questions undermine employee commitment to the change initiatives and their allegiance to you and possibly the company. Additionally, these leadership questions may ripple out to your customers, partners and stakeholders.

"Be the Change You Want to See

"Don't abdicate change management to others, such as human resources, or leave it to chance because you think people will "get it" the first time. You have to take full responsibility, understand the mindset of your team, enlist their support and hold them accountable.

The role of leadership in change management requires care, communication and commitment. As the leader, you are the bridge between your organization and the envisioned change. If you understand your role and the expectations around it, clarify your vision, communicate effectively, and hold yourself and others accountable throughout the change process, you can successfully navigate even the most disruptive change" (Deshler, 2016).

1.3 PSOCM® Schedule

Now it's time to develop the preliminary *schedule* of events which is subject to *change*. The *schedule* is the PSOCM® Phases, Steps and Activities that manifests itself as your basic project management Gantt chart. Project management solutions that integrate Gantt charts give managers visibility into team workloads, as well as current and future availability, which allows for more accurate scheduling. Gantt charts have been around for nearly a century, having been invented by Henry Gantt, an American mechanical engineer, around 1910.

A Gantt chart is a project management tool assisting in the planning and scheduling of projects of all sizes, although they are particularly useful for simplifying complex projects. Project management timelines and tasks are converted into a horizontal bar chart, showing start and end dates, as well as dependencies, scheduling and deadlines, including how much of the task is completed per stage and who is the task owner. This is useful to keep tasks on track when there is a large team and multiple stakeholders when the scope changes.

As it's in a bar chart format it is possible to check on progress with a quick glance (Figure 5.2). You can easily see:

+ a visual display of the whole project,

+ timelines and deadlines of all tasks,

+ relationships and dependencies between the various activities,

+ project phases

Gantt charts are a staple of the project management toolbox and is a **graphic depiction of scheduled tasks.** All your activities should be on the left, with your schedule on the right. You can also plan for **the duration of each activity** with bars. This way, you can see how different tasks overlap.

You can create them with basic software like Microsoft Project, as well! As such, they're great tools for tracking project progress. Keep in mind that these charts work best when you've already planned out your projects. They're primarily a project scheduling tool – they're not meant for project planning. Another huge advantage of Gantt chart is that you can manage time and teams with more ease. In general, any tool that gives you the transparency you need to understand who's doing what at a given time is a tool you need in your stack. They don't inundate you with information. Instead, you can accurately schedule tasks, handle responsibilities, and make sure your team is doing their best work consistently.

The **PSOCM® Schedule** is what makes this model different from all the other change management models. It is tangible and it is measurable in time and activities (See Appendix A).

A Gantt chart is a type of bar chart that illustrates a project schedule. This chart lists the tasks to be performed on the vertical axis, and time intervals on the horizontal axis. The width of the horizontal bars in the graph shows the duration of each activity. Gantt charts illustrate the start and finish dates of the terminal elements and summary elements of a project. Terminal elements and summary elements constitute the work breakdown structure of the project. Modern Gantt charts also show the dependency (i.e., precedence network) relationships between activities.

The entire length of the PSOCM process is between 3 and 5 years, depending on the need for organizational change. The time frame is dependent on the type of industry involved and the need to address change. The time frame is shorter for more high technology organizations and longer for more traditional organizations. However, this longer phase (3-5 years) is for the monitoring (10.4). Most of the OCM development activities (1.1-10.3) should occur within an 18-month time frame.

People Sustained Organizational Change Management (PSOCM) Gantt Chart

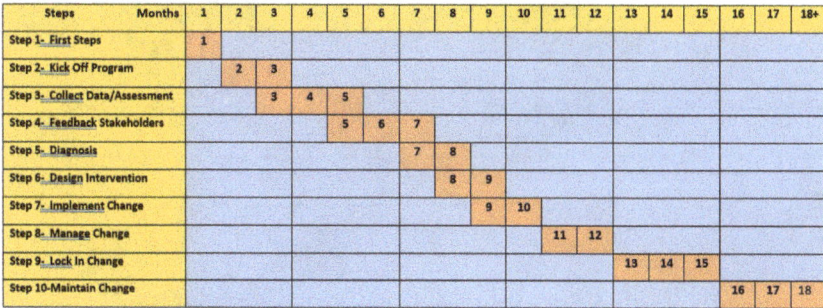

Steps / Months	1	2	3	4	5	6	7	8	9	10	11	12	13	14	15	16	17	18+
Step 1- First Steps	1																	
Step 2- Kick Off Program		2	3															
Step 3- Collect Data/Assessment			3	4	5													
Step 4- Feedback Stakeholders					5	6	7											
Step 5- Diagnosis							7	8										
Step 6- Design Intervention								8	9									
Step 7- Implement Change									9	10								
Step 8- Manage Change											11	12						
Step 9- Lock In Change													13	14	15			
Step 10-Maintain Change																16	17	18

Figure 5.2

The PSOCM Schedule is portrayed in the Gantt chart here (Figure 5.2). Steps 1-4 (Phase 1) requires seven months, Steps 5-9 (Phase 2) requires nine months, and Step 10 (Phase 3) requires three to five years. The Gantt Chart shown here is highly simplified showing just the 10 Steps. A Gantt Chart with all 39 Activities would need to be tailored to your specific project. The chart here would take 18 months to complete. However, I have had jobs take both longer and shorter depending on unanticipated events, people issues, and financial and available resources. I have provided you with a Gantt Chart template that lists all the Activities (see Appendix A).

1.4 HUMAN DYNAMIC

Human beings don't like change and organizations consist of humans. So, you identified the problem. You took it to top management and sold them on the need for change. But before you do anything to manage the change process, remember you have a problem within a problem. It's the fact that people don't like change. The immediate response will be, "But we always did it this way."

Mary Shelley, the English writer of the book *Frankenstein*, said that "Nothing is so painful to the human mind as a great and sudden change (Shelley, 1818)." Accept the fact you, as the change agent, and your ideas are not going to be accepted *carte blanche*. In fact, people's automatic response will be to reject your proposition because it interrupts their daily routine! In the following article the author says, "The companies that emerge from the crisis with a strong balance sheet *and* a functioning, high-value talent pool will be the ones with leaders who do something more. They deal effectively with both the structural side of leading change and the human dynamic too."

"Nowadays, Leadership Means Being More Human.

"As the economic crisis strikes ever deeper, executives, managers and employees everywhere face wrenching decisions. Of course, immense business skill and personal resolve are required to reduce costs, implement complex changes and direct scaled-back business operations. But that is only half the story.

"In turbulent times, we need our leaders to be more human than ever too.

"Confronted by change, particularly layoffs and restructuring, people go through times that are rarely easy. Uncertainty at work triggers all kinds of behavioral and emotional reactions. Instead of being loyal, productive and enthusiastic, employees grow insecure, fearful and skeptical--and rightly so. Seismic shifts of the magnitude we're experiencing today test the resiliency of everyone in an organization.

"The depth of this economic crisis is unparalleled in our lifetimes, but we can draw on lessons from similar, if less pervasive, episodes in the past. We need to remember them.

"I first experienced how employees and organizations struggle to recover from traumatic change when I was working at AT&T in the 1970s and 1980s. I was an organizational psychologist studying stress when the deregulation and break-up of the telecom industry led to thousands of job losses. 'Downsizing' emerged as the remedy of choice. I remember vividly the futile attempts executives made to dispose of all feelings of loss and grief in a one-day program--so that we could move on to the real work, as we saw it, of reshaping the business and generating new sources of revenue. Alas, gathering people together and imploring them to grieve on command simply didn't work. It still won't.

"Since then, I've spent a significant portion of my career helping leaders guide their organizations through painful, dramatic change--and survive with something left that is worth having. Here's a short version of what I tell leaders now:

"Managers today have more or less mastered the structural side of leading change. They can understand the practical situation, make the case for change and take action. Reorganizing, restructuring and pushing for leaner organizations has all been institutionalized in our business models. Yet for all our operational savvy, 75% of change initiatives fail-- even in the best of times--and in today's tough times, successful change is harder than ever.

"The companies that emerge from the crisis with a strong balance sheet *and* a functioning, high-value talent pool will be the ones with leaders who do something more. They deal effectively with both the structural side of leading change and the human dynamic too. They keep a focus on maintaining and building trust.

"This is not a time to take your talented people for granted. Those who remain on the payroll now see few external options. They are happy to still have jobs. But a captive audience is always vigilant. They are well aware of how they and their co-workers are being treated.

"Of course, tending to the human side of change does not prevent plant closings, layoffs or tough work realities. But when you balance the structural, technical aspects of managing change with attention to the personal side of transition, you become a more credible and trustworthy leader. To strengthen your ability to lead your people as you run the business, focus on these six areas:

"--Manage the change, but lead the transition. Of course, you need to communicate the business reasons for change and the specific actions you have to take to right the ship. But you also need to acknowledge that people are experiencing loss and grief. If you ignore the personal and psychological elements of the process, you will appear callous, arrogant or disconnected. The ability to cope with the emotional fallout of change is especially important if you have been or will be reducing your workforce.

"--Balance the drive to keep things moving with the need to give people time to catch up. People react in different ways to change and adapt at various paces. Be patient, over-communicate, coach people who are struggling and understand that performance may initially lag. But don›t go to extremes--this is not an excuse to be indulgent of chronically poor performers and complainers.

"--Know when to empathize and when to be tough. Effective leaders know to be tough and assertive in terms of goals, accountability, focus and perseverance. However, they are also empathetic. Listen with an open mind and without judging. Tell people--repeatedly--that you value them, and acknowledge the emotional impact of seeing colleagues and friends escorted out the door.

"--Balance realism and optimism. Nobody wants to be around a boss who radiates gloom and doom 24/7. But don›t overdo the optimism, either. Tell people the truth, acknowledge mistakes and be clear about your situation and prospects for the future. You can be resolute and hopeful without sugarcoating the challenge.

"--Trust yourself, and trust others. Self-reliance, confidence and willingness to do the hard work are essential. But you also need to involve others in efforts to change and maintain the business. You cannot fix the company or implement a new process or come up with a new strategy all on your own. You need the support of peers and subordinates, not only to get the work done but also as fellow travelers on a challenging journey.

"--Know your strengths, and try new things. Draw on your personal and organizational strengths and skills, and confidently apply them to new situations and circumstances. But keep in mind that your old strategies and solutions may not work today. Lead the way with a willingness to learn and try new things--even when the process is difficult or painful.

"Leadership isn't about finding the right business model or crafting the ultimate set of competencies. It's about being honest, authentic and human, even--and especially--in turbulent times" (Bunker 2009).

Conclusion

So now what? You have identified the problem (Step 1.1), sold the leadership (Step 1.2), and are sensitive to the human nature to resist change (Step 1.4). Now you need to sell the need for change to the organization. You need a Communication Plan (Step 1.5).

1.5 COMMUNICATION PLAN

"A communication plan is a policy-driven approach to providing stakeholders with information. The plan formally defines who should be given specific information, when that information should be delivered and what communication channels will be used to deliver the information.

"An effective communications management plan anticipates what information will need to be communicated to specific audience segments. The plan should also address who has the authority to communicate confidential or sensitive information and how information should be disseminated (email, websites, printed reports, and/or presentations). Finally, the plan should define what communication channels stakeholders will use to solicit feedback and how communication will be documented and archived.

"Communication plans play an important role in change management. An effective communication strategy can help break down resistance to change by getting everyone on the same page and helping stakeholders become engaged and endorse the need for change and the steps being taken to bring it about.

"In project management, the communications plan may include a glossary of common terms that will be used during the project. This glossary may also define and include samples of templates, reports and forms that the project manager will use to communicate information.

"A communication plan for emergency situations must address ways both electronic and non-electronic communication channels should be used to disseminate information. This includes announcements over a building paging system, automated text message, email alerts, prerecorded robocalls and phone trees. Should electronic communication channels be available, social media and the organization's website can also be used to communicate emergency information" (WhatIs.com, 2021).

"Developing a Plan for Communication

"What is a plan for communication? Planning is a way to organize actions that will lead to the fulfillment of a goal. Your goal in this case is to raise awareness about your initiative's long-term benefits to your community.

To develop a plan for communication of any sort, you have to consider some basic questions:

- Why do you want to communicate with the community? (What's your purpose?)
- Whom do you want to communicate it to? (Who's your audience?)
- What do you want to communicate? (What's your message?)
- How do you want to communicate it? (What communication channels will you use?)
- Whom should you contact and what should you do in order to use those channels? (How will you actually distribute your message?)

"The answers to these questions constitute your action plan, what you need to do in order to communicate successfully with your audience. The remainder of your communication plan, involves three steps:

- Implement your action plan. Design your message and distribute it to your intended audience.
- Evaluate your communication efforts and adjust your plan accordingly.
- Keep at it

"Communication is an ongoing activity for any organization that serves, depends upon, or is in any way connected with the community. The purpose, audience, message, and channels may change, but the need to maintain relationships with the media and with key people in the community remain. As a result, an important part of any communication plan is to continue using and revising your plan, based on your experience, throughout the existence of your organization.

"Why should you develop a plan for communication? A plan will make it possible to target your communication accurately. It gives you a structure to determine whom you need to reach and how.

- A plan can be long-term, helping you map out how to raise your profile and refine your image in the community over time.

- A plan will make your communication efforts more efficient, effective, and lasting.

- A plan makes everything easier. If you spend some time planning at the beginning of an effort, you can save a great deal of time later on, because you know exactly what you should be doing at any point in the process.

"When should you develop a plan for communication? As soon as your organization begins planning its objectives and activities, you should also begin planning ways to communicate them; successful communication is an ongoing process, not a one-time event.

Communication is useful at all points in your organization's development - it can help get the word out about a new organization, renew interest in a long-standing program, or help attract new funding sources.

"How do you develop a plan for communication? One way to look at planning for communication is as an eight-step process. The steps are:

1. Identify the purpose of your communication

2. Identify your audience

3. Plan and design your message

4. Consider your resources

5. Plan for obstacles and emergencies

6. Strategize how you'll connect with the media and others who can help you spread your message

7. Create an action plan

8. Decide how you'll evaluate your plan and adjust it, based on the results of carrying it out" (Community Toolbox, 2021).

"Creating a Change Communication Plan. Like the process outlined in the Standard for Change Management, creating a change management communication plan starts with a deep understanding of the organization, stakeholders and change impacts. The goal is to support the business objective by helping stakeholders understand the change, how they will need to adapt their day-to-day responsibilities and what is expected of them.

By ensuring a consistent flow of information, engaging stakeholders and continually managing feedback, change communication helps people feel more comfortable as they move to the future state and adopt new ways of working.

The communications planning process involves the following steps similar to the change management process described above:

"Step 1: Assess the Situation, People, Channels and Needs. If you are working with change management partners, they are likely responsible for a Stakeholder Analysis, which summarizes the levels and types of impacts on different roles and functions. If a Stakeholder Analysis is not available, you should work with the change sponsor or subject matter expert in each function to uncover the critical information needed for communications planning.

As you assess the situation, people, channels and needs to prepare for developing a change communications plan, be sure to:

+ Know your employee audience and who will be most affected – You need details of the changes happening to each audience and when to be able to plan appropriate customized communication.

+ Understand what's changing and why and document the case for change – The "what" and "why" of the change are key components of your messaging to all audiences.

+ Define the vision for the future and how it aligns with the business plan – The organization has a reason for making the change and the vision explains this in terms employees will understand.

+ Identify the "pain points" that the change plan addresses – The difference between how people operate today vs. the "future state" should be reflected in your messaging to help people understand areas that will change the most.

+ Identify communications channels needed to reach the audiences – Keep in mind that any touchpoints stakeholders may have with their leaders or the organization, including face-to-face huddles and operational meetings, can be used to deliver and reinforce key messages.

"Step 2: Create the Change Communications Plan. Most change communication is designed to drive engagement that results in behavior change and new ways of working. Any communication plan can create awareness of what is happening and promote its benefits. Change communications plans must do that and more – they must help people see where they fit and provide answers to their deepest concerns:

"What does this mean to me and what do I need to do?"

"Behavior change happens one person at a time and the more your communication can connect on a personal level, the more effective it will be.

"This doesn't mean your communications team should offer therapy or coaching to every employee! However, you will be most successful with an approach focused on individual needs as well as overarching general communications. Consider:

+ What do front-line employees need to know as they experience and deal with the expectations of change?

+ What will help their leaders answer their questions and connect team members to their roles in attaining the ultimate goal?

+ What framework can you use to ensure your communications and messages can adapt to audience needs as transformation moves forward and continues to evolve along the way?

"At the end of the day, your plan should support the behavior change with communication that gives stakeholders the information they need *when* they need it and equips leaders to help in the process. The change communication plan includes the following key sections:

- Objectives based on the business goals (what success looks like) – Like any communications effort, change communication plans should align closely with the business objectives for the change. These objectives can be explained in a story or graphic to help everyone connect with the vision for success.

- Desired behaviors for employees – These may vary by role or function, and should be observable (ideally measurable, e.g., use of a new tool or software) to demonstrate adoption of the change.

- Key messages – You'll need core messages explaining the overarching change and vision, as well as audience-specific messages to support key milestones. For example, customized messages for field engineers would be timed to the rollout of a new process, to explain training plans, rollout timing and expectations of their role in consulting with the field.

- Communication strategies and tactics – This section summarizes the key activities you'll implement to support the change for all categories of stakeholders. It might be organized by target audience (e.g., leaders/front-line employees), or by change initiative (e.g., phases of a software rollout).

- Editorial calendar – An overview of your plan for delivering relevant information to stakeholders at key points in the change effort. It summarizes the message themes and the channels used to deliver them, aligning timing with key milestones in the program.

- Formal and informal two-way feedback channels – Whether you use existing channels or create new ones, this "must have" could include online mailboxes, suggestion boxes in a field office (formal), or a defined process for front-line leaders/change champions to invite and respond to employee feedback (informal). The organization must actively respond to feedback from all channels and use it to guide communication (often through the communications team).

- Cadence of measurement – Key performance indicators (KPIs) measure business progress, and the communications team should regularly report on measures such as engagement with tools, participation in key events, feedback received and responded to, etc.

+ Input and ongoing feedback – Be ready to evolve your activities to meet changing needs and continuously evaluate the effectiveness of communications efforts. This will be easier if you engage regularly with those on the front lines of the change – whether through focus groups, surveys or periodic input meetings with a cross-functional work team.

+ Action plan – A game plan outlining specific activities and timing for executing tactics in the change communications plan. It details the deadlines and people responsible for steps including leader and legal review of content and design, printing or other production, mailing, distribution, and delivery of presentations or information to employees.

"Step 3: Prepare Key People for Their Critical **Influencer Role.** All leaders – from front-line supervisors to middle managers and senior executives – serve as role models and champions for new behaviors and change. For any change to be successful, leaders from every stakeholder group must be active and visible in leading their teams and reinforcing progress. Best practice research confirms that employees want to hear from leaders during change:

1. They want to hear about business reasons for the change, risks and competitive information from senior leaders who are responsible for the change.

2. They want to hear about the personal impacts of the change and what it means to them from their immediate supervisors.

"In addition, employees often turn to influential peers because of strong relationships, experience, skills and commitment. These influencers can be recruited as "change agents" (or part of a "change network"), trained as communicators, equipped with information and asked to share feedback that they hear from their coworkers.

"These Official and Unofficial Leaders are the Drivers of Change

"In best-practice organizations, the communication responsibility assigned to these leaders is clearly articulated by their direct supervisors, who set expectations and hold them accountable for delivering information and gathering feedback.

To set leaders and change agents up for success, change sponsors and communication teams collaborate to define their communication role and ensure they are equipped with information, tools, training and support. These key steps should be a component of every change communication plan.

+ Evaluate communication capabilities of leaders – Consider their communications experience and knowledge when choosing the tools and training to help prepare leaders for their change role. For example, supervisors with minimal experience may be best served by a more basic approach, while senior leaders will find messages and toolkits familiar.

+ Assemble a network of change agents, including peer influencers – Early in your planning, define what this group will be asked to do, how much time it will take, and the support to be provided. Share this information with managers and supervisors in each stakeholder group and ask them to nominate influential employees to participate. With leader approval, invite the individuals to participate, starting with a kick-off meeting to share expectations.

+ Create tools to help them deliver critical messages – Develop a toolkit for leaders and change agents with communication tools suited for their specific situation and audience. Core messages, communication tips, slides, handouts, infographics, posters, FAQs and even communication content (e.g., email announcements) can be provided to support communication with their teams. Toolkits can be customized and updated periodically as the program progresses.

+ Brief them on the tools and provide more training if needed – Conduct a briefing or webinar that explains the change, key tools in the toolkit and how to use them. This will have the greatest impact if their senior executive reinforces the importance of their communication roles. Keep in touch with participants to understand how they are using the tools and what is most helpful (gathering input to guide future activities). Provide coaching as needed on key communication concepts and tools.

+ Identify feedback channels and reinforce response expectations – Responding promptly to employee questions and feedback is one of the most important change communication responsibilities. Leaders and change agents need to know which feedback channels employees can use, the response process being followed, and specific expectations for them to answer employee questions. If a response process doesn't exist, create and implement one. Be sure this information is in the toolkit and reinforced consistently.

Step 4: Execute the Communications Plan. When you receive input and approval on your change communications plan and messages, it's time to take action. Be sure to brief key communication contacts (such as internal communications editors, intranet managers and video resources) about your plans so they are ready to provide support when needed. Also give a heads up to anyone who will be tapped to deliver messages to employees, so they know their role, what's coming and when.

"Because of the nature of change programs, expect to evolve your plans and adapt your materials to the changing needs of the projects and stakeholders. Your efforts are more likely to be successful if you follow a few guiding principles:

+ Be consistent and purposeful about messaging – Ensure everyone receives the same core messages and understands the importance of using them. Reflect the same information in internal communications materials, graphics and intranet content.

+ Keep leaders at the forefront – Employees are closely watching their leaders and it is up to the communication team to provide leaders with the latest information and tools to keep employees informed.

- Communicate often with a focus on what employees want to know — Be sensitive to the concerns of front-line employees and what they need to know to deal with uncertainty and changing circumstances. Provide updates when available and be clear about what is in progress. Address myths or rumors with facts and share information in channels most likely to reach them (including providing updates that leaders can share with their teams).

- Listen carefully and respond religiously — Monitor feedback channels and ask employees what they're thinking to uncover questions and concerns to address in communication. Set a standard for responding to employee questions or feedback within 48 hours, even if it's just to let them know their input was received and you are working on finding an answer. Guidance and talking points for handling feedback should be provided to leaders and change agents as well.

- Celebrate work done in the previous system and highlight successes — While it is good to communicate about the "future state," it's also important to acknowledge the achievements of the past. This can help employees feel their efforts are appreciated here and now. As changes roll out and successes are identified, be sure to highlight people who are adopting new ways of working and the positive outcomes they are achieving. Ask change agents and leaders to be on the lookout and bring you success stories you can share.

- Plan for recognition and ongoing engagement — Work with different functions as needed to align on ways to recognize and reinforce progress and adoption of change. The communications team can provide visibility through internal communications channels, for example, but recognition programs and engagement surveys may be owned by human resources or another team.

- Remember that it takes time and consistent reinforcement to achieve lasting change — Your communications and recognition activity should continue long after the rollout. By reinforcing key concepts and successes through updated messages and leader tools, you'll help employees see the change is taking hold and their efforts are successful.

"Step 5: Evaluate What Should Be Stopped, Started or Continued. Gather input from leaders, change agents and your cross-functional team of advisers to understand what communication is working well and what could be done to better meet employee needs. Ask the tough questions and probe to understand how employees are feeling, what challenges they are facing and what they are worried about.

"You can uncover important information in day-to-day conversations, input meetings, follow-up surveys or stakeholder interviews. Consider using these tips to help you listen for what's not being said and ask questions to ensure understanding.
In addition to anecdotal feedback and insights from people on the front lines, some of the things you can use to evaluate your efforts include:

+ Communication metrics – What tools are employees using most (e.g., intranet pages or software tools), which activities are most popular? What is the most used feedback loop?

+ How are employees handling the change? – Use a pulse survey of approximately five questions to consistently poll employees on their knowledge, acceptance and adoption of the change. Compare your results across employee groups and locations to identify topics of concern and adjust communications accordingly.

+ What is getting in the way – Watch for trends in questions asked, information requested, or comments made and probe with leaders and change agents to understand issues people are facing. Share information with project leaders to prompt possible adjustments to address issues and communicate updates as appropriate.

+ Lessons learned – Many change efforts are done in the spirit of continuous improvement and learning, and your communications plans should be no exception. Learn from your evaluation and adjust your messages, tools and communication cadence to respond to stakeholder needs" (Grossman, 2020).

INTRODUCTION

Not everything that is faced can be changed.
But nothing can be changed until it is faced.
– James Baldwin

You are ready to "rock and roll." It's time to engage the people of the organization in the process of organizational change management. Never forget that it's not about the process. It's about the people who actually make the organization exist! Sometimes we tend to get so caught up and involved in the process work that we lose sight of them. I am the first to admit my own tendency to be distracted from this truth. I created the 10-Step **process.** But that is why I named it the *People Sustained Organization Change Management* (PSOCM®) process. I intentionally put the word *People* first. So, should you.

In Step 2.0 there are the following Actions:

Action 2.1 Initial Group Meeting

Action 2.2 Setting Ground Rules

Action 2.3 Employee Involvement

2.1 Initial Group Meeting

The initial group meeting is important because it sets the tone for everything that happens next and throughout the OCM program. It is also called the roll out. Most of the change management tomes promote the multi-message approach to make sure to get the employees attention. I think that approach is important, but it also tends to diffuse and dilute the message. I am advocating for an attention getting, all hands event, where everyone is invited on a given day at an exact time. And the first person to present the message is *numero uno, el hefe*, the boss! It is also the perfect opportunity for the boss to introduce the change management team that has been personally picked to carry out this important organization mission.

You will want to address everyone in the organization involved together at one time. It needs to be communicated as personal as possible. Your venue depends on the scale. Let's say it's a group of up to 200. Find a nice location and venue to deliver the message. It needs to be a location where people feel at ease and not intimidated. Perhaps it's a lecture hall at a local college or even some sort of community theater. If it is a larger audience with satellite offices, then you can either breakup the presentation using a combination of tele video of organization's leader and then on-site folks to handle the in-person presentation. If it's the satellite or branch office, then have a role for the local leader to play. This reinforces the team approach.

In any case, the entire series of events need to be carefully choreographed with consistent messages tied to the Communication Plan. The meeting is important because you want everyone to be on the same page on the same day. Every employee involved needs to be able to walk away to the same understanding about what is happening. Because they are going to talk about it. They will discuss it formally in their individual smaller teams or groups, and informally either one on one, through social media, or in other extracurricular, off-site social activities.

What should you not do? Do not make it a webinar with people at their desk. It would make sense to record the event so people could playback the event if interested or if they missed the event. Speaking of people missing in action, don't allow it. Make attendance at the event mandatory. All work ceases during the event. **It is that important!**

2.2 SETTING GROUND RULES

Change is upsetting because people don't know what is going to happen next. One way to help people in the change process is to explain the rules of engagement. You need to use the initial group meeting to explain what you expect of them both during the meeting and after. In other words, tell them how they should behave. As the "change agent" you have a great deal of power because you have knowledge that others don't. They will look to you and the leadership to explain how you want them to act.

It is important that you establish how the employees will be involved in a meaningful way. This depends on the magnitude and type of change (positive/negative). They have to come away knowing and believing that the final change process will not only involve them but will be driven by them. If you plan to present them with the change product as having already been decided, then you have lost half the battle because the employees won't have any ownership or stake in the change process.

"Here is a set of eight research-inspired ground rules that can help teams improve their performance, working relationships, and individual well-being.

+ **State views and ask genuine questions.** This enables the team to shift from monologues and arguments to a conversation in which members can understand everyone's point of view and be curious about the differences in their views.

+ **Share all relevant information.** This enables the team to develop a comprehensive, common set of information with which to solve problems and make decisions.

+ **Use specific examples and agree on what important words mean.** This ensures that all team members are using the same words to mean the same thing.

+ **Explain reasoning and intent.** This enables members to understand how others reached their conclusions and see where team members' reasoning differs.

+ **Focus on interests, not positions.** By moving from arguing about solutions to identifying needs that must be met in order to solve a problem, you reduce unproductive conflict and increase your ability to develop solutions that the full team is committed to.

+ **Test assumptions and inferences.** This ensures that the team is making decisions with valid information rather than with members' private stories about what other team members believe and what their motives are.

+ **Jointly design next steps.** This ensures that everyone is committed to moving forward together as a team.

+ **Discuss undiscussable issues.** This ensures that the team addresses the important but undiscussed issues that are hindering its results and that can only be resolved in a team meeting.

"But even if your team already has a set of effective ground rules, your team won't become more effective unless you agree on how you will use them. Here's how to do that:

+ **Explicitly agree on the ground rules and what each one means.** A set of behaviors aren't your team's ground rules until everyone on the team agrees to use them. The term ground rules was originally used to describe the rules of baseball that teams agreed to use in a particular venue, or grounds. Those rules were — and still are — necessary for playing baseball fairly across venues that are not exactly the same. Similarly, when your team members take time to discuss and develop a common understanding of what your rules mean, you increase the chance that the rules will be implemented consistently and effectively in different situations.

+ **Develop a team mindset that's congruent with the ground rules.** The behaviors your team uses are driven by the mindset (that is, values and assumptions) you operate from. If you adopt effective ground rules but operate from an ineffective mindset, the ground rules won't work. For example, if you assume that you are right about Bob being off topic, you won't test your inference — you'll just tell him to get back on topic. But if you assume that you might be missing something that Bob sees, you will be curious about the connection Bob sees between his comment and the topic at hand.

+ **Agree that everyone is responsible for helping each other use the ground rules.** Teams are too complex to expect that the formal leader alone can identify every time a team member is acting at odds with a ground rule. In effective teams, all members share this responsibility, meaning teams should agree on how individuals will intervene when they see others not using a ground rule.

+ **Discuss how you are using the ground rules and how to improve.** Take five minutes at the end of each team meeting to discuss where you used the ground rules well and where you can improve. If you find yourself having these conversations outside the team, you're not building a better team." (Schwarz, 2016).

2.3 EMPLOYEE INVOLVEMENT

Any organizational change management process must have employee involvement -- or it will fail. You cannot dictate change. If you created a sincere and authentic communication plan, then the employees will understand the gravity of the situation and the need for change. It also has to be a serious effort at involving the employees in the actual change and not just window dressing. It is human nature to resist change. However, it is also human nature to want to survive and better themselves. They also feel important if asked to participate in the OCM process and given some clearly defined responsibilities.

The most effective involvement process is to set up work teams who are assigned to tackle specific elements of the OCM plan activities. It is important to give a group some level of autonomy to deliver a product. The group's ownership of the activity is critical to their becoming enthusiastic. Just make sure that you have given them clear instructions regarding:

+ What they need to achieve, as in what is the deliverable,
+ When the deliverable is due,
+ What authority they have to compel others to assist them, and
+ What resources they have at their disposal.

They should also have a liaison person who is on the executive management team to provide them with guidance when asked, secure resources or compliance from other individuals or units. Picking the right team leader is also critical. The person might even be a critic of the endeavor. People's perspective changes when they have to take personal and professional ownership of a task or activity.

"What is employee involvement?

So, what exactly is employee involvement and how can organizations benefit from it? Employee involvement can be defined as:

When employees participate directly to help an organization fulfill its mission and meet its objectives by applying their ideas, expertise, and efforts towards problem solving and decision making.

More specifically, employee participation can be broken into representative participation (through unions), direct communication, and upward problem solving. To simplify, we will focus on the latter two categories because, although unions do help ensure that the employee "voice" is heard, this blog article is more about understanding outcomes, tools, and methods. Employee involvement is something that can be present at varying degrees within an organization, and is reinforced by leadership, culture and environment.

Changing an organization from a strict top-down hierarchy to one that engages employees at all levels to make decisions is not an easy thing to do- it involves not only structure and policy changes but also *cultural change*, which takes time, effort, and expertise. That being said, organizations from every industry are applying the concepts of employee involvement to drive the continual improvement of their processes and performance.

"Outcomes & Benefits.

To understand the benefits of employee involvement, let's take a look at what the research has to say. The following outcomes of employee involvement initiatives have been identified through empirical organizational research:

- Increased **employee productivity** across industries, even for low-skilled employees that do routine tasks.
- In manufacturing, employee involvement programs are a long-term investment, but one that leads to increased **plant performance** over time
- Improved **organizational decision-making** capability
- Improved **attitude** regarding work
- Substantially improved **employee well-being**
- **Reduced costs** through elimination of waste and reduced product cycle times

+ Leads to employee **empowerment, job satisfaction, creativity, commitment,** and **motivation,** as well as **intent to stay** [secondary effect].

"How to 'get' employee involvement

In order for an employee involvement process to be effective, **three things need to be present:**

1. Employees need to be given the authority to participate in substantive decisions

2. Employees need to have the appropriate decision-making skills

3. Incentives to participate (whether implicit or explicit) must be present

Like I said earlier, sustaining an entire employee involvement process is no easy task. It would require the work of highly trained internal or **external consultants** with expertise in assessment, training, management education, and evaluation. A formal process involves manager and employee training, support from the highest levels, and the application of specific measures to increase employee participation. These can include quality circles, self-directed/self-managed work teams, gainsharing programs, employee ownership, problem solving teams, and cross-functional task-forces." (Powell, 2011).

Introduction

Change begets change. Nothing propagates so fast.
– Charles Dickens

This step is probably the most boring of all the activities you will undertake. However, it is also the most foundational. For the consultant or objective third-party observer, this is where you learn about your client and inform your analysis. Even if you are doing an internal review process, which is not recommended, you will be surprised about what you can learn. Not everyone has both a detailed and broad-based, comprehensive understanding of what makes your organization tick. Indeed, you might be surprised to find out that your own biased view of the organizational zeitgeist is misplaced or misunderstood.

So, what might come from this phase?

+ First and foremost, you and the process team, are going to come to a *common understanding* to what consists of and drives the corporate or organizational "culture." In the later phases of interviews and other investigative tools, you will be able to ask, solicit and discern *relevant* facts about the organization.

+ It might be that the organization is not adhering to its stated goals. Nothing undercuts an organization more than taking people through goal setting sessions that are pointless. They only serve to undercut the staff belief that their opinion matters or that such lofty goals matter. One should always allow for opportunistic thinking. However, the outcomes still need be accepted by the organization through the change management process. Change may be a constant factor in your organization attaining its stated goals. However, too much self-inflicted change can be both debilitating and disconcerting to the organization's employees.

+ Failure to follow through on stated goals and objectives service to undercut the employee's belief that they even matter. If the CEO or leadership routinely ignores the strategic plan, then why should the rank and file? I had a good "lesson learned" in this when I ran a large organization. I was talking to my executive team about this great idea that I had. I was really very excited about it. At the end of what I thought was a really motivating and inspirational presentation, I was informed by my head of strategic planning that it was already in the strategic plan to be implemented and resources in the third quarter of year three.

3.1 EXISTING VISION AND MISSION

This step should be relatively simple. It involves doing a document search to come up with the relevant information on the organizational vision, mission and/or strategy. These can often be found in annual reports or on the organization's website. The level of detail and sophistication may vary greatly. For example, all of this may exist as a single page of information. On the other hand, it could be part of a 3- to 5-year strategic plan that is very detailed in terms of activities, accountabilities and due dates. Also, the terminology may be inconsistent in terms of what is a vision versus a mission, strategy versus a tactic, a goal versus and an objective, or a task versus and an action item. The problem with inconsistency could be a lack of definition regarding the terminology being used.

If you are creating this from scratch, then it is important to understand what you need to create. The vision statement focuses on tomorrow and what the organization wants to become. The mission statement focuses on today and what the organization does. While companies commonly use mission and vision statements interchangeably, it's important to have both. One doesn't work without the other, because having purpose and meaning are critical for any business.

3.2 DOCUMENT REVIEW

The document review builds on 3.1. However, the amount of documentation will be vastly greater. In order to make the document review manageable and useful, it will be important to collect documentation considered *relevant* to the organizational change management (OCM) process. Documentation could include:

Management

+ Mission, Goals, Objectives (3.1)
+ Communication Plans
+ Organizational Charts/Structure
+ Flyers, Pamphlets, Advertising
+ Internal/External Newsletters (print or electronic)
+ Strategic Plan
+ Staff Reports

Budgetary

+ Preliminary or Adopted Annual Budgets
+ Annual Reports
+ Fees, Charges
+ Purchasing Manuals
+ Capital Improvement Plans
+ Performance targets/measurements (see 3.3)

Human Resources

+ Policies and Procedures Manuals

+ Wage/Salary Schedules

+ Personnel Manuals

+ Position Descriptions

+ Training Manuals/Programs

Technological

+ Websites

+ Process Systems

Regulatory/Legislative

+ Local, State, Federal Laws/Regulations/Guidelines

Other Relevant Documents

+ The types of documentation vary from one organization to the next. Look for items not on this list. For example, some larger organizations which have been established may have created a history document. Occasionally, the founder may have written an autobiography or there may be a biography. A little Google research on the name of the organization or its famous or infamous founders might be useful.

This list is meant to give you some ideas on what kind of documentation you might look for. In creating the Document Review List, some documents only need to be referenced. The key is to collect or note every written document that the organization relies on to function. One final note. Make a note of any documentation that might help inform the Step 3.4 Cultural Assessment.

3.3 PERFORMANCE MEASUREMENTS

Every organization function with sets of performance measures or targets. Every individual position, team, and unit/division has a set of performance expectations, implicit or explicit, that come with the job. You need to focus on the existing performance measures. We will deal with the introduction of possible new ones later. Deming famously said that *What gets measured, gets done* (Walton, 1986). So, it will be important to establish what is being measured and why early on because that may be a key indicator as to what the problem is that needs to be fixed or changed.

The most comprehensive description of these are what Cummings and Worley (2005) call *Unobtrusive Measures*. These are found in company records and archives. They include "records of absenteeism or tardiness; grievances; quantity and quality of production or service; financial performance; meeting minutes; and correspondence with key customers, suppliers or governmental agencies." They further include "market share and return on investment," as well as "quantity and quality of the outputs of work groups and individual employees." There are also "work systems, control systems, and human resource system…management information systems, operating procedures, and accounting practices."

I have intentionally pulled this out and made it separate from the 3.2 Document Review process because of its importance. Change management is about improving "performance efficiency and cost-effectiveness."

"What is Performance Measurement?

Performance Measurement can be best understood through considering the definitions of the words 'performance' and 'measurement' according to the Baldrige Criteria:

- Performance refers to output results and their outcomes obtained from processes, products, and services that permit evaluation and comparison relative to goals, standards, past results, and other organizations. Performance can be expressed in non-financial and financial terms.

◆ Measurement refers to numerical information that quantifies input, output, and performance dimensions of processes, products, services, and the overall organization (outcomes). Performance measures might be simple (derived from one measurement) or composite.

The challenge for organizations today is how to match and align performance measures with business strategy, structures and corporate culture, the type and number of measures to use, the balance between the merits and costs of introducing these measures, and how to deploy the measures so that the results are used and acted upon.

"Who uses Performance Measurement?

All organizations measure performance to some extent. However, there is a large disparity among organizations in terms of which performance measures are used with many primarily focusing on financial measures. There has however, been a general move away from financial measurement since the early 1980's. This was accelerated in the 1990's and 2000's by the worldwide acceptance of business excellence models and performance measurement frameworks that address all stakeholders' needs.

"Performance measurement is one of the cornerstones of business excellence. Business excellence models encourage the use of performance measures, but in addition and more importantly, they consider the design of performance measurement systems to ensure that measures are aligned to strategy, and that the system is working effectively in monitoring, communicating, and driving performance.

"A recent report presented by the Performance Measurement Association (PMA) on one of the new performance measurement frameworks, the Balanced Scorecard, demonstrated the popularity of this particular method. The PMA presented evidence that 39% of FTSE 100 companies were actively using the scorecard, and other researchers have reported that between 40% and 60% of Fortune 1000 companies have attempted to implement the Balanced Scorecard. With the movement away from financially based measurement systems only gaining momentum in the early 1990's this represents a significant change in organizational practices in such a short space of time.

"What are the common challenges associated with the Performance Measurement approach?

The performance measurement revolution has seen a move away from the problems of past measurement systems. Five common features of outdated performance measurements systems were:

+ Dominant financial or other backward-looking indicators
+ Failure to measure all the factors that create value
+ Little account taken of asset creation and growth
+ Poor measurement of innovation, learning and change
+ A concentration on immediate rather than long-term goals

"The focus in performance measurement is now on achieving a balanced framework that addresses the issues described above. Examples of these new frameworks are Kaplan and Norton's Balanced Scorecard, Skandia's navigator model and the Performance Prism. Others recommend that the results sections of business excellence models should be used to generate a balanced set of performance measures.

+ There are a number of challenges that are faced when designing an effective Performance Measurement System, these include the following:
+ How to measure non-financial performance
+ What measures to choose and why
+ How to use them - what to do with the results
+ Who should be responsible for using the results
+ How and to whom, to communicate the results
+ The resources needed to consider the above and design and deploy the measurement system

"There are other major requirements that an organization needs to consider before an effective performance measurement system can be designed or installed. Apart from lower-level measures that may be vital for the operation of processes, all measures need to be chosen to support the attainment of specific performance or behavior identified by the organization's leaders as important or necessary to work towards the organizational goals. This being the case, there must be clearly defined goals/objectives and strategies chosen to reach them before measures can be chosen to support their attainment. Similarly, the key processes, drivers of performance, and the core competencies required by employees need to be identified before effective performance measurement can be achieved.

"How can the BPIR help?

The BPIR will help you to understand and select the most appropriate performance measures for your organization.

"The BPIR's database, accessible to members only, contains almost ONE THOUSAND financial and non-financial measures. However, do not be daunted! - you can sort these by commonly used processes and the categories of business excellence models. This means that you will be able to quickly select appropriate ones for your organization. Not only do we provide examples of the measures but for the most popular we provide a commentary on how to use them and for all measures we provide examples of formulae used to calculate performance.

"In addition, linked to most measures we provide performance benchmarking data showing how organizations perform relative to the measure. Such data will help your organization to improve once you have established a Performance Measurement System.

"What is the track record of Performance Measurement use?

Performance measurement is fundamental to organizational improvement. The importance of performance measurement has increased with the realization that to be successful in the long-term requires meeting (and therefore measuring performance against) all stakeholders' needs including customers, consumers, employees, suppliers, local community stakeholders, and shareholders. While the importance of performance measurement is difficult to quantify it is evident that in virtually all texts, research, and case studies on organizational improvement, that performance measurement plays a central role. It is worth noting that performance measurement is a requirement for benchmarking and business excellence" (BPIR.com, 2021).

3.4 CULTURAL ASSESSMENT

Each organization's culture is unique. It is like a personality fingerprint in that no two corporate cultures are alike. In some cases, the culture itself may be the cause of problems that are inherent in an organization's problems. So, what is "culture?"

The cultural assessment process outlined here is taken from Edgar H. Schein's book "Organizational Culture and Leadership." In his book he defines culture as:

A pattern of shared basic assumptions that was learned by a group as it solved its problems of external adaptation and internal integration, that has worked well enough to be considered valid and, therefore, to be taught to new members as the correct way to perceive, thin, and fell in relation to those problems.

He employs a 10-step "cultural deciphering process" (Schein, 2004). It is important that the organizations employees "identify important assumptions" that help or hurt organizational change. You start with what the leadership thinks the culture is and then test that assumption through the assessment. The fact that there is a cultural perception gap between the leadership and the staff could be a problem in and of itself. However, the primary purpose of the cultural assessment is to gauge the level of acceptance the proposed organizational change may have or not have and why.

The purpose of the cultural assessment is to bring together identified groups within the organization and ask them to think about and identify the visible structures and processes, known goals, and unknown or taken for granted assumptions. The latter being that culture is shared assumptions of the members of the organization. The point of the assessment is to sort out those assumptions that help the organization achieve its goals and the organizational change, as opposed to those that do not.

+ Step One: Obtaining Leadership Commitment. It is as important to have the organization's leadership by into the cultural assessment as it is to have them buy into the organizational change itself. In the process of getting the buy in, is getting the leadership view on what they think the culture is.

+ Step Two: Selecting Groups for Interviews. Groups can be homogenously grouped or heterogeneously segmented, sized from three to thirty people. The group needs to be given the task of addressing the organizational change at hand.

+ Step Three: Selecting an Appropriate Setting for the Group Interviews. The room or venue chosen should be sized to comfortably accommodate the group with wall space for hanging flip charts. Additional breakout rooms should be easily accessible.

+ Step Four: Explaining the Purpose of the Meeting. The introduction of the meeting's purpose needs to come from someone in leadership who blesses the exercise and introduces the change agent.

+ Step Five: Short Lecture on How to Think About Culture. This pep talk is an explanation about the importance of culture to the organizational change process and the need to decode the culture at the level of visible structures and processes, known goals, and unknown or taken for granted assumptions.

+ Step Six: Eliciting Descriptions About Visible Structures and Processes. Start with the most recent hires and ask about their first takes. Examples are dress codes, expected or observed behaviors, arrangement of spaces, rewards and punishments, and how people get ahead.

+ Step Seven: Identifying Espoused Goals. Ask what people value in the workplace, what they believe, if there are differing values between work groups or levels of management.

+ Step Eight: Identifying Shared, Underlying Assumptions. What are the values that aren't espoused are talked about openly? Are there values that aren't talked about that might conflict with state goals. For example, that business should be socially significant, a need for clear guidance or rules, the lack of immediate feedback, or unspoken negative behaviors.

+ Step Nine: Identifying Cultural Aids and Hindrances. Set up subgroups to refine assumptions according to whether the aid or hinder to changes being proposed or being observed. Have identify these differing perspectives in writing.

+ Step Ten: Reporting Assumptions and Joint Analysis. The subgroups need to work together to reach a consensus on how these shared assumptions can be addressed considering the changes. How do the consensus assumptions aid in the advancement or hinderance of the change goals?

Conclusion. Culture can only be assessed through human interaction and discussion. Surveys and questionnaire cannot elicit the kind of information this process can. The value of the assessment is its providing insight into the organizational change in question. The assessment should first identify the cultural assumptions and discuss whether they help or hinder the organizational change process. Again, culture must be described in terms of the visible structures and processes, known goals, and unknown or taken for granted assumptions (Schein, 2004).

Introduction

If you don't like something, change it. If you can't change it,
change the way you think about it.
— Mary Engelbreit

This is the most important step in the process. It is here, in the feedback phase, where you find out what the problem really is. You could call it the truth of the matter. The basic process is Assessment (Phase 1), Implement (Phase 2), and Maintain (Phase 3). But you must start with understanding what problem has to be changed. However, it may not have been what you or your client's *information bias* said it was. Sometimes the "problem" isn't what the people who hired you said it was. The latter can be a problem because your new client may not like the answer. The problem could be them or their *leadership bias*. For example, they may think that a person/group needs to be fired, disciplined or retrained because he, she, or them is the problem.

This could be called the investigative phase. One of my personal quirks is that I like detective novels. Much like its sister genres of the mystery or international intrigue novels, the lure of the novel is to find out what the real truth is. And the truth will set you free. But free from what? The truth could also lose your business. The lure of the investigative novel is that your bias/prejudice misleads you. You always seem to pick the wrong culprits.

The Problem. The problem is generally about people. Even in the rare case where there is a software problem, someone bought the software for some reason – however, misplaced. Sometimes it is an outdated process (we always did it this way) created by a person long gone. Times change, but the process may not be kept up. Sometime there is an entire dysfunctional unit led by one dysfunctional person – who someone mistakenly hired. I freely admit that I am guilty of all of these. If you live long enough, then you make a lot of mistakes that you hopefully learned from. As a consultant that is what have paid me for. It's called experience.

For example:

1. I once hired a very intelligent, engaging and attractive looking individual who I thought had a lot of potential. But I didn't know that they were bipolar and had two sides to their personality.

2. I once bought software from a salesperson who convinced me it would do things it couldn't.

3. I once had a brilliant idea that really wasn't.

4. I once inherited a person or group of people who made mistakes that I had to correct.

This is why you hire a consultant like me to help you. However, putting these types of experience in a resume is not exactly inspiring. "Hire me because I made a lot of mistakes!" The tag line being, "And learned from them."

There are five types of stakeholder feedback: participant observation, interviews, focus groups, open houses, and surveys. They need to occur in this order so the information becomes more and more refined and focus. It is important to link a basic set of questions for the purpose of data charting. The questions should occur in all feedback venues.

Have at least five questions that occur in the participant observation, interviews, focus groups, open houses, and surveys. Stage and phase the feedback venues so that one informs the next one. Stage them so that the more general information gathering informs the more specific informed. You need to "drill down" on some key answers to get to the root of the problem(s). The quest for information must be phased so that the survey is conducted last. Participant observation informs the individual interview. The individual interviews inform the focus group questions which informs the survey questionnaire. Also, there are four phases in terms of these types of qualitative research. They are planning, observation, analysis, and reporting.

4.1 PARTICIPANT OBSERVATION

Participant observation is an unobtrusive method of direct data collection. The researcher meets with the person or group to be observed, outlines the observation process, and then spends some amount of time observing what the "participant" does. The "observer" should spend more time observing than asking questions. In the case of the participant interacting with the public, the observer won't interrupt the participant while interacting.

This form of feedback is important because it provides firsthand experiential information. The information is detailed since the observer can ask questions about each step in a process. This type of information could also be "chain observation" because you could observe a process that goes from the CEO to middle management to a frontline supervisor to the final employee activity. It might also reveal some miscommunication about a desired outcome and the real outcome. For example, the CEO tell the Vice President that some new activity needs to be implemented. However, by the time it gets to the front line work it becomes quite the opposite outcome.

This is not unlike the "pass-it-on" game where the first person writes down a message and then whispers the message in someone's ear and it is passed along through several people. When a message is passed along it eventually is lost in translation to 180 degrees from its original meaning. This is a form of qualitative research. You could also review the message and how it was interpreted by several people in the same job classification. You might find that the five people working at the front counter have five different takes on the message.

There are four types of participant observation (Sauro, 2015):

1. Complete Observer. The observer is not seen or noticed by the participant. With the ubiquity of video cameras, remote observation remains a viable option.

2. Observer as Participant. The observer is known and recognized

by the participant. There is some interaction with the participants, but the interaction is limited. The researcher's aim is to play a neutral role as much as possible.

3. Participant as Observer. The observer is fully engaged and participates in the activity of the participant. While there is full interaction with participants, they still know that this is a researcher.

4. Complete Participant. In customer research, this is like a "secret shopper." The observer fully engages with the participants and partakes in their activities. However, the participants aren't aware that observation and research is being conducted, even though they fully interact with the researcher.

Prepare your questions in advance and select the appropriate site(s) where you are to observe any activities (Mack, 2011).

4.2 Interviews (Structured and Unstructured)

To me this is the most fascinating part of the OCM process. I am always amazed at what people tell the interviewer in confidence. People talk about how their great ideas were ignored or that their boss promoted an employee after a "relationship." I had one very sad experience where a department director of a very large group told me an amazing story in confidence. It was about one of the organization's board members. Quite frankly, I was completely astonished at what he told me. However, I found out later that this director was a pathological liar and mentally ill. His story was a total fabrication. So be prepared to hear some amazing stories. Be prepared to fact check such stories. When possible, ask the interviewee for detail and/or documentation of any serious allegations.

Interviews are the most commonly used methodology in the organizational change process (Burke, 1982). One of the benefits of doing one-on-one interviews is that it generates trust. It provides the change agent an opportunity to interact, in complete confidentiality, with the organization's employees. But who do interview? You want a representative sample of people both at different levels and different groups within the organization. It is important to have two or more people from each. You do this to avoid having very biased pre-established answers. Have a serious discussion with the leadership about the best people to interview and why. You should try to ferret out the why from other sources within the organization to anticipate the leadership leading you with intentional or unintentional biased personalities. You cannot rule out that the leadership is the problem.

The interview may or may not be taped (Mack, 2011). The former may intimidate the interviewee. If you use the latter, then have a second person participate as note taker (Mark 2011).

If the change agent is perceived as a completely independent and unbiased researcher, then people will be inclined to confide in them. As

I noted above, people will provide their personal biased take on things.

Anticipate that the interviewee may ask you questions about the interview process, the change be considered, etc. (Mack, 2011).

There are two methods used in interviewing techniques. They are structured and unstructured.

Structured Interviews. The structured interview, also called *quantitative interview*, have a fixed number of prepared questions with preestablished response choices and preset number of issues. The primary advantage is the ability to code and statistically compare respondent choices. Questions should focus on organizational structure, measurement systems, human resource systems, and organizational culture (Cummings, 2005).

Unstructured Interviews. The unstructured interview, also called *qualitative interview*, consists of open-ended questions generated from previous questions. The primary advantage is you get more discovery of issues you may have missed. Questions are more general and are "about organizational functioning:

+ "What are the major goals or objectives of the organization or department?

+ "How does the organization currently perform with respect to these purposes?

+ "What are the strengths and weaknesses of the organization of department? [see SWOT in glossary]

+ "What barriers stand in the way of good performance? (Cummings, 2005)."

Mixed Method. I recommend using a mixed method. You start with prepared questions that allow for statistical comparison, but then you create another set of questions based on the unexpected responses to the preset answers (Rothwell, 1985).

4.3 FOCUS GROUPS

Focus groups are a form of qualitative research where you are doing group interviews. They provide an important perspective in the quest to define and solve the problem statement. Individuals give the singular perspective that, although it may provide insight, does not speak for the group or groups. What is it that the major stakeholder groups think? What is it that they truly want to happen?

The survey as an instrument can help do this for you, but the survey is static. It can only respond to your information bias, which means the questions you come up with. The focus groups can provide insight that you haven't thought of.

Selecting the groups is also important. Creating like-minded groups means information may come out of the group dynamic.

Groups need to be drawn from external stakeholders who are critical to your organization achieving its mission. These are people who represent themselves, but some group type. Since they are like-minded it is important that you find and create internal and external groups with their alternative motives.

These are primarily major customers and secondarily vendors/suppliers, etc. To start with you are one of three groups:

+ Private sector: Retail customers, wholesale buyers, vendors/suppliers, government regulators, special interest groups.

+ Public-sector: Business, developers, manufacturers, special interest groups, neighborhood associations, inter-agency elected and appointed, citizens.

+ Non-profit: customers, inter-agency elected and appointed, citizens.

For example, a private-sector company that manufactures a product may have direct buyers or bulk wholesale buyers.

For example, a federal governmental agency like the Internal Revenue

Service is funded by taxpayers, with oversight by the three branches of government (i.e., executive, legislative, judicial) and has customer taxpayers.

Create three to five focus groups.
The focus group outline:

+ Two persons conduct focus group. One is moderator who asks questions and mark up the tear sheets that are put on wall. The second person who is the note taker and timekeeper.

+ Group size: 6-10 participants. Consider balancing the group according to gender, race, social status, and age. Overestimate the recruitment by 20 percent because of "no shows."

+ Time: 90-120 minutes. Tell people the session will run 90 minutes but leaves a 30-minute cushion.

+ Mid-morning of 9:00-11:00 AM or mid-afternoon of 2:00-4:00 PM. This allows people time to tend to their primary business at the start or end of day. It also takes into account their lunch meetings.

+ The meeting should be taped recorded. Creating actual transcripts is useful, but it is really a function of cost.

+ Moderator: Start with introductions, explain purpose and ground rules, turn off cell phones.

+ Moderator: Ground rules are respectful of other opinions, one person speaking at a time, no side discussions, don't dominate discussion, turn cell phones off.

+ Moderator: Is there to lead the discussion, to facilitate and not dominate discussion. Start by saying the moderator is there to lead the discussion, learn from it, and not to interject their expertise or bias. Start with a brief introduction of self.

+ Moderator: Note the topics. Have 5 topics noted after the explanation of change topic. However, the moderator needs the freedom to ask follow-up questions for the purpose of clarification or to explore some ideas not originally contemplated.

+ Moderator: After the selected topics have time for an open discussion about their thoughts on the topic. For example, is there anything you should have asked but didn't. Then questions.

- Moderator: Final summary statement of what to expect in terms of process timeline and products. Thank them for their participation.

Do some follow-up calls with individuals if you need clarification on the topics. You may want to make some of the participants part of a distinct follow up interview process for persons you overlooked and didn't include in the earlier interview process.

Much of the information here comes from *Focus Groups as Qualitative Research*, 2nd Edition, Qualitative Research Methods Series 16, a Sage University Paper by David L. Morgan, Portland State University. Professor Morgan was an early academic mentor of mine.

4.4 OPEN HOUSES

This technique is optional and provides a chance to both collect information and to disseminate information. It is designed to be an informal gathering of the organization's staff, and/or vendors and customers. Depending on the audience, either (1) For internal customers, hold it during work hours in a facility that is on site such as a lunchroom, or (2) for external customers hold it after hours at some neutral facility such as a library, school, or community center.

Create a brochure to hand out that outlines both the changes contemplated, resources available to get information (website, interview times), and contact information.

One alternative is to create a virtual open house where internal and external stakeholders can access information via the Internet or an organization's intranet. One advantage of this is you can add on the survey questionnaire. Just make sure that you ask the leading questions. You can have one or more stations for different types of information depending on the size of the organization. If the organization is small (less than 20 employees), then just use one location. If the organization is larger, then create additional stations. Each station within the same facility should represent one change management question.

4.5 Surveys

Surveys are the most effective way to accumulate generalized statistical information from your stakeholders. However, you should hold off on creating a survey until you have collected information about what the problem is and what the post-change concerns are. The structured and unstructured interviews, focus groups, and open houses should all have preceded the survey and informed it.

Survey Process. The survey process has five steps:

1. The survey development should involve members from all sections of the organization from the front counter to the top floor. In other words, from customer service to the management team.

2. The survey should be administered to everyone in the organization.

3. The survey analysis is done only by the change agent, be it a consultant or an in-house person/group. This keeps *confirmation bias* out of the analysis.

4. The data feedback starts at the and filters down to the frontline customer service function. This follows the "no surprises" rule.

5. Feedback meetings are scheduled with individual work groups to discuss the survey's findings. (Cummings, 2005).

If you have the time and budget, then consider doing both a pre-implementation survey and a post-implementation survey of internal and external stakeholders. This is one method of gauging the success of the perceptions regarding the change implemented (Carter, 2001).

Survey Instrument. There are five types of survey instruments: mail out, telephone, web based, in person, and intercept. I am not going to spend time explaining and weighing the pros and cons of these. Suffice it to say that the web-based survey is the most cost effective and efficient method for the purposes of soliciting information in and from an organization. Web based surveys have the advantage of convenience, rapid data collection, cost-effectiveness, confidentiality, and specialized population. The normal disadvantages really do apply here. These are limited respondent base, self- selection, and lack of interview involvement.

The limited respondent base and self-selection are not problematic because 100 percent participation can be mandated and monitored. The lack of interviewer involvement is mitigated because in person interviews will have preceded and informed the survey. The actual development and administration of the survey depends on the IT capability of the organization. A trained consultant can manage the survey development and work with the organization's IT group to field a more robust Statistical Package for the Social Sciences (SPSS). However, the use of readily available instruments like Survey Monkey can be used for a cheap alternative.

The primary advantage is to require all members of the organization to participate. This can be monitored by tracking the individual employee's login. I can be initiated by having the survey link sent via email directly to each and every employee. The email will provide both instructions and a deadline. The latter should be 10 workdays or two calendar weeks. You should be prepared to have follow-up with the few recalcitrant employee holdouts. The primary resistance to such a survey is the fear of reprisals from either the immediate supervisor or upper management. This can be dealt with by doing the important prep work of reassuring employees that the survey is confidential and that their answers are secure. It is also important to communicate the need for the survey and how it will inform how the organization will address the changes in question.

Question Types. The survey should be structured so that it starts with easy to answer *introductory* questions that are straightforward, uncomplicated and not sensitive in nature. The *sensitive* questions should be placed later in the survey. These are questions that get to the heart of the change in question. It is important to get valid answers once the person is comfortable answering questions. Finally, you may want to introduce *related* questions. These are questions that don't address the specific change but give you an opportunity to collect other information you may want for future or other use.

Survey Structure. The survey should have a series of unbiased, well-structured questions that will systematically address the information identified. There can be both fixed-answer and open-ended questions. It is important to create a logical sequence to the questions (Rea, 2014).

Survey Pretesting/Coding. If possible, the survey should be pretested to weed out poorly worded questions and overall quality. It is important that the survey be formatted so that data can be easily put into data processing.

Closed- and Open-Ended Questions. Closed-ended questions allow for a uniformity of responses, comparative analysis, and data charting. Open-ended questions allow the survey to capture ideas that the analyst had not thought of and is a venting mechanism that makes the respondent feel better (Rea, 2014).

PHASE II – IMPLEMENT ORGANIZATIONAL CHANGE

Now that you have identified both the quantitative and qualitative data in Phase I, it is time to do something about it. In Phase II you implement the change through a process of diagnosis, interventions, process mapping/reengineering, change restructuring, and locking in change.

"Locking in Change!"

5.0 Introduction

Be the change that you wish to see in the world.
– Mahatma Gandhi

You now have assembled a lot of quantitative and qualitative data related to the *preliminary problem statement*. It is time to create the *final problem statement* and begin the diagnosis.

Final problem statement. You started this process by creating a *preliminary problem statement* based on the information provided by the organization's leadership. Now that you have completed the organizational assessment you need to determine if the *preliminary problem statement* is still correct. You now need to create a *final problem statement* based on the hard data (facts) and the soft data (opinion). You will review the data and will reach one of three conclusions:

+ The *preliminary problem statement* is wholly supported by the assessment facts and can be moved forward as is.

+ The *preliminary problem statement* is partially supported by the assessment facts and needs to be modified.

+ The *preliminary problem statement* is wholly not supported by the assessment facts and needs to be rejected.

What if the leadership's assumption about the problem is intentionally wrong? The latter is a worst-case scenario where you realize you were brought in as a *stalking horse*. The latter being defined as *a false pretext concealing someone's real intentions* (OxfordLanguages.com). This, of course, is a worst-case scenario where you are faced with making an ethical decision that impacts your business or job.

You, the change agent, now need to present this to your client for their approval before you can move on to the diagnosis phase. This may or may not present a problem. One of the advantages of hiring a consultant is that the consultant brings with them the patina of professional/subject matter expert (SME) objectiveness.

However, let us assume the stalking horse scenario is not the case. In which case you are faced with advising your client that their premise was wholly or partially correct, or incorrect. With any luck your client will realize that addressing the issues embedded in the final problem is paramount and will benefit their organizational mission statement. That being said, the problem statement will either be found to be correct or modified in order for the diagnosis phase to begin. You create the *final problem statement* for diagnosis.

5.1 Problem Statement

A problem statement is a statement of the problem that requires timely action to improve the situation. This statement concisely explains the barrier the current problem places between a functional process and/or product and the current state of affairs. This statement is objective, focusing on the facts of the problem and leaves out subjective opinions. To make this easier, it's recommended to ask who, what, when, where and why to create the structure for your problem statement. This will also make it easier to create and read and makes the problem at hand more comprehensible and solvable.

According to Indeed.com, there are a few key elements to keep in mind when crafting a problem statement that can have a positive impact on the outcome of the project.

1. Describe how things *should* work.
2. Explain the problem and state why it matters.
3. Explain your problem's financial costs.
4. Back up your claims.
5. Propose a solution.
6. Explain the benefits of your proposed solution(s).
7. Conclude by summarizing the problem and solution.

Writing a problem statement is essential because it can help you focus your research and create a more cohesive and guided project. In science or other areas of research, it is easy to get sidetracked by the wealth of knowledge and information that is available. By writing a problem statement, you can force yourself to remain focused on answering a specific question at hand. This allows you to ultimately achieve better results and not to waste time pursuing unnecessary avenues or detours from your main goal.

"What is a problem statement?

A problem statement is a statement of a current issue or problem that requires timely action to improve the situation. This statement concisely explains the barrier the current problem places between a functional process and/or product and the current (problematic) state of affairs. This statement is completely objective, focusing only on the facts of the problem and leaving out any subjective opinions. To make this easier, it's recommended that you ask who, what, when, where and why to create the structure for your problem statement. This will also make it easier to create and read and makes the problem at hand more comprehensible and therefore solvable. The problem statement, in addition to defining a pressing issue, is a lead-in to a proposal of a timely, effective solution.

"Why is a problem statement important?

A problem statement is a communication tool. Problem statements are important to businesses, individuals and other entities to develop projects focused on improvement. Whether the problem is pertaining to badly needed road work or the logistics for an island construction project; a clear, concise problem statement is typically used by a project's team to help define and understand the problem and develop possible solutions. These statements also provide important information that is crucial in decision-making in relation to these projects or processes.

"Problem statements have multiple purposes

The problem statement has other purposes, too. One is to identify and explain the problem in a concise but detailed way to give the reader a comprehensive view of what's going on. This includes identifying who the problem impacts, what the impacts are, where the problem occurs and why and when it needs to be fixed. Another purpose of the problem statement is to clarify what the expected outcomes are. Establishing what the desired situation would look like helps provide an overarching idea about the project. The proposed solution and scope and goals of the solution are made clear through this statement.

"Problem statements help guide projects

The problem statement provides a guide for navigating the project once it begins. It is continually referenced throughout the duration of the project to help the team remain focused and on track. Near the completion of the project, this statement is again referred to in order to verify the solution has been implemented as stated and that it does indeed solve the initial problem. This can help in making sure that proper steps are being taken to prevent the same problem from happening again in the future.

Bear in mind that the problem statement does not attempt to define the solution, nor does it outline the methods of arriving at the solution. The problem statement is a statement that initiates the process by recognizing the problem.

"How to write a problem statement

A problem statement is a tool used to gain support and approval of the project from management and stakeholders. As such, it must be accurate and clearly written. There are a few key elements to keep in mind when crafting a problem statement that can have a positive impact on the outcome of the project.

1. Describe how things *should* work.
2. Explain the problem and state why it matters.
3. Explain your problem's financial costs.
4. Back up your claims.
5. Propose a solution.
6. Explain the benefits of your proposed solution(s).
7. Conclude by summarizing the problem and solution.

"1. Describe how things should work

To begin, you'll want to provide some context that will make it easier to understand the problem. Start by explaining how this particular process *should* work. Concisely describe how the process would function if the current problem didn't exist before mentioning the problem, keeping the end-user in mind. For example, let›s say that you have an idea of how to increase efficiency in a process to maximize the best use of resources. You might begin by describing a theoretical situation in which the system is more efficient and working toward your proposal from there, always keeping in mind who, what, when, where and why to keep yourself on track.

"2. Explain the problem and state why it matters

The problem statement should address not only *what* the problem is, but *why* it›s a problem and *why* it›s important to solve it. This will wrap the other ‹W› questions in organically, in most cases. For example: *Why* should we fix this problem? Because it affects the efficiency of departments X, Y and Z, wasting resources and driving prices up for consumers. This addresses what the problem is, who is affected and why the problem should be fixed. You may also consider including what attempts have already been made to solve the problem and why they didn't work out. As concisely as possible, explain everything you know about the current problem.

"3. Explain your problem's financial costs

When you state the problem to decision-makers, you'll want to explain the costs of not fixing it. Seeing as money is the language in which businesspeople speak, it's easiest to frame the problem and proposed solution in terms of financial costs. For example, if the problem is actively costing unnecessary money, preventing the company from making more money or damaging the company's public image (indirectly costing money) make sure you explain it specifically and clearly in terms they understand. Try to pinpoint exact dollar amounts for the problem's cost.

"4. Back up your claims

Once you claim the problem is costing the company money, you must be prepared to support your claims with evidence. If you neglect this step, you may not be taken seriously. Do your research, cite your sources and have the data ready to present.

"5. Propose a solution

The Problem Statement should describe your proposed solution(s) to the problem. At this point, you won't be focused on finding a single solution, but you should have a solid grasp on the causes of the problem and be prepared to propose practical approaches to understanding and remedying it. State your objectives by suggesting well-thought-out plans for attacking the problem.

"6. Explain the benefits of your proposed solution(s)

Now, you've described an ideal scenario in which the problem doesn't exist. You've pointed out the problem, explaining the ramifications of choosing not to fix it (using dollars and solid data) and proposed some realistic approaches to finding a solution. Now is a very good time to demonstrate why this solution will work, again focusing on efficiency and the financial impact of your solution. Address what expenses the solution will decrease, how this solution will free up revenue streams and what intangible benefits, such as increased client satisfaction, your solution will bring. This should all fit into a single short paragraph.

"7. Conclude by summarizing the problem and solution

Now you'll move onto your conclusion. This should consist of the problem, why it needs to be fixed and a summarized argument of why your solution is the best answer to the problem.

"Following this format will help all parties who read it to understand the problem and be open to considering the best solution" (Indeed, 2020).

5.2 DIAGNOSE PROBLEM

Diagnostic Methods. There are numerous problem-solving, diagnostic methodologies. I am not going to create countless pages of a new academic literature review to analyze the various methodologies. Let us just say, I came to realize that selecting a diagnostic method was as difficult as selecting the correct OCM modeling process. What I found were a preponderance of models that were not rigorous enough and did not systematically lead to a conclusion. The processes I found were often very obtuse in describing elemental relationships with no systematic conclusion.

I did find a good description of the "problem solving process" described in *The Universal Traveler* (Koberg 1991). It is states that the,

> "Process makes it clear 'where to begin': we start by "analyzing" the situation in order to uncover its facts and details with the intent to identify "what need fixing." Then, after considering the facts and determining what the true issue(s) is (are), we "synthesize" by eliminating, replacing, or changing parts or relationships according to the 'insight' found in analysis. Once you understand problem-solving and goal-seeking as a process (of applying the results of analysis to what is done in synthesis), what remains is simply the details and enjoyment of your work."

What you want is a problem-solving, diagnostic method that clearly allows you to take your qualitative and quantitative data, create the *final problem statement*, design the intervention, and implement change. What I found was a lot of diagnostic models that resulted in some very interesting bubble diagrams with some very interesting components, which delivered nothing useful. They were for the most part *black box models*. The product of black box models is a little like delivering mystery meat. It is like the quotation attributed to Germany's first chancellor Otto von Bismarck: "If you like laws and sausages, you should never watch either one being made."

I was also leery of the predetermined bubble diagram labels. It was like being told to look at the heart, liver, lungs, etc. and their relationships. That seemed dangerous to me. It was telling me what the solution was before it was diagnosed. However, in medicine the diagnosis is not so prescribed as it is organic in detecting the symptoms first. It is the confluence of symptoms that lead to the discovery of the diseased organ.

What I wanted and selected was a diagnostic method that clearly delineated the steps and process of creating a defensible set of implementation actions.

The Diagnostic Method. In my field of doctorate research, organizational psychology, there is always the organization as individual metaphor. In other words, organization is made up of individuals so there are psychological corollaries. So, I started to wonder if the same were true for the diagnosis. Are there also medical corollaries? What if we diagnosed the organization in the same manner as the individual? How would the medical diagnosis look if the change agent were in the medical doctor role.

The medical diagnostic process is "A complex, patient-centered, collaborative activity that involves information gathering and clinical reasoning with the goal of determining a patient's health problem" (Balogh, Miller, Ball, 2015). Substitute the word "organization" for "patient" and it reads quite well.

Think of yourself, the change agent, as the medical practitioner examining the organization. In medicine, the dual process theory is used. The patient comes in with a complaint about an ailment and you immediately work to create two possible tracks. Track "A" is *symptom recognized* and Track "B" is *symptom not recognized*. There are requisite tests to make in the initial screening (e.g., temperature, blood pressure, weight, height). And then it is important to actively listen to the patient's description of the ailment symptoms. A common maxim in medicine attributed to William Osler is: "Just listen to your patient, he is telling you the diagnosis" (Gandhi, 2000, p. 1087).

The medical diagnostic model has several defined stages (Figure 5.4).

Figure 5.4. *Improving Diagnosis in Healthcare*, National Academy Press, Washington, D.C. (2015)

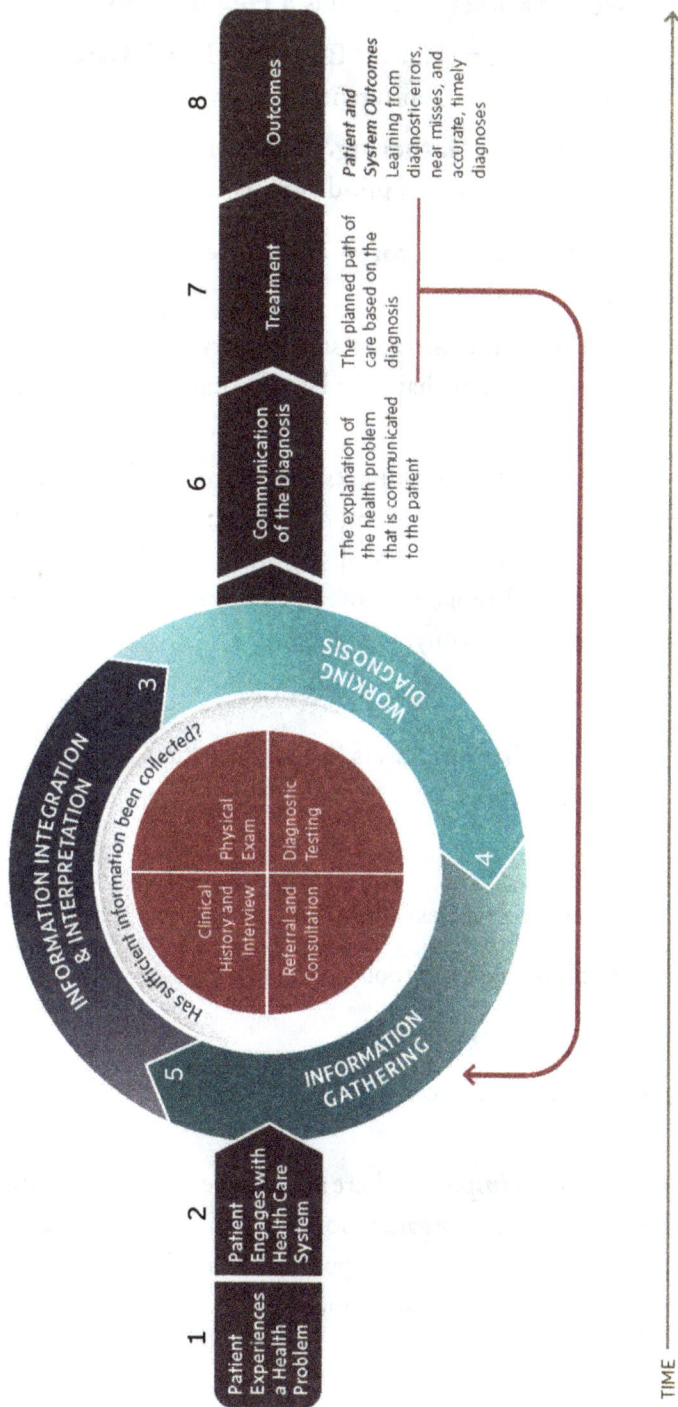

1. **Organization** (Patient) **has a Health Problem**

2. **Organization** (Patient) **Engages Health Care System** (Change Agent/Consultant)

3. **Information Gathering.** At the center of the medical model there are four central pre-diagnosis activities:

3.1. **Clinical history and interview** (Data Collection/ Stakeholder Feedback)

3.2. **Physical exam** consists of observation and review of internal and external factors that may be affecting the overall organizational health.

Internal Change Impacts. There are six types of internal change impacts on the individual and the organization. They are the physical layout/assets, organizational culture, rules/procedures/processes, technology and tools, employee resources, and financial resources. I have created the acronym for them.

PORTEF

+ Physical Layout/Assets (buildings, offices spaces, parking, satellite offices)

+ Organizational Culture

+ Rules/Procedures/Processes

+ Technologies and tools

+ Employee resources

+ Financial resources

External Change impacts. There are six types of external change impacts on the individual, the organization, and on humanity. They are socio-cultural, technology, economic, political, pandemic, and environment. I have created the acronym for them.

STEPPE

+ <u>S</u>ocio-cultural (gender, race, nationality)

+ <u>T</u>echnological (artificial intelligence, technological advances, pharmaceutical, medical)

+ <u>E</u>conomic (recession, depression, trade wars, monetary devaluations, economic systems)

+ <u>P</u>olitical (elections, *coup d'état*, regulatory/legislative)

+ <u>P</u>andemic (global diseases such as COVID-19, AIDS, Ebola, Zika, H1N1, SARS)

+ <u>E</u>nvironmental (volcanic, tsunami, weather, flooding, earthquakes, climate change)

3.3. **Diagnostic Testing** (i.e., third party evaluations such as cultural assessment, performance evaluation, fiscal auditing)

3.4. **Referral and consultation** (Outside consultation with respective subject matter experts in the fields of human resources, financial analysis, legal assessment, etc.)

The corollary here is that you as the medical doctor are the change agent. You have listened to the patient/organization describe what they think is the problem (*preliminary problem statement*) and you have done your due diligence by reviewing the four pre-diagnosis criteria.

4. **Information Integration and Interpretation.** Involves hypothesis generation, updating prior probabilities, communication among all levels (i.e., internal and external stakeholders).

Clinical Reasoning. This is the "cognitive process that is necessary to evaluate and manage the patient's [organization's] medical [curative] problem" (Barrows, 1980, p. 19). Clinical reasoning occurs within the clinician's mind and facilitated by the clinician's work system. This is called *hypothetico-deductivism* which is an analytical reasoning model that describes clinical reasoning as hypothesis testing. The steps involved in hypothesis testing are:

4.1. **Acquisition.** Change agent obtains contextual information by taking history, performing organizational examination, administering diagnostic tests, or consulting with other subject matter experts (SMEs).

4.2. Hypothesis generation (working diagnosis). Change agent formulate alternative diagnostic possibilities.

4.3. Interpretation (diagnostic modification and interpretation). Change agent interpret the consistency of information with each of the alternative hypothesis under consideration.

4.4. Hypothesis evaluation (diagnostic verification). The data are weighed and combined to evaluate whether one working diagnosis can be confirmed. If not, then further information gathering, hypothesis generation, interpretation, and evaluation is conducted until verification is achieved (Balogh, Miller, Ball 2015).

5. **Working Diagnosis.** You begin by creating a single Working Diagnosis based on the Information Gathering, and Information Integration and Interpretation. Throughout the diagnostic process, there is an ongoing assessment of whether sufficient information has been collected. If the diagnostic team members are not satisfied that the necessary information has been collected to explain the organization's health problem or that the information available is not consistent with a diagnosis, then the process of information gathering, information integration and interpretation, and developing a working diagnosis continues. When the change agent/team judge that they have arrived at an accurate and timely explanation of the organization's problem, they communicate that explanation to the organization's leadership as the final diagnosis. In the medical model you are now ready to prescribe the intervention or therapy.

6. **Communication of the Diagnosis.** This is accomplished in Step 1.0 First Step, 1.5 Communication Plan. Use the same venues and techniques to update your employees. You are not ready to communicate the intervention strategies, but you can set the stage by talking about the issues that need resolution.

7. **Treatment** (Implementation). This is accomplished in Step 7. Implementation.

8. **Outcomes.** This is accomplished in Step 10. Maintain, 10.1 Monitoring Performance.

Introduction

The significant problems we face cannot be solved at the same level of thinking we were at when we created them. — **Albert Einstein**

L et me start by explaining how I am using the term *intervention*. I am using it because the word in the accepted terminology in the field of social studies. It refers to decision making where intervening is done effectively in a situation in order to secure desired outcomes. Unfortunately, the word "intervention" later became used in the field of psychology as a pejorative word for a carefully planned process by which friends and family of a drug addict may confront that person about their addiction. What we are really talking about is taking action to bring about positive organizational change. The use of the word intervention carries a negative connation and is meant to imply the need for the change to cause a cessation of an activity and the substitution of a new activity. I prefer to characterize this next step as a *transformation*. Kurt Lewin's three-step model labeled the process as *transformation*.

6.1 OCM Interventions

The term intervention refers to planned programmatic activities aimed at bringing changes in an organization. These changes are intended to make improvements to the functioning of the organization in terms of its performance efficiencies and cost effectiveness. The changes are brought through the employees in the organization with the help of the change agent or consultants who facilitate the change process. Any intervention involves close interaction between the change agent and the organization.

Intervention basically refers to an intended activity to bring change in the organization and the consequent activities within the organization. The intervention can be brought by an external consultant who acts in consultation with the client members. A member within the organization, acting as the in-house consultant can also make the intervention. The organization itself could plan the intervention without employing either an internal or external consultant. Where a consultant is employed, any intervention is a collaborative activity between the client and the consultant.

French & Bell (1994) state that, "intervention are sets of structured activities in which selected organizational units (target groups or individuals) engage in a task or a sequence of tasks where the task goals are related directly or indirectly to organizational improvement. Interventions constitute the action thrust of organization development; they "make things happen" and "what is happening."

Organizational change management (OCM) interventions are structured programs designed to solve a problem, thus enabling an organization to achieve the goal. These intervention activities are designed to improve the organization's functioning and enable managers and leaders to better manage their team and organization cultures. These OCM interventions are required to address the issues that an organization might be facing ranging from process, performance, knowledge, skill, will, technology, appraisal, career development, attrition, top talent retention and the list can actually be pretty exhaustive.

"Specific OD intervention methods include:

"a) **Role Playing.** This is an integral part of training used to act out a realistic situation that involves two or more people, purposes to enable participants handle a given situation given a pre-medicated background. Role-playing is a contingency method of preparing group members to perform without intervention from superiors once a given situation develops. Role analysis is a prescribed way of behaving.

"b) **Team Development.** As an important OD process team development (or team building) has come to be regarded as the very foundation of developing work group maturity and effectiveness. It covers such areas as diversity training and structured exercises (formulation of strategic work plans by a group). The basic objectives of team development are: i) To set goals and/or priorities. ii) To analyze or allocate the way work is performed. iii) To examine the way a group is working (its norms, decision-making, communication). iv) To examine relationships among the people doing the work.

"c) **Survey Feedback Information** gathered through personal interviews and/or survey questionnaires are analyzed, tabulated into understandable form and then shared with those who first supplied the information. It is expected that effective feedback should be relevant, understandable, descriptive, verifiable, limited, controllable, comparative, and inspiring Recipients "must see feedbacks as a stimulus for action rather than a final statement." (Nadler, 1997:147-148).

"d) **Inter-Group Problem-Solving.** When inter-group conflicts develop, holding joint meetings is often regarded as a step in the right direction. During such meetings, members of each group are allowed to view themselves as members of a larger family. They are urged to minimize their differences and maximize what holds them together – their corporate existence.

"e) **Process Consultation.** OD consultants take delight in consulting two or more disputing parties, initially, separately, and later jointly. The purpose is to help participants air their views to the hearing of their warring partners. At times, it is discovered that what was heard or reported was not what was actually meant. The process of consultation roughens the edges of conflict and sharpens the sword of peace.

"f) **System Four Management.** In the process of solving problems in the work environment, OD experts often advocate the adoption of system four management approach. Categorizing management philosophies into four major systems, Rensis Likert developed the following: i) System 1: Exploitative – automatic management: Superior has no confidence and trust in subordinates. ii) System 2: Benevolent – autocratic management: Superiors have subservient confidence in subordinate. This is master-servant style of management. iii) System 3: Consultative – democratic management: Superiors have substantial but not confidence and trust in the subordinates. iv) System 4: Participative democratic management: There is complete confidence and trust in subordinates. 5 As an intervention process, system from management style can be used to diffuse tension and create a congenial atmosphere in the work environment.

"g) **MBO Approach Management** by objectives seeks to involve subordinates in the decision-making mechanism of the enterprise. Its objective is to ensure managerial effectiveness while encouraging peaceful approach to solving interpersonal problems.

"h) **The Grid Training.** In order to ensure minimum resistance to a change, OD experts often resort to the use of the Grid management system. First developed by Blake and Moulton (1964), the managerial grid has helped workers to voluntarily submit themselves to the winds of change. Key coordinates in the concern for people, concern for production facsimile is the country club management (1,9), Do-nothing management (1,1), Organization man (5,5), Production Pusher (9,1) and the team builder (9,9) – this being the ideal grid for solving organization conflicts and effecting a change."

"i) **Third Party Meeting.** When it becomes necessary to invite a third party to a dispute, it is expedient to select a third party that is impartial, judicious and having a human face. The Industrial Arbitration Panel is such a third party. Parties to the dispute are expected to respect and uphold the decisions of the third party." (Uwah, 2009).

INTRODUCTION

It must be considered that there is nothing more difficult to carry out, nor more doubtful of success, nor more dangerous to handle, than to initiate a new order of things. – **Niccolò Machiavelli**

Change occurs by undertaking all three phases, ten steps, and 30 activities that are provided here. However, the heart of the change process is the determination of what is the problem and how to fix it. Once the problem is diagnosed, then the next step is fixing the problem. This is done through a combination of process mapping and business process reengineering.

7.1 Process Mapping

Business Process Mapping came about through The American Society of Mechanical Engineers (ASME). In 1921, Frank and Lillian Gilbreth introduced the "flow process chart" in a presentation that they gave called, *Process Charts, First Steps in Finding the One Best Way to Do Work.* The tools that they presented quickly became engineering standards and continued to be shown through the 1940s, having been sanctioned by the American Society of Mechanical Engineers (ASME). And in 1947, the ASME adopted a symbol system for consistency in this type of chart.

The manufacturing industry also adopted process maps to identify value-added activities and inefficiencies. These maps often took days to create and were static. More recently, business process mapping has evolved with software development. Businesses can use software tools to create their maps quickly, evolve them over time, and make them accessible to all team members, facilitating a culture of improvement. Most business process mapping software integrates with business process management software systems, so that you can draw the maps and have them come to life within your business.

Business process mapping refers to defining what a business entity does, who is responsible, to what standard a business process should be completed, and how the success of a business process can be measured.

The purpose behind business process mapping is to assist organizations in becoming more effective. A clear and detailed business process map or diagram allows outside firms to come in and look at whether or not improvements can be made to the current process.

Business process mapping takes a specific objective and helps to measure and compare that objective alongside the entire organization's objectives to make sure that all processes are aligned with the company's values and capabilities.

A process map is a planning and management tool that visually describes the flow of work. Using process mapping software, process maps show a series of events that produce an end result. A process map is also called a flowchart, process flowchart, process chart, functional process chart, functional flowchart, process model, workflow diagram, business flow diagram or process flow diagram. It shows who and what is involved in a process and can be used in any business or organization and can reveal areas where a process should be improved.

Business process mapping is intended to be cross-functional and highly participatory, so that all business units involved gain a shared understanding of key business processes and can work together to improve them. The method is both top-down and bottom-up and supports more detailed analysis such as as-is workflow modeling, proposing a to-be process, and defining functional requirements for a solution.

Types of Business Process Maps

Many different types of business process maps exist, and range from planning activities, details, documents, products, roles, locations, strategies, and interactions. Also, various levels of detail are available for mapping. The following are some examples of map types for business processes.

+ **Flowcharts:** These are graphic illustrations of your process (Figures 7.1-7.5). Three types of flowcharts are popular: top-down flowcharts, deployment flowcharts, and detailed flowcharts. Top-down flowcharts show the steps of a process, clustering them together in a single flow. Deployment flowcharts are a top-down flowchart expanded to include who is performing each task. Detailed flowcharts are an expansion of both the top-down and deployment flowcharts, showing as many details as possible.

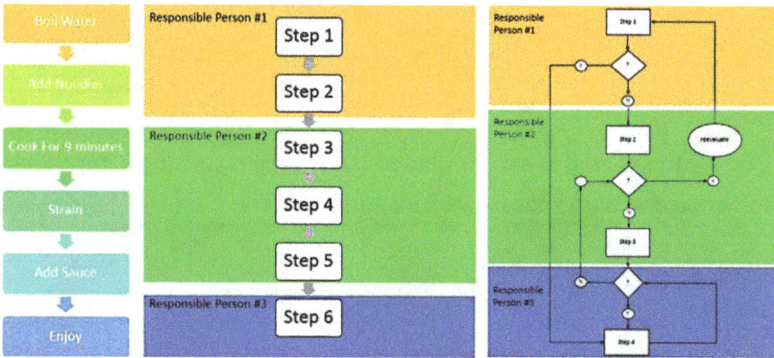

Figure 7.1

+ **Swimlane Diagrams:** These diagrams, also known as cross-functional maps, detail the sub-process responsibilities in a process.

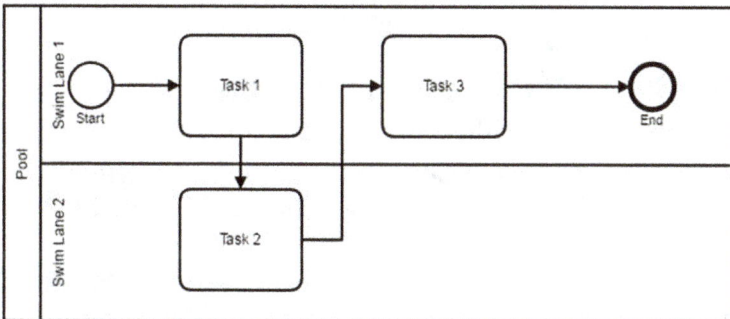

Figure 7.2

+ **State Diagrams:** These diagrams show the behavior of

systems in the Unified Modeling Language (UML), describing the states of component.

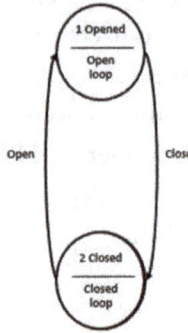

Figure 7.3

+ **Data Flow Diagram:** Similar to a flowchart, this diagram focuses solely on the data that flows through a system.

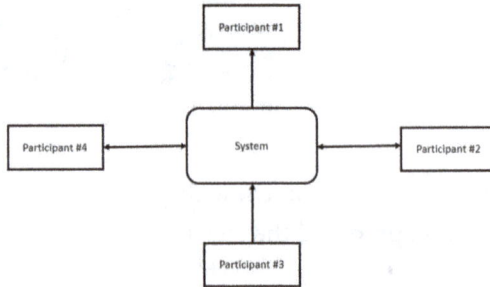

Figure 7.4

+ **Value Stream Mapping:** Some of Lean Manufacturing principles, value stream mapping demonstrates the current state and helps to design the future state of a process, focusing on taking products and services from their beginning to their completion (Eby, 2017).

Figure 7.5

7.2 BUSINESS PROCESS REENGINEERING (BPR)

Business process reengineering (BPR) is a business management strategy, originally pioneered in the early 1990s, focusing on the analysis and design of workflows and business processes within an organization. BPR aimed to help organizations fundamentally rethink how they do their work in order to improve customer service, cut operational costs, and become world-class competitors.

According to Inteqgroup, the six steps of business process reengineering are:

1. **"Define Business Processes.** Map the current state (work activities, workflows, roles and reporting relationships, supporting technology, business rules, etc.).

2. **Analyze Business Processes.** Identify gaps, root causes, strategic disconnects, etc. in the context of improving organizational effectiveness, operational efficiency and in achieving organizational strategic objectives.

3. **Identify and Analyze Improvement Opportunities.** Identify, analyze and validate opportunities to address the gaps and root causes identified during analysis. This step also includes identifying and validating improvement opportunities that are forward facing – often strategic transformational opportunities that are not tethered to current state process.

4. **Design Future State Processes.** Select the improvement opportunities identified above that have the most impact on organizational effectiveness, operational efficiency, and that will achieve organizational strategic objectives. Make sure to select opportunities for which the organization has the budget, time, talent, etc. to implement in the project timeframe. Create a forward-facing future-state map that comprehends the selected opportunities.

5. **Develop Future State Changes.** Frequently overlooked (and a key root cause in failed BPR initiatives), this is where the above opportunities are operationalized before implementation. New workflows and procedures need to be designed and communicated, new/enhanced functionality is developed and tested, etc. Changes and opportunities cannot be implemented until they are operationalized.

6. **Implement Future State Changes.** Classic implementation based on dependencies among changes/opportunities, change management, project management, performance monitoring, etc." (Inteqgroup, 2021).

"What Is Business Process Reengineering?

Business process reengineering is a structured approach to improving a company's performance in areas such as cost, service, quality, and speed through changes in (appropriately) processes. This radical change methodology starts at the highest level of a company and works down to the most minute details to overhaul the system in a short time. As a complete redesign, BPR differs from other methodologies where incremental improvements result from regular process updates. Companies undergoing BPR must reassess their fundamentals and reform their processes with the goal of standardization and simplification.

Ambitious companies that implement BPR start with the intent of doing whatever it takes to improve performance across the business. Examples of company-specific goals through BPR include:

+ Taking a decentralized process and making one person responsible for it

+ Redeveloping the company's goals so improvement plans are consistent

+ Taking a department-specific process and assigning it to coordinate and integrate cross-functionally

+ Going from a product perspective to a process perspective

The term "reengineering" suggests that an item has already been developed and is now being redeveloped. In this case, the business's processes are undergoing redevelopment. Business processes are the sets of activities that lead to specific goals or outcomes. Usually, they are performed regularly and systematically. In most businesses, changes to a pre-existing process happen relatively slowly and incrementally. With BPR, however, the most modern tools are put to use from the ground up as the business rethinks the fundamentals of existing processes, ideas, and designs.

The term "process" focuses on how work is done, not on the specific people, their job descriptions, or the tasks they perform. BPR is more interested in the series of steps that produce the product or service, from conception through creation.

BPR can bring dramatic business improvements in quality and productivity. However, because extensive employee input and engagement are required, BPR can be very expensive and time-intensive to implement. An alternative to the traditional approach of constant meetings is group decision support software (GDSS), which helps solve unstructured or semi-structured issues by providing collaboration platforms for idea generation and organization, conflict resolution, priority setting, and solution generation.

Another term for a GDSS is a *computerized collaborative work system.* BPR is also known as *business process redesign, business transformation,* or *business process change management.*

"Business Process Reengineering Methodology Overview

Michael Hammer, an original promoter of BPR in the 1990s, preached 'reengineering work: don't automate, obliterate.' At the time, investments in technology were expected to return dramatic results to improve process performance. However, new technologies are often applied after a process had been in place for many years, so they are incapable of doing more than moderately speeding performance. Hammer recommended challenging the ingrained assumptions and rules, so real improvements could be made.

Early on, the field of BPR discovered numerous recommendations:

+ Organize around the outcome, not the specific task. One person owns a whole process, performing or coordinating all steps.

+ Those closest to the process should perform the process. Instead of farming out different types of easily managed work, the people who need the quick outcomes from simple tasks take ownership.

+ Have the people who produce the information process it. This streamlines the outcome of the information gathered into usable data.

+ Centralize resources. Databases and other technology systems can consolidate resources to cut down on redundancies and increase flexibility.

+ Integrate corresponding activities, not merely their results. This keeps the content cohesive, without the gaps and miscommunication that could cause delays.

+ Control the decision points and where the work is done. Built-in controls enable the employees who perform the work to self-manage, so managers can become supportive rather than directive.

+ Information should be collected once and at the source. You can erase data redundancies when processes are connected in a central database.

"BPR Frameworks: INSPIRE, PRLC, and More

Due to the unique nature of every company and its distinctive challenges, there is no universal framework for BPR. Instead, BPR should adapt to not only the company, but also the customers and stakeholders. Consultants in business process management have tried to make easy guidelines. They often use proprietary frameworks based upon the experience and philosophy, then tailor the methodology to the specific company they are working with. For example, Bhudeb Chakravarti developed the INSPIRE (Initiate, Negotiate, Select, Plan, Investigate, Redesign, and Ensure) framework, and M'hammed Abdous and Wu He developed a framework specifically for higher education with four steps: initiation, analysis, reengineering, and implementation and evaluation. William J. Kettinger, Subashish Guha, and James T. C. Teng developed the Process Reengineering Life Cycle (PRLC) Methodology, which will be detailed below.

All of the suggested frameworks take into account basic guiding principles for BPR. These can make the process more advantageous and increase the chances for successful outcomes. They often differ in their emphasis in designing new processes versus redesigning old processes and the sequence of steps. Michael Glykas and George Valiris strongly recommend a multidisciplinary approach that encompasses both process improvement and innovation. Regardless of how an organization undertakes BPR, they must have a deep understanding of their business culture and a clear vision, and they must use the most suitable, relevant information technology. They should ask several core questions before adopting BPR:

+ Who are the customers?

+ What value do we offer the customer?

+ Do the current processes deliver the expected value?

+ Do the processes need to be redesigned or completely redefined?

+ Do the current processes sync with the company's long-term goals?

+ If we started over from scratch, would we still use the existing processes?

Common guiding principles for the stages of BPR are as follows:

"BPR Step 0: Preparation and Coordination

Although all the steps in a BPR plan are important to a successful product, you will have the best chance for success when you properly lay the foundation. The company vision and mission statements should already be developed, and you should have an idea of where the current processes fall short of meeting customer needs.

"BPR Step 1: Set the Vision

Companies must be clear on why they want or need to reengineer their processes and why they aren't where they have to be. A business-needs analysis could help start the process and convince stakeholders with clearly defined and measurable objectives. The organization must understand that their current processes require changes and invest in a vision for the future. Understanding the reasons are critical because they ensure employee buy-in. Otherwise, the employees may feel that their work life is threatened. They may obstruct the change, especially the necessary radical alterations that come with BPR. Since absolute support is critical, a clear vision of the intended consequences can give the employees a goal to rally.

Another option is to design an organizational learning agenda, which is a set of questions that your project team develops ahead of the project plan. They help identify what your company needs to learn before the start of the decision-making phase, especially when you have a very large agency or a project that cuts across many departments.

"BPR Step 2: Assemble the Team

Next, the company gathers a team that can consist of internal employees, consultants, or a mix of to conduct the reengineering. Depending on the project scope, the business should consider these factors choosing a team:

+ Should an initial team consider the reengineering?
+ Should the team be responsible for the BPR in its entirety?
+ What experience and background should team members have with respect to the company or the field?
+ Should the team be a smaller core group or a larger contributor group?
+ How much autonomy does the team have with decisions?
+ Should the team include members outside of the company?

Hammer and Champy discuss five specific roles that should comprise the BPR team: the leader, the process owner, the reengineering team, the steering committee, and the reengineering czar. They cite that the core

176

reengineering team ideally includes five to 10 people. A truly effective BPR team has representatives from each group:

+ Top management
+ The area that the process addresses
+ Information technology
+ Finance
+ End process users' group

Your BPR team should be diverse and include members that could add value with their contextual knowledge. These members may not be obvious choices, but consider them for their objectivity and expertise:

+ Staff who do not know the process at all
+ Staff who are experts in the process
+ Customers
+ Staff from the affected department
+ Technology experts
+ External professionals

An effective BPR team is competent, motivated, credible within the company, empowered, well-led, organized, and complementary in its composition, and it has specific goals.

"BPR Step 3: Determine the Processes

This portion of BPR requires a comprehensive study of the company itself, looking at its mission, goals, the needs of its customers, and how the company is meeting those demands. Through this lens, the team reviews and analyzes current performance of the processes, rooting out weaknesses and non-value-add tasks, while asking what each process is trying to accomplish. It is imperative at this step to choose which process(es) to initially evaluate, starting with a small amount so as not to overwhelm the company. Hammer and Champy discourage *benchmarking* — measuring your company's performance against similar but best-in-class companies — because it can restrict innovative thinking.

"BPR Step 4: Redesign

This is the portion of BPR where the team gets to flex its creative muscle and craft the main principles that will be applied to the reengineering effort. These include figuring out what biases and assumptions that the team works under and looking for opportunities to integrate technology. Team members should remember that they are not only making the old processes better, but completely redesigning how they are performed. Also, no specific rules govern the redesign.

Consider using a process analysis checklist to identify efficiencies and inefficiencies in existing process maps. This helps get the process reviewers to think about the questions they need to ask of each process. For a BPR project, the process analysis checklist would look for ways to:

- ✦ Reduce the number of handoffs
- ✦ Centralize the data
- ✦ Decrease the number of delays
- ✦ Release resources quicker
- ✦ Combine related activities

"BPR Step 5: Include the Whole Company

Companies should remember that BPR does not work well if it is done in a bubble. Not only should companies get employee feedback, but they should also review the other portions of the company that will evolve because of the changes. The company is managing change, thus ensuring maximum benefits and minimal negative impact. This may include organizational and management structures, as well as logistics, operations, customer case managers, production, manufacturing, corporate, and different management levels. Experts in reengineering techniques can help design ways to communicate with a variety of project stakeholders. Further, continued communication about the reengineering process itself, the results, and the employees' part in it is essential and empowers the workers. Reinforcing the reengineering method through performance incentives keeps them positive and engaged" (Smartsheet, 2021).

Introduction

Nothing is so painful to the human mind as a great and sudden change. – **Mary Wollstonecraft Shelley**

The final implementation phase is to create a 3 to 5-year strategic plan with commensurate multi-year budgets. The multi-year budget is often overlooked in many organizational change programs. They assume that an annual budget is all that is reasonable, and even practical. But the multi-year budget is important because not everything can be accomplished in a one-year period. Also, much of today's financing is done through multi-year instruments, which end up in the year-to-year budget ledgers. It is no different that preparing the household monthly budget factoring in the 30-year home mortgage payment and the 60-month car loan.

8.1 Cultural Change

Cultural change is a fundamental change in the way you function and do business. It is much like brain transplant – easier said than done. Culture is really the heart and soul of the organization. It is as close to being the "brand" as anything else. There have been some cases where the culture of the organization was so toxic, so dysfunctional that the organization had to been dismantled. This extreme form of cultural change has occurred in some inner-city schools where the teaching culture is deemed unsavable.

In recent years, attempts to turn around failing schools are most closely linked to the Obama Administration's supercharged School Improvement Grant (SIG) program. Between 2010 and 2015, the federal government spent $7 billion in efforts to turnaround low-performing schools. In exchange for these funds, grantee schools pledged to implement prescribed interventions, such as replacing personnel or changing instructional practices. However, some political pundits have called for school closure instead of throwing more money at them. In the case of for-profit and nonprofit organizations, shutting down some dysfunctional units might be advisable. However, shutting down the entire organization is more problematic.

The most common solution is to replace some or all of top management. In the private sector, this is usually accomplished by replacing the CEO and his immediate management team. This is less of an option in the nonprofit sector because the top position is usually the founder.

According to David Shedd, in Wharton Magazine (2011), the nine keys to cultural change are:

"1. Clearly Define the Culture: Define the new culture clearly, fully explaining the attributes of the culture and the acceptable behavior in the new culture.

"2. Over Communicate: Through teaching and training, communicate your picture of the new culture and the required change in values and goals. Communicate repeatedly; however, many times you speak about the new culture, some team member will be hearing and understanding it for the first time.

"3. Leadership Example: As the leader, embody the new culture in your actions, words, and behaviors. Anything less will be perceived as hypocrisy and a lack of commitment to the cultural change. If you want to create an improved customer service mindset, then be customer-oriented and customer-focused yourself.

"4. Relentless Follow-up: Continue with relentless and ongoing follow-up, support and encouragement. Start every meeting discussing the progress towards the new culture. When managing by walking around, clarify and confirm with employees their understanding of the new cultural mindset.

"5. Create Conditions to Align with Culture: Change the physical environment to reflect and allow for the acceptance of the new culture. If teamwork is the theme, re-arrange the office to induce better teamwork; if safety is the theme, spend the money to make the physical conditions in the office, the factory or the service vehicles safe. Likewise, align the incentives to match the culture.

"6. Share Good and Bad Examples: Share the success stories about individuals or teams that have fully embraced the new culture. Also, share the failures; describe the times when you or others did not live up to the new values and goals.

"7. Involve the Individual: Involve the employees, encouraging their new ideas and putting them into practice. When appropriate, have individual employees teach and/or evaluate each other. Any involvement of the individual employee gives them a stake in realizing the cultural change. Ken Blanchard says it well:

People often resent change when they have no involvement in how it should be implemented. So, contrary to popular belief, people do not resist change, they resist being controlled.

"8. Accountability: There needs to be accountability. Expel those employees who do not accept the new cultural values and goals. Since they do not fit with the new culture, they will just be an impediment to the full implementation of the culture.

"9. Patience and Persistence: Changing the culture involves changing the mindset and instincts of each person in the company. This does not happen overnight. So, patience and persistence are necessary for continuing down the path for the one to three years usually required" (Shedd, 2011).

STEP 8.0 MANAGE CHANGE/RESTRUCTURING

8.2 STRATEGIC PLANNING

Introduction

You may or may not already have a strategic plan in place. So, it may not be necessary to replace it. However, if you do have one, then you may want to revisit its structure and utility based on the discussion here. If nothing else, you need to incorporate the change being made into the plan.

A strategic plan helps you accomplish several things. First, it is essentially your short-term business plan. By Short-term means your annual budget. Long-term means 3 to 5-years. It really is impossible to see out further than that in today's quickly changing landscape of Internal Change Impacts and External Change Impacts (see Chapter 1). Second, it allows you to spread out your activities over time. You simply don't have the time or resources to do everything at once. Many activities need to occur in phases and that linear progression takes time. Finally, the strategic plan needs to be revisited at least annually. I say "at least" because you can really revisit anytime you need to.

The strategic plan needs a shadow document which is a multi-year budget. You already have your annual budget process. However, the staging of activities needs a corollary

> "Strategic planning is an organizational management activity that is used to set priorities, focus energy and resources, strengthen operations, ensure that employees and other stakeholders are working toward common goals, establish agreement around intended outcomes/results, and assess and adjust the organization's direction in response to a changing environment. It is a disciplined effort that produces fundamental decisions and actions that shape and guide what an organization is, who it serves, what it does, and why it does it, with a focus on the future. Effective strategic planning articulates not only where an organization is going and the actions needed to make progress, but also how it will know if it is successful."
>
> – Balanced Scorecard Institute

financing mechanism. You may have an ongoing stream of financing in place. But you may also envision further alternative financing in the future. You also are faced with the reality of having more activities now than you have financial resources now. Short of finding the additional financing, you just have to wait for it to happen.

When you revisit your strategic plan is a matter of the nature of your business. In the private sector the implementation of the plan is tied to the calendar year for tax purposes. So, if the first year of the reoccurring plan starts on January 1st, then revisit the plan roughly 3 months prior that date or say early October. In the public-sector the budget cycle is different and divided into two groups. The first are state and local government agencies (e.g., city and county). These budgets cycles start on July 1st and end on June 30th of the following year. The federal budget cycle starts on October 1st and ends on September 30th of the following year. If you are a private sector firm with a preponderance of federal or state contracts, then your planning cycle may become bifurcated in order to remain cognizant of their budget cycles and your tax cycle. Many private sector firms are essentially sub-contractors to government agencies and as such have to adjust to the government budget cycles.

The strategic planning process needs one person to own it. In a large organization it is possible to have one or more persons do this. If you are large enough, then you may even have the luxury of creating a strategic planning group or unit. The strategic planning point person or group then in turn has an established strategic planning committee that involves people from working units in the organization. In a small organization it becomes the duty of the CEO or COO to take on this task. If you are a small mom and pop shop, then mom or pop needs to take on this task. The bottom line is you need to have a strategic plan to guide the future of your organization and a person who is accountable to make it happen.

I have observed numerous strategic planning sessions. Quite frankly many of them were a pointless exercise. Many organizations hire a facilitator to walk the leadership through what is an organizational annual goal setting process. I don't have a problem with this step, but it is often a very shallow exercise in futility. The process of revisiting your mission, vision, goals, objectives and task activities needs to be a serious, comprehensive look at that entire linkage. Are each of these still valid? The strategic planning process needs to be made real by assigning each *task* or *activity* to a *specific person* who is accountable to a *timetable* with *deliverables* and appropriate *resources*.

Four final notes. (1) It is imperative that you hire an outside facilitator to take you through this process. Anyone drawn from within the organization will be seen to have some form of bias or allegiance. This facilitator will not and cannot contribute to the strategic plan creation. Their job is to facilitate its creation. It would be worthwhile to create a job description and shop that. Hopefully, you will find someone with experience in strategic planning facilitation. (2) Think about who should participate from staff. The top leadership team must participate. Also consider including the lead managers of any specific divisions or groups within the organization. (3) Another item is about how long the strategic planning event should be. It can't be done as a one-time morning, afternoon or evening event. It will take at least 1-2 full days. (4) Finally, it is best to hold the planning session offsite. This will stop staff from running back and forth to take care of business in their office. The rule is no one leaves, and no cell phone calls except on breaks and before or after lunch – not during lunch. You hold the event from 9:00 AM to 4:00 PM. This gives participants additional time to communicate with their home groups in the morning and afternoon. This schedule and requirements should be in writing and in advance of the strategic planning event.

Strategic Planning Model

One would think that there would be dozens of great strategic planning models to choose from. At least that's what I thought. I was amazed at what I didn't find. I could not find a straightforward strategic planning model. What I found through my literature review was that authors would either give several models to choose from or present a model with no real identifiable progression. I am sure you have seen the models with arrows going up, down, left, right, and in a circle. I could not believe that anyone could not provide me with a coherent, logical, start to finish model. One publication that did have a fairly coherent approach was "Strategic Planning for Dummies." I could buy a used copy for $4.19 from

Thriftbooks.com. Truthfully, I would be embarrassed to present a model with that citation. So, I decided that I would create my own model. My model has five Steps: 1. Formation, 2. Information, 3. Communication, 4. Implementation, and 5. Evaluation.

Strategic planning team. Take some time to consider who should participate in the creation of the Strategic Plan and how they participate. There should be a core leadership team that works on Steps 1-3, and 5. However, Step 4. Implementation needs to be divided up between individual work groups/divisions that encompass all of the organization's employees. This is critical to achieving organizational change management "buy-in." People who help craft the Strategic Plan have reason to "buy-in" to the plan.

Step 1. Formation. Strategic planning begins with the process of establishing the direction of the organization, of both where you are and where you want to go. The purpose of goal setting is to clarify the vision for your business. This stage consists of identifying three key facets: Define the short- and long-term objectives. Identify the process of how to accomplish your objectives. Your goals need to be detailed, realistic and match the values of your vision.

+ **Vision statement. A vision statement is brief and speaks to what an organization wants to ultimately become in the long-term.** This is the statement(s) that describes why the organization exists, i.e., its basic purpose. Describe what your company stands for and aims to be. Visioning is intentionally the first step and a goal-setting strategy used in strategic planning. You need to articulate a vision for the future and the outcomes you would like to achieve.

+ **Mission statement.** The mission statement is brief and speaks to what the immediate, present-day organization is about. What do you do? Whom do you serve? How do you serve them? **A mission statement focuses on today and what an organization does to achieve it.** It is similar to a vision statement but includes more specific details and actions. It details what your company is about, what it does and explains to stakeholders why the organization exists. It is also important to consider how you reinforce and reward positive performance, and how you prevent and penalize negative performance. The latter could be withholding the rewards.

+ **Values.** These describe the way you want your organization to behave in order to achieve your Vision. Explain what your business stands for. Values embody and explain the culture of your organization. Values also explain the ethics you wish to embrace. For example, you can provide financial incentives to a private sector stakeholder. But you should not do this with a public-sector stakeholder.

+ **Goals.** Goals clarify the vision. Goals are the **outcome** you intend to achieve, whereas objectives are the **actions** that help you achieve a goal.

+ **Objectives.** Strategic objectives define the short-term and long-term (3-5 year) actions you want to achieve.

+ **Action Items.** These are specific things done to achieve the Objectives. Develop **action plans for each Action Item. Also, assign each action item to a person who is wholly accountable for managing the action item. Also, action items must have sufficient resources to accomplish them. They also must be performance measurable.**

+ **Strategies.** These facilitate and support the mission. Strategies are the "how to accomplish" each goal. Determine what resources the organization has to reach the goals and objectives. The first step in forming a strategy is to review the information from the analysis. Determine what resources the organization has that can help support the goals and objectives. Identify areas where the organization needs to seek external resources.

Step 2. Information. Analysis is a key stage because the information gained in this stage will shape the next stages. In this stage, gather as much information and data relevant to accomplishing your vision. The focus of the analysis should be on **understanding the needs of the business** as a sustainable entity, its strategic direction and identifying initiatives that will help your organization grow. Examine any external or internal issues that can affect your goals and objectives. Make sure to identify both the strengths and weaknesses of your organization as well as any threats and opportunities that may arise along the path.

SWOT Analysis. Use SWOTs to help identify possible strategies by identifying and building on the Strengths, resolving Weaknesses, exploiting Opportunities and avoiding or mitigating Threats (Figure 8.1).

+ Strengths. Perform internal organizational internal audit to identify key strengths. These are the internal advantages of the organization that encourage the success of the mission and vision.

+ Weaknesses. Perform internal organizational internal audit to identify key weaknesses. These are internal factors that inhibit the success of the mission and vision.

+ Opportunities. Perform external environmental audit to identify key opportunities. These are the external variables an organization should capitalize on to achieve the mission and vision.

+ Threats. Perform external environmental audit to identify key threats (see STEPPE/PORTEF in Chapter 5). These are the external variables an organization should minimize or eliminate in order to achieve the mission and vision.

S	W	O	T
Strength (Internal)	Weakness (Internal)	Opportunity (External)	Threat (External)
Physical Layout/Assets	Physical Layout/Assets	Socio-Cultural	Socio-Cultural
Organizational Culture	Organizational Culture	Technological	Technological
Rules/Procedures/Processes	Rules/Procedures Processes	Economic	Economic
Technologies and Tools	Technologies and Tools	Political	Political
Employee Resources	Employee Resources	Pandemic	Pandemic
Financial Resources	Financial Resources	Environmental	Environmental

Figure 8.1 SWOT Analysis

Step 3. Communication. After the plan has been developed, it must be shared and communicated clearly, convincingly, and consistently. This is the primary responsibility of the leader, but there must also be a key person or persons within the organization who will communicate the essential plan with internal and external stakeholders. The message is developed and embodied in the Communication Plan.

The Communication Plan is a vehicle used to announce the Strategic Plan process at the beginning and to share the outcome of the process at the end. It is imperative that everyone in the organization feels they are an informed participant in the exercise. Communication is one aspect of creating employee "buy-in" to the organizational change management process.

It is also important to include messaging to external stakeholders who were not part of the process. Achieving change is important as both real change and perceived change. Make sure that external stake holders are aware of any changes that will affect them directly or indirectly. The more directly the external stakeholder is impacted, the more you should consider including them in the strategic planning process.

Step. 4 Implementation. Successful strategy implementation is critical to the success of the organization. This is the action stage of the strategic management process. Everyone within the organization must understand their responsibilities and duties, and how their role fits in with the strategy. Resources for the strategic plan must be in place at this point. Once the funding is in place and the employees are ready, execute the plan. Establish both establish both short-term, Annual Objectives and Long-Term Multi-Year Objectives.

Implementation is managed through the development of an Annual Action Plan. This is a step-by-step plan for implementing the Strategic Plan. Annual Action Plans are prepared for the annual short-term. One major function of the Annual Action Plan is to allocate resources for getting the plan implemented. If resources are not available or there is an excess of resources, then the Strategic Plan should be re-evaluated. Annual Action Plans need to cover the functional areas which are required for implementation. Each functional area will submit detailed budgets and plans for inclusion within the Annual Action Plan.

Sample Annual Action Plan Outline
Vision
Mission (Fiscal Year)
    Goal 1 – Technology Upgrades
        Objective 1.1
            Action 1.1.1 (Purpose, Person, Schedule, Resources, Budget)
            Action 1.1.2 (Purpose, Person, Schedule, Resources, Budget)
        Objective 1.2
            Action 1.2.1 (Purpose, Person, Schedule, Resources, Budget)
            Action 1.2.2 (Purpose, Person, Schedule, Resources, Budget)
    Goal 2 – Human Resources Reclassification
        Objective 2.1
            Action 2.1.1 (Purpose, Person, Schedule, Resources, Budget)
            Action 2.1.2 (Purpose, Person, Schedule, Resources, Budget)
        Objective 2.2
            Action 2.2.1 (Purpose, Person, Schedule, Resources, Budget)
            Action 2.2.2 (Purpose, Person, Schedule, Resources, Budget)
    Goal 3 – Facilities Expansion/Upgrades
        Objective 3.1
            Action 3.1.1 (Purpose, Person, Schedule, Resources, Budget)
            Action 3.1.2 (Purpose, Person, Schedule, Resources, Budget)
        Objective 3.2
            Action 3.2.1 (Purpose, Person, Schedule, Resources, Budget)
            Action 3.2.2 (Purpose, Person, Schedule, Resources, Budget)

Figure 8.2

Step 5. Evaluation. Strategy evaluation includes performance measurements of the goals, objectives and actions. Any successful evaluation of the strategy begins with defining the parameters to be measured. Monitoring internal and external issues will enable you to react to any change in your operating environment.

You should review your strategic plan every year. When you review your strategic plan, you're looking at the vision, mission, goals and objectives and checking to see where your organization stands in relation to them. What you thought would be opportunities and threats to your organization a year ago may not be the same.

Don't spend the time creating a strategic plan and then put it on the shelf to collect dust. Live by it. And regularly update your strategic plan. Successful implementation requires monitoring the progress of Action steps within the Annual Action Plan. Evaluation should be done on a regular basis (i.e., daily, weekly, monthly, quarterly, annually) depending on the activity with an emphasis on the following (Figure 8.2):

+ How much progress has been made in accomplishing the Actions?

+ What prevents you from moving forward?

+ Is there a need to go back and revise the strategic objectives?

+ What adjustments need to be made to the Annual Action Plan?

8.3 TAKING ACTION

A strategic plan outlines of who will do what, when and how. However, the how is an important variable in the success of the implementation. Up to now, I have taken you through creating the problem statement, the diagnosis of the problem and the strategic planning to solve the problem. But now it's time to implement the solution.

There are reams of published methods on implementation. It would take another literature search and meta-analysis to provide you with a best management practice for the implementation. Instead, I am going to give you what think is a practical, tried and true methodology. That is project management using the critical path method.

"The critical path method (CPM), also known as critical path analysis (CPA), is a scheduling procedure that uses a network diagram to depict a project and the sequences of tasks required to complete it, which are known as paths. Once the paths are defined, the duration of each path is calculated by an algorithm to identify the critical path, which determines the total duration of the project.

"The critical path method (CPM) is used in project management to create project schedules and helps project managers create a timeline for the project. The critical path method includes:

+ Identifying every task necessary to complete the project and the dependencies between them

+ Estimating the duration of the project tasks

+ Calculating the critical path based on the tasks' duration and dependencies to identify the critical activities

+ Focusing on planning, scheduling and controlling critical activities

+ Setting project milestones and deliverables

+ Setting stakeholder expectations related to deadlines

"After making these considerations, you gain insight into which activities must be prioritized. Then, you can allocate the necessary resources to get these important tasks done. Tasks you discover that aren't on the critical path are of a lesser priority in your project plan, and can be delayed if they're causing the project team to become overallocated.

"Projects are made up of tasks that have to adhere to a schedule in order to meet a deadline. It sounds simple, but without mapping the work it can quickly get out of hand and you'll find your project off track.

"When you're analyzing the critical path, you're looking closely at the time it will take to complete each task, taking into account the task dependencies and how they'll impact your schedule. It's a technique to find the most realistic project deadline. It can also help during the project as a metric to track your progress.

"Therefore, when you're doing critical path analysis, you're finding the sequence of tasks that are both important and dependent on a previous task. Less important tasks aren't ignored and are part of the analysis; however, they're the ones you know can be jettisoned if time and money won't permit" (ProjectManager, 2021).

Introduction

Mistakes are the portals of discovery. – James Joyce

The process of locking in organizational change is a matter of training (executive, employee, cross-functional, customer service, team), which is embedded in a procedures manual, then applied with performance measurements, with an appraisal system, and with total quality management. The organizational change is locked in at the time of implementation, but organizational change is an iterative process over time. Organizational change is implemented and revisited through a 3 to 5-year strategic plan. The plan itself can be revised on an annual basis in terms of making minor adjustments.

9.1 CARROT AND STICK

What is motivation?

Carrot and stick motivation are a motivational approach that involves offering a "carrot" (a reward—for good behavior) and a "stick" (a negative consequence for poor behavior). It motivates staff by creating actionable goals and desirable rewards for employees who can alter their behavior and performance. It is a simple and effective form of feedback for employees.

The carrot and stick theory can be applied effectively in the workplace with a reward and consequence system as motivational tools for staff members. Using the carrot and stick approach in the workplace can be an effective form of extrinsic motivation. Set the goal you would like your employees to achieve, then create a carrot and a stick related to that goal.

For example, if you want your sales team to sign contracts with five new clients per month, you need a reward for those who do so and a consequence for those who don't. Your reward could be an increased commission on those five sales, and the consequence could be taking a percentage off of the commission of the employee with the lowest number of new clients that month.

The carrot and stick approach can work very well to modify the behavior of your employees, guiding them to avoid the actions that are punishable and engage in the actions that will earn rewards. As long as your reward is attractive enough and your consequence is undesirable, this method can help motivate employees to achieve your preferred outcomes.

"How to implement a carrot and stick policy

Use these steps to begin a carrot and stick motivational policy for your team:

1. Set a goal.
2. Create an incentive.

3. Decide who should receive the carrot.

4. Outline a consequence.

5. Decide who should receive the stick.

6. Choose your carrot and stick policy carefully.

"1. Set a goal

When you first implement a carrot and stick policy, you need to set a goal for your employees. It should be measurable and achievable within a deadline. You need to be specific about what you want your staff to accomplish and have a date by which you expect the goal to be achieved.

By beginning with a series of small, attainable goals, your employees are more likely to reach your desired objectives and earn their rewards. It is important to begin with small goals that you are confident your staff will be able to achieve. This will make it easier to implement your carrot and stick policy.

Your objective should be a goal that can be measured, such as a certain production output, a sales total or another common metric used by your employees. Opt for a goal such as 'Increase sales by 5% by the end of this quarter' instead of simply setting the goal to 'Increase sales.

"2. Create an incentive

The key to the carrot and stick approach is using an incentive that interests or appeals to employees. Decide on a reward you can offer for reaching the goal. There are four general types of rewards you could give your staff members:

+ Compensation

+ Benefits

+ Recognition

+ Appreciation

Choose a reward that you believe your employees would want to receive. In a large company, a company-wide email recognizing the employees who achieved the objective could be a highly sought-after reward. For a small startup with only a few employees who often work closely together, company-wide recognition might not be as attractive as a reward, and a small stipend or gift might be more appreciated. Consider what might be valuable to your employees, and use your company culture and structure to help you determine potential rewards.

If you notice that not many employees can reach your goal, try offering a different reward to see if that helps with motivation. Alter your rewards as needed by choosing a new reward if there doesn't seem to be enough interest, or by creating larger rewards for bigger, more challenging goals.

"3. Decide who is eligible to receive the carrot

You will also need to decide who is eligible for the reward and clearly outline any qualifications to all employees. If everyone surpasses your goal, you may decide to give a small reward to each employee. Alternatively, you could choose to give a larger reward to the employee who performed the best. For example, if you have set a sales goal for your employees and they reach the goal, you could give everyone a small reward such as a staff party or a catered lunch or choose to reward the top employee with a larger personal prize, such as a monetary bonus.

"4. Outline a consequence

Choose a consequence for employees who do not meet the stated goal or have the lowest performance, and clearly communicate it. When your staff reaches its goals and you consistently follow through on providing the "carrot," your staff members will be more inclined to believe that you will also follow through on the "stick" as well. Once they see that you are serious about your carrot and stick motivation policy, they will be more motivated to avoid the punishment and receive the reward.

"5. Decide who is eligible to receive the stick

Just like with the incentive, you will need to decide who receives a consequence. You could choose a small punishment for those who were unable to reach your goal, or you could have a more serious punishment for the employee who performed the worst at the task.

For example, if your goal is to reach a certain production output and only half of your employees can reach that goal, you could choose to have the employees who failed assist with inventory, or you could select the employee with the lowest output and give them the responsibility of tidying up the break room for the next two weeks.

"6. Choose your carrot and stick policy carefully

If you choose to reward all staff members who can reach or surpass your goal, then your consequence should be applied only to the employee with the worst performance. Similarly, if you are singling out the employee who performed the best, apply a small punishment to all who were unable to reach your goal. This can help you avoid dividing your employees into those who got a small reward and those who got a small punishment.

You should unify your staff in achieving the goals you set out, while still allowing for them to compete. If everyone either gets a reward or a punishment, there will be little motivation to surpass the goal or avoid group punishment. Instead, single out either the employee with the best performance or the worst performance to motivate staff to be the one who avoids the stick and receives the carrot.

"Carrot and stick examples

Using rewards and consequences that employees are actually motivated by is the key to having the carrot and stick approach work successfully. If you offer a reward that nobody desires or a consequence that no one minds, employees will not have a reason to work toward achieving the goals you set.

Examples of rewards for staff members include:

+ Taking the employee out for dinner or buying a group lunch

+ Allowing them to work from home for a pre-arranged length of time

+ Gifting a personalized mug, water bottle or another frequently used item

+ Adding a bonus to their next paycheck

- Upgrading their desk, office chair or another piece of equipment that is used daily
- Going out for a group activity
- Giving paid time off
- Publicly thanking the employee(s), either in a company-wide email, in-person or with a hand-written note
- Giving a gift card to a service, subscription or activity that the employee would be interested in
- Increasing their sales commission

Your company culture can help determine what rewards will be the most desirable. If your team values health and wellness, for example, consider a spa day, a gym membership or a massage.

Be sure to keep your carrot and your stick balanced. Obtaining the reward should be just as motivating as avoiding the punishment. You need both in place to inspire your staff members to shape their behavior and achieve the goals you have set.

The possible consequences that could be used in a carrot and stick approach will vary widely based on the job. Here are some examples:

- Loss of a portion of the employee's commission
- Having to work an unfavorable shift
- Missing out on a company-wide reward
- Having to complete a disliked task, such as assisting with inventory or cleaning the break room" (Indeed, 2020).

9.2 EXECUTIVE LEADERSHIP TRAINING

The first level of organizational change management training starts at the top with the executive team. Training includes understanding the change in question, being able to communicate the need for the change, and the individualized training on how to implement the change. The executive team needs to embrace the change process with a deep understanding of the need for it.

"Dynamic leadership comes from a combination of the right personal qualities **and** the right leadership training. Leadership training allows organizations to nurture and cultivate the managers, motivators, and big thinkers who will carry the organization into the future.
"Training in effective supervisory skills arms your current and future team members to:

+ **Increase productivity:** To motivate your people to do their best, you have to understand them. Leadership training fosters empathy and emotional intelligence and helps leaders assess what a teammate needs to succeed and then give it to them.

+ **Retain employees:** Most people quit bosses, not jobs. When employees feel like they are being guided in the right direction, they happily stay engaged. This saves organizations a fortune in turnover costs.

+ **Improve decision-making:** Strategic vision is learned, not born. With leadership training, the people you put in charge can better manage risk and see projects through to the end.

+ **Implement the best leadership style:** There is more than one way to steer a ship. Leadership training helps identify the right *kind* of leadership for your organization. It also teaches how to know when to try a different approach.

+ **Support succession:** Eventually, even top directors move on to their next phase in career and life. The longevity of your organization depends on cultivating the talent that will take over.

"Without leadership training, the loudest voices and flashiest personalities tend to get put in charge. These people tend to talk a good game but ultimately lack leadership and management skills.

"With leadership training, you can identify the people with leadership potential and prepare them for the kind of success that lifts up *everyone* including the team, the customer, and the organization as a whole.

"10 Leadership Training Topics

Leadership training is an ongoing process, with enough leadership meeting topics to keep employees busy for months or even years. A list of leadership topics for discussion might include:

"Leadership Topics for Managers

1. **Delegation & empowerment:** No leader can do everything themselves. Understanding when to delegate, and then standing by your delegation, is one of the most critical executive leadership training topics.
    Subtopics to Consider: Defining and clearly communicating tasks, selecting the right employee or team, agreeing on objectives and resources, setting deadlines, and supporting the assignee's work.

2. **Conflict resolution:** Organizations are made up of people, and people come into conflict. Learning to resolve conflict in a way that honors both sides belong to every management training topic list.
    Subtopics: Clarify disagreements, establish common goals, identify and circumvent barriers to teamwork, and build consensus around a resolution.

3. **Change management.** An organization's staying power depends on its managers' ability to cope with and communicate change.

Subtopics: Lead with the culture, starting at the top and involving every layer, make the emotional and rational case for change, leverage formal and informal solutions, and engage, adapt, and assess.

4. **Influence.** Why do some people command respect without ever giving commands?
   Subtopics: Belief in your team, servant leadership, giving and earning trust, investing in others, autonomy, and leading with character.

5. **Motivation and engagement.** People aren't machines. Understand what motivates them, and they can exceed your wildest expectations.
   Subtopics: Fostering a pleasant working environment, encouraging happiness, setting clear goals, micromanaging, collaboration, and self-development.

"Leadership Training Topics for Employees

6. **Interpersonal relationships:** Businesses are not built on technology; they are built on relationships. Train leaders to cultivate relationships with others on their team and across departments.
   Subtopics: Cultivating a positive outlook, managing emotions, Active listening, and empathy.

7. **Decision skills:** Employees' ability to make the right decision and stand by it nurtures confidence and streamlines the whole organization.
   Subtopics: Understanding reactions and tolerances, first principles, risk-taking, and leverage the perspective of others.

8. **Time and energy management:** Many distractions vie for managers' time and tend to sap the energy the fuels productivity in the time they have. Therefore, effective leadership training includes tips and tips for time and energy management.
   Subtopics: Distractions, Organization, and open-mindedness.

9. **Self-awareness:** Before leaders can manage others, they must effectively manage ourselves. Self-awareness training asks leaders to self-reflect on their emotions, strengths, and weaknesses. **Subtopics:** Feeling feelings, giving and receiving feedback, keeping an open mind, and mindfulness.

10. **Communication skills:** Mistrust springs from misunderstanding. Effective communication is critical to effective leadership. **Subtopics:** Establishing trust, speaking with precision and clarity, using body language and tone, avoiding assumptions, and how to have difficult conversations.

"Your management team may brainstorm other leadership topics for presentation. These are also great training topics for managers and supervisors" (Lessonly, 2021).

9.3 EMPLOYEE TRAINING AND DEVELOPMENT

"Training and development describes the formal, ongoing efforts that are made within organizations to improve the performance and self-fulfillment of their employees through a variety of educational methods and programs. In the modern workplace, these efforts have taken on a broad range of applications—from instruction in highly specific job skills to long-term professional development. In recent years, training and development has emerged as a formal business function, an integral element of strategy, and a recognized profession with distinct theories and methodologies. More and more companies of all sizes have embraced 'continual learning' and other aspects of training and development as a means of promoting employee growth and acquiring a highly skilled work force. In fact, the quality of employees and the continual improvement of their skills and productivity through training, are now widely recognized as vital factors in ensuring the long-term success and profitability of small businesses. 'Create a corporate culture that supports continual learning,' counseled Charlene Marmer Solomon in *Workforce*. 'Employees today must have access to continual training of all types just to keep up. If you don't actively stride against the momentum of skills deficiency, you lose ground. If your workers stand still, your firm will lose the competency race.'

"For the most part, the terms 'training' and 'development' are used together to describe the overall improvement and education of an organization's employees. However, while closely related, there are important differences between the terms that center around the scope of the application. In general, training programs have very specific and quantifiable goals, like operating a particular piece of machinery, understanding a specific process, or performing certain procedures with great precision. Developmental programs, on the other hand, concentrate on broader skills that are applicable to a wider variety of situations, such as decision making, leadership skills, and goal setting.

"Training in Small Business

Implementation of formal training and development programs offers several potential advantages to small businesses. For example, training helps companies create pools of qualified replacements for employees who may leave or be promoted to positions of greater responsibility. It also helps ensure that companies will have the human resources needed to support business growth and expansion. Furthermore, training can enable a small business to make use of advanced technology and to adapt to a rapidly changing competitive environment. Finally, training can improve employees' efficiency and motivation, leading to gains in both productivity and job satisfaction. According to the U.S. Small Business Administration (SBA), small businesses stand to receive a variety of benefits from effective training and development of employees, including reduced turnover, a decreased need for supervision, increased efficiency, and improved employee morale. All of these benefits are likely to contribute directly to a small business's fundamental financial health and vitality.

"Effective training and development begin with the overall strategy and objectives of the small business. The entire training process should be planned in advance with specific company goals in mind. In developing a training strategy, it may be helpful to assess the company's customers and competitors, strengths and weaknesses, and any relevant industry or societal trends. The next step is to use this information to identify where training is needed by the organization as a whole or by individual employees. It may also be helpful to conduct an internal audit to find general areas that might benefit from training, or to complete a skills inventory to determine the types of skills employees possess and the types they may need in the future. Each different job within the company should be broken down on a task-by-task basis in order to help determine the content of the training program.

"The training program should relate not only to the specific needs identified through the company and individual assessments, but also to the overall goals of the company. The objectives of the training should be clearly outlined, specifying what behaviors or skills will be affected and how they relate to the strategic mission of the company. In addition, the objectives should include several intermediate steps or milestones in order to motivate the trainees and allow the company to evaluate their progress. Since training employees is expensive, a small business needs to give careful consideration to the question of which employees to train. This decision should be based on the ability of the employee to learn the material and the likelihood that they will be motivated by the training experience. If the chosen employees fail to benefit from the training program or leave the company soon after receiving training, the small business has wasted its limited training funds.

"The design of training programs is the core activity of the training and development function. In recent years, the development of training programs has evolved into a profession that utilizes systematic models, methods, and processes of instructional systems design (ISD). ISD describes the systematic design and development of instructional methods and materials to facilitate the process of training and development and ensure that training programs are necessary, valid, and effective. The instructional design process includes the collection of data on the tasks or skills to be learned or improved, the analysis of these skills and tasks, the development of methods and materials, delivery of the program, and finally the evaluation of the training's effectiveness.

"Small businesses tend to use two general types of training methods, on-the-job techniques and off-the-job techniques. On-the-job training describes a variety of methods that are applied while employees are actually performing their jobs. These methods might include orientations, coaching, apprenticeships, internships, job instruction training, and job rotation. The main advantages of on-the-job techniques is that they are highly practical, and employees do not lose working time while they are learning. Off-the-job training, on the other hand, describes a number of training methods that are delivered to employees outside of the regular work environment, though often during working hours. These techniques might include lectures, conferences, case studies, role playing, simulations, film or television presentations, programmed instruction, or special study.

"On-the-job training tends to be the responsibility of supervisors, human resources professionals, or more experienced co-workers.

Consequently, it is important for small businesses to educate their seasoned employees in training techniques. In contrast, off-the-job tends to be handled by outside instructors or sources, such as consultants, chambers of commerce, technical and vocational schools, or continuing education programs. Although outside sources are usually better informed as to effective training techniques than company supervisors, they may have a limited knowledge of the company's products and competitive situation. Another drawback to off-the-job training programs is their cost. These programs can run into the multi thousand dollar per participant level, a cost that may make them prohibitive for many small businesses.

"Actual administration of the training program involves choosing an appropriate location, providing necessary equipment, and arranging a convenient time. Such operational details, while seemingly minor components of an overall training effort, can have a significant effect on the success of a program. In addition, the training program should be evaluated at regular intervals while it is going on. Employees' skills should be compared to the predetermined goals or milestones of the training program, and any necessary adjustments should be made immediately. This ongoing evaluation process will help ensure that the training program successfully meets its expectations.

"Common Training Methods

While new techniques are under continuous development, several common training methods have proven highly effective. Good continuous learning and development initiatives often feature a combination of several different methods that, blended together, produce one effective training program.

"Orientations

Orientation training is vital in ensuring the success of new employees. Whether the training is conducted through an employee handbook, a lecture, or a one-on-one meeting with a supervisor, newcomers should receive information on the company's history and strategic position, the key people in authority at the company, the structure of their department and how it contributes to the mission of the company, and the company's employment policies, rules, and regulations.

"Lectures

A verbal method of presenting information, lectures are particularly useful in situations when the goal is to impart the same information to a large number of people at one time. Since they eliminate the need for individual training, lectures are among the most cost-effective training methods. But the lecture method does have some drawbacks. Since lectures primarily involve one-way communication, they may not provide the most interesting or effective training. In addition, it may be difficult for the trainer to gauge the level of understanding of the material within a large group.

"Case Study

The case method is a non-directed method of study whereby students are provided with practical case reports to analyze. The case report includes a thorough description of a simulated or real-life situation. By analyzing the problems presented in the case report and developing possible solutions, students can be encouraged to think independently as opposed to relying upon the direction of an instructor. Independent case analysis can be supplemented with open discussion with a group. The main benefit of the case method is its use of real-life situations. The multiplicity of problems and possible solutions provide the student with a practical learning experience rather than a collection of abstract knowledge and theories that may be difficult to apply to practical situations.

"Role Playing

In role playing, students assume a role outside of themselves and play out that role within a group. A facilitator creates a scenario that is to be acted out by the participants under the guidance of the facilitator. While the situation might be contrived, the interpersonal relations are genuine. Furthermore, participants receive immediate feedback from the facilitator and the scenario itself, allowing better understanding of their own behavior. This training method is cost effective and is often applied to marketing and management training.

"Simulations

Games and simulations are structured competitions and operational models that emulate real-life scenarios. The benefits of games and simulations include the improvement of problem-solving and decision-making skills, a greater understanding of the organizational whole, the ability to study actual problems, and the power to capture the student's interest.

"Computer-Based Training

Computer-based training (CBT) involves the use of computers and computer-based instructional materials as the primary medium of instruction. Computer-based training programs are designed to structure and present instructional materials and to facilitate the learning process for the student. A main benefit of CBT is that it allows employees to learn at their own pace, during convenient times. "Primary uses of CBT include instruction in computer hardware, software, and operational equipment. The last is of particular importance because CBT can provide the student with a simulated experience of operating a particular piece of equipment or machinery while eliminating the risk of damage to costly equipment by a trainee or even a novice user. At the same time, the actual equipment's operational use is maximized because it need not be utilized as a training tool. The use of computer-based training enables a small business to reduce training costs while improving the effectiveness of the training. Costs are reduced through a reduction in travel, training time, downtime for operational hardware, equipment damage, and instructors. Effectiveness is improved through standardization and individualization.

Web-based training (WBT) is an increasingly popular form of CBT. The greatly expanding number of organizations with Internet access through high-speed connections has made this form of CBT possible. By providing the training material on a Web page that is accessible through any Internet browser, CBT is within reach of any company with access to the Web. The terms 'online courses' and 'web-based instruction' are sometimes used interchangeably with WBT.

"Self-Instruction

Self-instruction describes a training method in which the students assume primary responsibility for their own learning. Unlike instructor- or facilitator-led instruction, students retain a greater degree of control regarding topics, the sequence of learning, and the pace of learning. Depending on the structure of the instructional materials, students can achieve a higher degree of customized learning. Forms of self-instruction include programmed learning, individualized instruction, personalized systems of instruction, learner-controlled instruction, and correspondence study. Benefits include a strong support system, immediate feedback, and systematization.

"Audiovisual Training

Audiovisual training methods include television, films, and videotapes. Like case studies, role playing, and simulations, they can be used to expose employees to 'real world' situations in a time-and cost-effective manner. The main drawback of audiovisual training methods is that they cannot be customized for a particular audience, and they do not allow participants to ask questions or interact during the presentation of material.

"Team-Building Exercises

Team building is the active creation and maintenance of effective work groups with similar goals and objectives. Not to be confused with the informal, ad-hoc formation and use of teams in the workplace, team building is a formal process of building work teams and formulating their objectives and goals, usually facilitated by a third-party consultant. Team building is commonly initiated to combat poor group dynamics, labor-management relations, quality, or productivity. By recognizing the problems and difficulties associated with the creation and development of work teams, team building provides a structured, guided process whose benefits include a greater ability to manage complex projects and processes, flexibility to respond to changing situations, and greater motivation among team members. Team building may include a broad range of different training methods, from outdoor immersion exercises to brainstorming sessions. The main drawback to formal team building is the cost of using outside experts and taking a group of people away from their work during the training program.

"Apprenticeships and Internships

Apprenticeships are a form of on-the-job training in which the trainee works with a more experienced employee for a period of time, learning a group of related skills that will eventually qualify the trainee to perform a new job or function. Apprenticeships are often used in production-oriented positions. Internships are a form of apprenticeship that combines on-the-job training under a more experienced employee with classroom learning.

"Job Rotation

Another type of experience-based training is job rotation, in which employees move through a series of jobs in order to gain a broad understanding of the requirements of each. Job rotation may be particularly useful in small businesses, which may feature less role specialization than is typically seen in larger organizations.

"Applications of Training Programs

While the applications of training and development are as various as the functions and skills required by an organization, several common training applications can be distinguished, including technical training, sales training, clerical training, computer training, communications training, organizational development, career development, supervisory development, and management development.

"Technical training describes a broad range of training programs varying greatly in application and difficulty. Technical training utilizes common training methods for instruction of technical concepts, factual information, and procedures, as well as technical processes and principles.

"Sales training concentrates on the education and training of individuals to communicate with customers in a persuasive manner. Sales training can enhance the employee's knowledge of the organization's products, improve his or her selling skills, instill positive attitudes, and increase the employee's self-confidence. Employees are taught to distinguish the needs and wants of the customer, and to persuasively communicate the message that the company's products or services can effectively satisfy them.

"Clerical training concentrates on the training of clerical and administrative support staff, which have taken on an expanded role in recent years. With the increasing reliance on computers and computer applications, clerical training must be careful to distinguish basic skills from the ever-changing computer applications used to support these skills. Clerical training increasingly must instill improved decision-making skills in these employees as they take on expanded roles and responsibilities.

"Computer training teaches the effective use of the computer and its software applications, and often must address the basic fear of technology that most employees face and identify and minimize any resistance to change that might emerge. Furthermore, computer training must anticipate and overcome the long and steep learning curves that many employees will experience. To do so, such training is usually offered in longer, uninterrupted modules to allow for greater concentration, and structured training is supplemented by hands-on practice. This area of training is commonly cited as vital to the fortunes of most companies, large and small, operating in today's technologically advanced economy.

"Communications training concentrates on the improvement of interpersonal communication skills, including writing, oral presentation, listening, and reading. In order to be successful, any form of communications training should be focused on the basic improvement of skills and not just on stylistic considerations. Furthermore, the training should serve to build on present skills rather than rebuilding from the ground up. Communications training can be taught separately or can be effectively integrated into other types of training, since it is fundamentally related to other disciplines.

"Organizational development (OD) refers to the use of knowledge and techniques from the behavioral sciences to analyze an existing organizational structure and implement changes in order to improve organizational effectiveness. OD is useful in such varied areas as the alignment of employee goals with those of the organization, communications, team functioning, and decision making. In short, it is a development process with an organizational focus to achieve the same goals as other training and development activities aimed at individuals. OD practitioners commonly practice what has been termed 'action research' to effect an orderly change which has been carefully planned to minimize the occurrence of unpredicted or unforeseen events. Action research refers to a systematic analysis of an organization to acquire a better understanding of the nature of problems and forces within it.

"Career development refers to the formal progression of an employee's position within an organization by providing a long-term development strategy and designing training programs to achieve this strategy as well as individual goals. Career development represents a growing concern for employee welfare and their long-term needs. For the individual, it involves the description of career goals, the assessment of necessary action, and the choice and implementation of necessary steps. For the organization, career development represents the systematic development and improvement of employees. To remain effective, career development programs must allow individuals to articulate their desires. At the same time, the organization strives to meet those stated needs as much as possible by consistently following through on commitments and meeting the employee expectations raised by the program.

"Management and supervisory development involve the training of managers and supervisors in basic leadership skills, enabling them to effectively function in their positions. For managers, training initiatives are focused on providing them with the tools to balance the effective management of their employee resources with the strategies and goals of the organization. Managers learn to develop their employees effectively by helping employees learn and change, as well as by identifying and preparing them for future responsibilities. Management development may also include programs for developing decision-making skills, creating and managing successful work teams, allocating resources effectively, budgeting, business planning, and goal setting" (INC., 2020).

9.4 Cross Functional Training

The traditional mass production model relies on specialization. However, a nimble and adaptive organization consists of people who can multi-task their job and that of other people. And it is also important that change embodies this philosophy. This is difficult to achieve in environments where there are unions who strive to make people's job descriptions very rigid. The refrain of "it's not my job" is exactly an example of the kind of inflexibility you need to overcome. The ability to do more than your personal job description is a kind of professional growth people should aspire to and not work to avoid.

"This is especially true for people who aspire to be managers. Managers must be able to manage a variety of people with different skill sets that the manager at a minimum understands. They need not be proficient in their employees' jobs. As a manager I managed people who were engineers. I did not have an engineering background, training or license. But I could read engineering plans and had learned the lexicon of the engineer so I could talk to them about any particular issue.

"A company's success is based on its performance, which is a factor of the kind of effort put in by its employees. It is a well-known fact that employee attrition or a poor-quality workforce can prove to be a major undoing for a company's efforts and could cost it a lot of money, time and other resources and also be the prime reasons for poor customer service and sub-standard products. In order to avoid these detrimental consequences, it is important for a company to train its staff and cross-functional training proves indispensable. Not only does cross-functional training increase efficiency in employees it also encourages professional development, team performance and overall cohesion in the workplace. At times, cross-functional training proves to be a more effective tool to enhance the company's productivity than any other method.

"While each employee is in their current role because they possess a particular skill set, cross-functional training provides them with additional skills and proficiency in roles that are outside of their core responsibilities and skill sets. *From a customer service perspective, for example, it would be required for the agents to also have product knowledge and some amount of trouble-shooting skills as well. They would be adept at marketing and selling also.* The purpose of cross-functional training in this case would ensure that the customer service agents are able to be more efficient when interacting with customers and be able to resolve the maximum number of queries at this level, thereby saving time and effort for the customer, raising their satisfaction and happiness levels and encouraging them to provide repeat business to the company.

"While running a business, one of the biggest hurdles to smooth processes and workflow often is absence of employees either due to illness or time off for other reasons. This becomes a huge problem during a critical project or a crucial time of the year for a company. At such times the benefits of cross-functional training can be truly appreciated. With suitably trained and multi-skilled staff work schedules will hardly ever go awry and neither would critical projects come to a standstill in the absence of a particular staff member. Lack of cross-functional training could lead to a shortfall of resources thereby drastically lowering the productivity levels of the company. Such training also raises the knowledge base and skill levels of all employees.

"We have earlier discussed that on-going training of employees is essential for any company and business. Through cross-functional training, employee morale gets a boost as they feel that they are being valued by the company by way of the investment being made to develop them professionally. Employees remain engaged and competitive and learn to appreciate the talents and skills of those they work with. Cross-functional training allows all employees to understand and appreciate the limitations and challenges of their co-workers thereby promoting a happy workplace with limited stress and conflicts.

"As competition increases and prices skyrocket, resources and manpower become scarce. All companies would benefit from having on their payroll, cross-trained employees. Irrespective of level or designation, the absence of any staff member can put a spoke in the smooth operations of the business. The situation can quickly turn grave and disastrous in case of extended absence or if people decide to quit for whatever reason. Rehiring or hiring temporary employees may not be ideal as they would take time to reach optimum efficiency or may not even have the required skill sets, knowledge base and attitude for the job.

"Cross-functional training significantly reduces recruitment costs and saves the company valuable time. If such training has been provided, any absences or vacancies can be immediately taken care of without worrying about productivity. Cross-functional training proves extremely useful in succession planning too – there would always be staff members ready and willing to take on new assignments and move into critical roles as soon as the need comes up. Of course, it does not imply that external hiring would never happen – however, the need would not be as much and as often. The existing employees would see the available opportunities within the company and be more willing to learn new skills and gain better and higher positions than leave to find other opportunities. Cross-functional training is also a major tool to attract some of the best talent present in the market as it provides a path for an individual's career growth.

"Cross-functional training promotes teamwork. When a team member is learning the complexities of another's role the person teaching becomes a mentor, guide and coach. This sort of 'support' promotes self-esteem and the overall quality of the jobs being performed. When employees join a company and stay with it for a long time, they not only expect monetary recognition but non-monetary appreciation – which is a great motivator. Cross-functional training and other kinds of training programs are great motivators – it lends a sense of security and faith for employees that their employer genuinely cares for them.

"Cross-functional training like all other training programs must have the required return on investment. There are definite costs for training programs and these costs must be offset by the results and benefits for each employee and the company as a whole. Cross-functional training also requires time and commitment and hence a company must weave it into the business plan, daily operations and overall culture of the company. As part of the strategy the company must also put in place incentive programs to encourage employees to take on new assignments and roles and also have a robust reward and recognition program for consistent and on-going efforts towards personal and professional development.

"Post training, it is necessary that, as all business strategies, the effects and benefits are measured. Measuring and monitoring will ensure that any deficiencies of the system will be removed and whatever is working well can be further improved. As programs get better and more employees get involved in the process of cross-functional training, the top management must be seen as providing complete support to the efforts. Cross-functional training commitment and investment also lets employees know that they have job security. They feel in control of their career and growth paths in the company and allow them to remain committed and engaged. They would also be more likely to provide creative and innovative ideas for improvement and be ready to do extra in order to achieve success for themselves and the company.

"While cross-functional training is not always easy to achieve given a number of challenges – employee resistance, compensation issues and other such obstacles – could inhibit the success of such an endeavor. One possible way could be to weave cross-functional training into the performance appraisal with clear guidelines as to its benefits and the kind of rewards and growth prospects that could come about. There must an incentive program and strategy that articulates what the employee can expect from the company if they are willing to expand their knowledge base and upgrade and add to their skills. This is a program that cannot be successful by coercion but will be highly efficacious when there is employee buy-in and a robust and well thought out strategy for its implementation" (Newman, 2015).

9.5 CUSTOMER SERVICE TRAINING

One of the basic tenets of retail is the 19th Century slogan, "The customer is always right." Coming from a public service background, I can tell you that this was a difficult sell to government employees who have a certain amount of personal entitlement invested in their power over the people they serve. I spent years training people to not say "No." This was especially true in the regulatory environment regarding property development. There was always an alternative path when it came to getting some particular permit approval. It might be horribly onerous, expensive, time consuming, with little chance of success. But it was a remotely possible alternative. If nothing else, I tried to train people to have some empathy for their customer wishes and desires.

Whatever the "change" you are creating or addressing, you need to train employees on how to implement it or deal with it. You might be able to use the same embedded teams who worked on managing and implementing the change in question.

"It's impossible for a business to place too much of an emphasis on its customers. If your customers are happy, your business will have a better chance of succeeding.

To make sure your business thrives, it's critical for you to guide your valuable customers through each stage of their journey with your company and help them get amazing results along the way.

However, keeping your customers happy isn't easy.

If you're going to keep your customers sweet, you'll need to build and nourish an amazing customer service team that works around the clock.

But are you investing in the right customer service training for your team?

In this post, we're going to guide you through the specifics of customer service training. To make you an expert in this subject, we'll cover the following:

1. The definition of customer service training
2. The main reasons to invest in customer service training
3. Tips for customer service training
4. Valuable materials for customer service training
5. Companies that excel at customer service training

Let's get started!

"What Is Customer Service Training?

As the name implies, customer service training is any type of activity aimed at teaching employees the knowledge, skills, or techniques they need to deliver effective and efficient customer service.

Customer service training comes in many shapes and sizes. Here are just some of the most common training methods:

+ In-person seminars and courses
+ Online interactive courses
+ Books and training materials
+ On-the-job mentorships

A range of factors will influence the training method you choose. Of course, the preferences of your team and your budget will be two of the most prominent.

"Why Should You Invest in Customer Service Training?

There are lots of reasons why it makes sense for your business to invest in customer service training. Here are the key rationales:

"Improved Customer Service Skills. The most obvious reason to invest in customer service training involves improving the customer service skills of your team members. This tactic will help make your customer service team more effective and efficient. And it will improve their productivity, as well as the results they're able to achieve for your customers.

"**More Engaged Employees.** Benefits of employee engagement are clear. If you're going to hold onto the best performers in your business, it's critical for you to make sure they're engaged and satisfied. One great way to boost employee satisfaction within your team is to invest in high-quality training. This tactic will show your team members that you care about their development and that you want to empower them to succeed.

"**Increased Customer Satisfaction.** With more skilled and motivated customer service team members, you're going to experience increased customer satisfaction. And these improved levels of customer satisfaction will allow you to reduce churn, elevate customer retention, and improve the lifetime value of your loyal customers.

"**Enhanced Profits.** Did you know that acquiring a new customer can cost five times more than retaining an existing one? With a legion of more satisfied customers, you can look forward to enhancing your profits and protecting the bottom line of your business.

"Training Tips for Teaching Customer Service

Before we dive into the most valuable training materials for customer service (and some examples of companies that get customer service training just right), let's outline some general training tips for customer service.

Here are the best practice tips to take your customer service training to the next level:

"**Make Your Training Interactive.** We all know what it feels like to find ourselves stuck in an uninspired training session. Our attention will quickly falter, and we'll struggle to stay engaged, which will reduce the effectiveness of the training.

The best customer service training grabs the attention of participants and engages them, in order to get amazing results. If you decide to invest in great customer service training, make sure you use the right delivery method, techniques, and personnel.

One surefire way to boost engagement within your training sessions is to make them interactive. Here are just a few pointers you can use to heighten the level of interactivity in your sessions:

+ Speak directly to your audience.

+ Use a blend of techniques.

+ Make good use of technology

"Deliver Purposeful Training. Before you host the training session itself, it's critical for everybody on your team to understand why it's happening, which goals you're hoping to achieve, and what each person can do to boost the effectiveness of the session.

If you fail to communicate these critical pieces of data, your participants will be thrown in at the deep end without the information they need. Since this ignorance will add an element of randomness to your session, your team won't know exactly what they should take from it.

To combat this outcome, make sure you clearly share the goals of your training session. You should articulate them in your invite to the training session, then re-emphasize this important message at the beginning and end of your session.

"Create Customized Training Content. If your training is going to truly resonate with your participants, it's important for you to create customized training content that speaks directly to them.

Before the session, you should invest an appropriate amount of time into customizing your training. Here are some of the areas you might want to alter to fit your business:

+ Branding / look and feel

+ Case studies / statistics

+ Messaging and tone

If you create a highly customized suite of training content, your team members will undoubtedly be more engaged and ready to learn.

"Provide Opportunities for Your Team to Practice. Theory is one thing, but it's also important to give your team members the chance to put their new skills to use. Since it's vital for you to incorporate practicality into your training, you should craft a roadmap that includes steps that encourage your team members, compound their learning, and put it to use.

For instance, you might decide to give your attendees new responsibilities after they've completed their training. Then you can monitor whether they've managed to effectively incorporate their learning.

"Assess the Impact of Your Training. Before you decide to deliver your training, it's important for you to plan the exact ways you're going to assess its impact. So, you'll need to outline a number of key metrics, such as:

+ ROI

+ Productivity

+ Individual results

You'll also need to plan out the ways you're going to measure those important metrics. For instance, you might decide to use a blend of the following techniques:

+ Data analysis

+ One-on-one interviews

+ Surveys and other feedback methods

One important step involves assessing the impact of your training. If you accurately gauge this assessment, you'll be able to determine whether it makes sense to invest in similar customer service training initiatives in the future.

"Valuable Customer Service Training Materials

Now we've established why customer training is important, as well as some of the tips you should keep in mind throughout the process. So, let's take a look at some of the best training materials you can use.

"Ideas, Games, and Exercises for Customer Service Training. If you decide to host your own session to energize and train your team, here are some great ideas for games and exercises:

1. Share best practice.

To create some energy in your session, you could challenge your team members to share their own experiences and best practices. To keep things interesting, you could throw a ball around the room from one speaker to the next, and use these talking points for inspiration:

+ Great customer service experiences

+ Biggest customer service challenges

+ Funniest customer service stories

This game will get your team into the habit of sharing their stories with each other and encourage them to learn from these experiences.

2. Do some detective work.

Ready to challenge the assumptions of your customer service team? In this exercise, you can break your participants up into groups and ask them to make a small purchase with one of your competitors. Then you can assess this competitor's customer service offerings.

This exercise is lots of fun, and it encourages your team members to think critically about customer service. Are they delivering excellent service?

3. Run roleplaying sessions.

For your more junior staff members, it might be helpful for you to coordinate roleplaying sessions that will sharpen their skills. For instance, if you have a new product or feature, you might want to help them prepare for some of the common issues they'll face.

These roleplaying sessions are easy to organize, and they can have a positive impact on the overall performance of your team members. They're also lots of fun and great ways to build team spirit.

4. Use suggestions to shape your sessions.

To make sure you choose the right exercises for your customer service training session, you should listen to your employees' suggestions. Take the time to speak with them and understand their priorities. For instance, you could leave out a suggestion box, in order to make sure your training is relevant.

If you respond to the immediate needs and priorities of your team members, you'll simultaneously provide them with effective training and show them you truly care.

5. Perform call reviews.

The best customer service teams should regularly record calls with customers and use those recordings as opportunities to reflect and improve. You could regularly go through call reviews with your team members and use them as opportunities for everyone to improve.

This exercise is often an exciting, engaging way for your team members to encourage reflection" (Davis, 2020).

9.6 TEAM BUILDING

Team building is the process of turning a group of individual contributing employees into a cohesive team. They become group of people organized to work together to meet the needs of their customers by accomplishing their purpose and goals.

Team building creates stronger bonds among the members of a group. The individual members respect each other and their differences and share their common goals and expectations.

Team building can include the daily interaction that employees engage in when working together to carry out the requirements of their jobs. This form of team building is natural and can be assisted if the group takes the time to come up with a set of team norms. These norms help group members know how to appropriately interact on the team and with the rest of the organization.

Team building can also involve structured activities and exercises led by team members. Or, with the proper budget and goals, managers can contract out for facilitation with an external resource. External facilitation by an experienced person can give your team building a boost.

"How to Build Highly Effective Teams

Too often, teams are formed merely by gathering some people together and then hoping that those people somehow find a way to work together. Teams are most effective when carefully designed. To design, develop and support a highly effective team, use the following guidelines:

"1. Set clear goals for the results to be produced by the team.

The goals should be designed to be "SMART." This is an acronym for:

+ Specific
+ Measurable

+ Achievable

+ Relevant and

+ Time-bound.

As much as possible, include input from other members of the organization when designing and wording these goals. Goals might be, for example, "to produce a project report that includes a project plan, schedule and budget to develop and test a complete employee performance management system within the next year." Write these goals down for eventual communication to and discussion with all team members.

"2. Set clear objectives for measuring the ongoing effectiveness of the team.

The objectives, that together achieve the overall goals, should also be designed to be "SMART." Objectives might be, for example, to a) to produce a draft of a project report during the first four weeks of team activities, and b) achieve Board-approval of the proposed performance management system during the next four weeks. Also, write these objectives down for eventual communication to and discussion with all team members.

"3. Define a mechanism for clear and consistent communications among team members.

New leaders often assume that all group members know what the leaders know. Consistent communication is the most important trait of a successful group. Without communication, none of the other traits can occur. Successful groups even over-communicate, such that:

+ All members regularly receive and understand similar information about the group, for example, about the group's purpose, membership, status and accomplishments.

+ These communications might be delivered through regular newsletters, status reports, meetings, emails and collaboration tools.

"4. Define a procedure for members to make decisions and solve problems.

Successful groups regularly encounter situations where they must make decisions and solve problems in a highly effective manner. Too often, the group resorts to extended discussion until members become tired and frustrated and eventually just opt for any action at all, or they count on the same person who seems to voice the strongest opinions. Instead, successful groups:

+ Document a procedure whereby the group can make decisions and ensure that all members are aware of the procedure.

+ The procedure might specify that decisions are made, first by aiming for consensus within a certain time frame and if consensus is not achieved, then the group resorts to a majority vote.

"5. Develop staffing procedures (recruiting, training, organizing, replacing).

Too often, group members are asked to join the group and somehow to "chip in." Unfortunately, that approach creates "chips," rather than valuable group members. Instead, if group members go through a somewhat organized, systematic process, then new members often believe that the group is well organized and that their role is very valuable in the group. Successful groups:

+ Identify what roles and expertise are needed on the group in order to achieve the group's purpose and plans – they staff according to plans, not personalities.

+ New group members go through a systematic process to join the group – they understand the group's purpose, their role, their next steps and where to get help.

"6. Determine the membership of the group.

Consider the extent of expertise needed to achieve the goals, including areas of knowledge and skills. Include at least one person who has skills in facilitation and meeting management. Attempt to include sufficient diversity of values and perspectives to ensure robust ideas and discussion. A critical consideration is availability – members should have the time to attend every meeting and perform required tasks between meetings.

"7. Determine time frames for starting and terminating the team, if applicable.

Now consider the expertise needed to achieve the goals of the team, and how long it might take to recruit and organize those resources. Write these times down for eventual communication to and discussion with all team members.

"8. Determine the membership of the team.

What expertise might the team need to achieve the goals of the group? For example, an official authority to gather and allocate resources, or an expert in a certain technology. Always consider if the members will have the time and energy to actively participate in the team.

"9. Assign the role of leader – to ensure systems and practices are followed.

The leader focuses on the systems and practices in the team, not on personalities of its members. For example, the leader makes sure that all team members: a) are successfully staffed, b) understand the purpose of the group and their role in it, c) are active toward meeting that purpose and role, and d) utilize procedures for making decisions and solving problems. (Note that the leader does not always have to be a strong, charismatic personality – while that type of personality can often be very successful at developing teams, it often can create passivity or frustration in other members over time, thereby crippling the group.)

"10. Assign role of communicator – communication is the life's blood of teams!

Communication is the most important trait of a successful team. It cannot be left to chance. Someone should be designated to ensure that all members receive regular communications about purpose, membership, roles and status. Communications should also be with people outside the team, especially those who make decisions or determine if the team is successful or not.

"11. Identify needs for resources (training, materials, supplies, etc.).

Start from analysis of the purpose and goals. What is needed to achieve them? For example, members might benefit from a training that provides a brief overview of the typical stages of team development and includes packets of materials about the team's goals, structure and process to make decisions. Consider costs, such as trainers, consultants, room rental and office supplies. How will those funds be obtained and maintained?

"12. Identify the costs to provide necessary resources for the team.

Consider costs, such as paying employees to attend the meeting, trainers, consultants, room rental and office supplies. Develop a budget that itemizes the costs associated with obtaining and supporting each of the resources. Get management approval of the budget.

"13. Contact each team member.

Before the first meeting, invite each potential team member to be a part of the team. First, send him or her a memo, and then meet with each person individually. Communicate the goals of the project, why the person was selected, the benefit of the goals to the organization, the time frame for the team effort, and who will lead the team (at least initially). Invite the team member to the first meeting.

"14. Early on, plan team building activities to support trust and working relationships.

Team building activities can include, for example, a retreat in which members introduce themselves, exercises in which members help each other solve a short problem or meet a specific and achievable goal, or an extended period in which members can voice their concerns and frustrations about their team assignments.

"15. Carefully plan the first team meeting.

In the first meeting, review the goals of the team, why each member was selected, the benefit of the goals to the organization, the time frame for the team effort, who will lead the team (at least, initially), when the team might meet and where, and any changes that have occurred since the individual meetings. Have this information written down to hand out to each member. At the end of the meeting, ask each person to make a public commitment to the team effort.

"16. Regularly monitor and report on status of team members toward achieving the goal.

It is amazing how often a team starts out with a carefully designed plan, but then abandons the plan once the initial implementation of the plan is underway. Sometimes if the plan is behind schedule, team members conclude that the project is not successful. Plans can change – just change them systematically with new dates and approval of the changes.

"17. Support team meetings and the members' processes in the team.

At this point, it is critical that supervisors of team members remain available to provide support and resources as needed. The supervisor should regularly monitor team members' progress on achieving their goals. Provide ongoing encouragement and visibility to members. One of the most important forms of support a supervisor can provide is coordination with other supervisors to ensure that team members are freed up enough to attend meetings.

"18. Regularly celebrate team members' accomplishments!

One of the best ways to avoid burnout is to regularly celebrate accomplishments. Otherwise, members can feel as if they are on treadmill that has no end. Keep your eye on small and recurring successes, not just the gold at the end of the rainbow" (McNamara, 2020).

9.7 PROCEDURES MANUAL AND STANDARDIZATION

The first step in the process to "lock in change" is to explicitly spell out how to implement the organizational change and thereby standardizing it. This is done by creating a procedures manual that addresses how the change is carried out by every job description in the organization from the CEO to the frontline customer service employee. This includes giving each employee the training and resources to carry out their individual role in the change.

"Policies, guidelines and procedures help your business to run systematically and efficiently. Having a written outline of how things should be done at your workplace ensures that every employee has the knowledge and vision to contribute to the growth of the business. Create a procedure manual to empower your employees to do their jobs to the best of their abilities.

"A procedures manual contains the policies, guidelines and processes for the whole organization. It exists to help employees do their jobs in an approved and consistent manner.

"Include Policies and Procedures for Your Business

Your procedure guide includes the policies and procedures for your overall workplace, as well as for each individual role. Policies reflect the **rules** you want your employees to follow, while procedures outline the **process** for following those rules.

Your business' procedure manual should include:

+ The vision, mission and core values of your business

+ Employee rights and regulations

+ Health benefits, sick days and vacation days

- Expenses, deductions and reimbursement
- Harassment and discrimination guidelines
- Online communication guidelines
- Overtime
- Breaks, mealtimes and rest periods
- Disciplinary action

"Having all of this information in writing ensures that your employees have a point of **reference** for anything they need to know regarding the rules of your workplace. This reduces miscommunication between the business and its employees. It also ensures there are processes in place for how to complete each action, and what to do in case disciplinary action is required.

"Outline Specific Instructions for Each Role

Each department in your organization should have a procedure manual where the tasks of each role within that department are outlined. For example, there should be an IT department manual, a customer service department manual and a sales department manual.

"Within each manual, be sure to list out each kind of role, such as IT manager, customer service representative and sales associate. Next, list **specific tasks** that each role is responsible for. Then, create step-by-step instructions for each task. For example, if one of the customer service representative's tasks is to close up the cash register each night, how should they do it? How should they count the cash and credit card transactions, where should they list them and what should they do with the cash at the end of the night?

"Having this kind of minute details documented ensures that there are no **knowledge gaps** for your staff. They have a reference they can check when they forget a process or are completing a new task. If an employee has to suddenly leave the company, you still have a record of all the tasks they are responsible for so that you can ensure **continuity** in your business.

"Use a Direct Writing Style for Your Procedure Manual

Writing a clear, coherent and useful process manual takes time. Start with drafting an outline of all of the information you need to include. Next, highlight the areas of priority, so you know which sections to start with. Complete the procedure manual section by section, instead of working on multiple sections at a time. This helps to reduce confusion and repetition.

"Use a **direct writing style** that makes it easy for your employees to follow the logical steps you offer. Include plenty of numbered step-by-step lists for processes that need to happen in a certain order. Use bulleted lists for procedures that can be completed out of order. Where possible, include images or graphics to aid in understanding.

"Implement Your Policies and Procedures

Always keep your procedure manual **up to date** by reviewing it each month. When necessary, revise the procedures that are out of date. Share the updated latest version of the procedure manual with your employees. Instead of having a printed version, consider having an online version of the manual, which makes it easier to ensure that your employees always have the latest content.

"Share the manual with all new employees and stress the importance of reading through each section to become familiar with the rules of your workplace and department. Reference the manual in meetings where questions about topics that are in the procedures come up. For example, if an employee wants to know what the policy is on taking sick days, answer their question and also remind them to review the information in the procedure manual" (Ahmed, 2019).

9.8 PERFORMANCE MEASURES AND EXPECTATIONS

Peter Drucker said that "What gets measured gets done." This means regular measurement and reporting keeps you focused — because you use that information to make decisions to improve your results. Both the performance measures and expectations or goals must be spelled out in the procedures manual and reinforced their employee training of same. You can't expect your employees to perform at their peak unless you have given them adequate resources and training to succeed in their individual part of the change management process. This included training them as to the need for the change.

"What is Performance Measurement?

Performance Measurement can be best understood through considering the definitions of the words 'performance' and 'measurement' according to the Baldrige Criteria:

+ Performance refers to output results and their outcomes obtained from processes, products, and services that permit evaluation and comparison relative to goals, standards, past results, and other organisations. Performance can be expressed in non-financial and financial terms.

+ Measurement refers to numerical information that quantifies input, output, and performance dimensions of processes, products, services, and the overall organisation (outcomes). Performance measures might be simple (derived from one measurement) or composite.

"The challenge for organisations today is how to match and align performance measures with business strategy, structures and corporate culture, the type and number of measures to use, the balance between the merits and costs of introducing these measures, and how to deploy the measures so that the results are used and acted upon.

"Who uses Performance Measurement?

All organisations measure performance to some extent. However, there is a large disparity among organisations in terms of which performance measures are used with many primarily focusing on financial measures. There has however, been a general move away from financial measurement since the early 1980's. This was accelerated in the 1990's and 2000's by the worldwide acceptance of business excellence models and performance measurement frameworks that address all stakeholders' needs. Today due to the advances of technology there are no limits in terms of the data that can be obtained for the use of performance measurement with the opportunities for analysing real-time data through performance dashboards.

"Whilst data is more readily available, it is critical that the design of a performance measurement system is appropriate otherwise the data and information can be overwhelming or unhelpful and lead to poor decision making. Measures to be useful need to be aligned to strategy, and be effective in terms of monitoring, communicating, and driving performance.

"A good overview of the different types of performance measures is provided by David Parmenter in his book Winning KPIs which describes three types of performance measures:

+ Key Result Indicators (KRIs). These include measures like customer satisfaction, net profit before tax, profitability of customers, employee satisfaction, return on capital employed. The common characteristic of these measures is that they are the result of many actions. They give a clear picture of whether you are travelling in the right direction. They do not however tell you what you need to do to improve these results. Thus, KRIs provide information that is ideal for the governance board, therefore to those not involved in day-to-day management.

+ Performance Indicator (PI). These tell you what to do. PIs lie beneath KRIs and could include profitability of the top 10% of customers, net profit on key product lines, % increase in sales with top 10% of customers, no. of employees using a suggestion scheme.

+ Key Performance Indicators (KPIs). Key performance indicators are a set of measures focusing on those aspects of performance that are the most critical for the current and future success of the organisation. They have six characteristics:

  + measured frequently e.g., daily or weekly

  + acted upon by CEO and senior management team

  + all staff understand the measure and what corrective action is required

  + responsibility can be tied down to an individual or team

  + significant impact (on more than one objective)

  + has a positive impact (on other performance measures)

"What are the common challenges associated with the Performance Measurement approach?

What are the common challenges associated with the Performance Measurement approach? The performance measurement revolution has seen a move away from the problems of past measurement systems. Five common features of out-dated performance measurements systems were:

+ Dominant financial or other backward-looking indicators

+ Failure to measure all the factors that create value

+ Little account taken of asset creation and growth

+ Poor measurement of innovation, learning and change

+ A concentration on immediate rather than long-term goals

"The focus in performance measurement is now on achieving a balanced framework that addresses the issues described above. Examples of these frameworks that support this are Kaplan and Norton's Balanced Scorecard, Skandia's navigator model and the Performance Prism. Others recommend that the results sections of business excellence models should be used to generate a balanced set of performance measures.

"There are several challenges that are faced when designing an effective Performance Measurement System, these include the following:

+ How to measure non-financial performance

+ What measures to choose and why

+ How to use them – what to do with the results

+ Who should be responsible for using the results

+ How and to whom, to communicate the results

+ The resources needed to consider the above and design and deploy the measurement system

"There are other major requirements that an organisation needs to consider before an effective performance measurement system can be designed or installed. Apart from lower-level measures that may be vital for the operation of processes, all measures need to be chosen to support the attainment of specific performance or behaviour identified by the organisation's leaders as important or necessary to work towards the organisational goals. This being the case, there must be clearly defined goals/objectives and strategies chosen to reach them before measures can be chosen to support their attainment. Similarly, the key processes, drivers of performance, and the core competencies required by employees need to be identified before effective performance measurement can be achieved" (BPIR, 2021).

9.9 Performance Appraisal/ Management

Adequate training and resources create the environment which facilitates the change in question. But then this performance must be measured by quantitative outputs and qualitative and individualized performance appraisals.

"Performance Appraisal is the systematic evaluation of the performance of employees and to understand the abilities of a person for further growth and development. Performance appraisal is generally done in systematic ways which are as follows:

1. The supervisors measure the pay of employees and compare it with targets and plans.

2. The supervisor analyses the factors behind work performances of employees.

3. The employers are in position to guide the employees for a better performance.

"Objectives of Performance Appraisal

Performance Appraisal can be done with following objectives in mind:

1. To maintain records in order to determine compensation packages, wage structure, salaries raises, etc.

2. To identify the strengths and weaknesses of employees to place right men on right job.

3. To maintain and assess the potential present in a person for further growth and development.

4. To provide a feedback to employees regarding their performance and related status.

5. To provide a feedback to employees regarding their performance and related status.

6. It serves as a basis for influencing working habits of the employees.

7. To review and retain the promotional and other training programs.

"Advantages of Performance Appraisal

It is said that performance appraisal is an investment for the company which can be justified by following advantages:

1. **Promotion:** Performance Appraisal helps the supervisors to chalk out the promotion programs for efficient employees. In this regards, inefficient workers can be dismissed or demoted in case.

2. **Compensation:** Performance Appraisal helps in chalking out compensation packages for employees. Merit rating is possible through performance appraisal. Performance Appraisal tries to give worth to a performance. Compensation packages which include bonus, high salary rates, extra benefits, allowances and pre-requisites are dependent on performance appraisal. The criteria should be merit rather than seniority.

3. **Employees Development:** The systematic procedure of performance appraisal helps the supervisors to frame training policies and programs. It helps to analyze strengths and weaknesses of employees so that new jobs can be designed for efficient employees. It also helps in framing future development programs.

4. **Selection Validation:** Performance Appraisal helps the supervisors to understand the validity and importance of the selection procedure. The supervisors come to know the validity and thereby the strengths and weaknesses of selection procedure. Future changes in selection methods can be made in this regard.

5. **Communication:** For an organization, effective communication between employees and employers is very important. Through performance appraisal, communication can be sought for in the following ways:

a. Through performance appraisal, the employers can understand and accept skills of subordinates.

b. The subordinates can also understand and create a trust and confidence in superiors.

c. It also helps in maintaining cordial and congenial labor management relationship.

d. It develops the spirit of work and boosts the morale of employees.

All the above factors ensure effective communication.

6. **Motivation:** Performance appraisal serves as a motivation tool. Through evaluating performance of employees, a person's efficiency can be determined if the targets are achieved. This very well motivates a person for better job and helps him to improve his performance in the future" (Management Study Guide, 2021).

9.10 Total Quality Management

Total quality management or TQM consists of organization-wide efforts to "install and make permanent climate where employees continuously improve their ability to provide on demand products and services that customers will find of particular value" (Ciampa, 1992). It is also another topic that has produced hundreds, if not thousands of books. If you Google the phrase, then you get "About 2,080,000,000 results (0.69 seconds)." I am going to start with the basics as spelled out by the father of TQM, W. Edwards Deming.

Deming's 14 Points on Quality Management, or the Deming Model of Quality Management, a core concept on implementing total quality management (TQM), is a set of management practices to help companies increase their quality and productivity.

W. Deming's 14 Points for Total Quality Management:

1. Create constancy of purpose for improving products and services.

2. Adopt the new philosophy.

3. Cease dependence on inspection to achieve quality.

4. End the practice of awarding business on price alone; instead, minimize total cost by working with a single supplier.

5. Improve constantly and forever every process for planning, production and service.

6. Institute training on the job.

7. Adopt and institute leadership.

8. Drive out fear.

9. Break down barriers between staff areas.

10. Eliminate slogans, exhortations and targets for the workforce.

11. Eliminate numerical quotas for the workforce and numerical goals for management.

12. Remove barriers that rob people of pride of workmanship and eliminate the annual rating or merit system.

13. Institute a vigorous program of education and self-improvement for everyone.

14. Put everybody in the company to work accomplishing the transformation (Walton, 1986).

"Primary Elements of TQM

TQM can be summarized as a management system for a customer-focused organization that involves all employees in continual improvement. It uses strategy, data, and effective communications to integrate the quality discipline into the culture and activities of the organization. Many of these concepts are present in modern quality management systems, the successor to TQM. Here are the 8 principles of total quality management:

1. **Customer-focused:** The customer ultimately determines the level of quality. No matter what an organization does to foster quality improvement—training employees, integrating quality into the design process, or upgrading computers or software— the customer determines whether the efforts were worthwhile.

2. **Total employee involvement:** All employees participate in working toward common goals. Total employee commitment can only be obtained after fear has been driven from the workplace, when empowerment has occurred, and when management has provided the proper environment. High-performance work systems integrate continuous improvement efforts with normal business operations. Self-managed work teams are one form of empowerment.

3. **Process-centered:** A fundamental part of TQM is a focus on process thinking. A process is a series of steps that take inputs from suppliers (internal or external) and transforms them into outputs that are delivered to customers (internal or external). The steps required to carry out the process are defined, and performance measures are continuously monitored in order to detect unexpected variation.

4. **Integrated system:** Although an organization may consist of many different functional specialties often organized into vertically structured departments, it is the horizontal processes interconnecting these functions that are the focus of TQM.

   + Micro-processes add up to larger processes, and all processes aggregate into the business processes required for defining and implementing strategy. Everyone must understand the vision, mission, and guiding principles as well as the quality policies, objectives, and critical processes of the organization. Business performance must be monitored and communicated continuously.

   + An integrated business system may be modeled after the Baldrige Award criteria and/or incorporate the ISO 9000 standards. Every organization has a unique work culture, and it is virtually impossible to achieve excellence in its products and services unless a good quality culture has been fostered. Thus, an integrated system connects business improvement elements in an attempt to continually improve and exceed the expectations of customers, employees, and other stakeholders.

5. **Strategic and systematic approach:** A critical part of the management of quality is the strategic and systematic approach to achieving an organization's vision, mission, and goals. This process, called strategic planning or strategic management, includes the formulation of a strategic plan that integrates quality as a core component.

6. **Continual improvement:** A large aspect of TQM is continual process improvement. Continual improvement drives an organization to be both analytical and creative in finding ways to become more competitive and more effective at meeting stakeholder expectations.

7. **Fact-based decision making:** In order to know how well an organization is performing, data on performance measures are necessary. TQM requires that an organization continually

collect and analyze data in order to improve decision making accuracy, achieve consensus, and allow prediction based on past history.

8. **Communications:** During times of organizational change, as well as part of day-to-day operation, effective communications plays a large part in maintaining morale and in motivating employees at all levels. Communications involve strategies, method, and timeliness" (ASQ, 2021).

Phase III – Maintain Organizational Change

You have recreated your organization. Now comes the long-term proposition of sustaining the changes over time.

"Sustaining the Changes!"

INTRODUCTION

To understand how something works, figure out how to break it. –
Nassim Nicholas Taleb

So, you have reinvented your organization. Congratulations! Now you need to *institutionalize* it. This is the one and only time I will use that word. That's because the organizational change management process is not static, but the overall institution must be. Lewin captured this best with his Unfreeze, Movement, Refreeze categories. Allowing for constant change is chaotic and detrimental to the psychological health of your employees. You need only look at the base of Maslow's Hierarchy of Needs. Your employees want safety and security. So, the 10th and final step is to maintain your hard-fought changes.

10.1 MONITOR PERFORMANCE

It is important that you either already have in place or have set up a new measurement and monitoring program. This accomplishes two things. First, there is the need to measure past versus future program performance. Second, it measures future performance alone. I assume that your organization already has a performance measurement program in place.

In the process of reviewing other change management authors and programs, I had to consider what I should recommend. Normally, I have some very strong views on how to do performance measurement. The old adage of "what gets measured gets done" is paramount. Using the right kind of measurement can influence people in terms of what they do.

The problem that I came to grapple with was if you have an existing performance measurement system, no matter how good or bad it is, there was no point in creating a new system that did not match the old one. You don't want to create and apples to oranges measurement situation. I am not going to dissuade you from building and using a better measurement system. However, you may need to create two separate measurement systems in the short-term in order to effectively measure the performance reality of the new reality created by the change management process.

It is difficult for me to make recommendations since I don't know if you are making and selling widgets or something else. Performance measurement is an entire field of its own and is not the purview of the change management process. However, it is important that you measure the before and after of change. It would be best to take a look at the performance metrics for the past three to five years before the changes were implemented and then track the change performance metrics for at least three years after the changes were implemented.

It would be best to not expect that the metrics will immediately change – especially in the first year. Change takes time to be fully realized because there are always bugs to be worked out. It may take 18-24 months to fully realize the benefits of the changes being implemented. Especially in the first year there may be a trial-and-error period where repeated, varied attempts are continued until success is achieved.

Measurement Systems. There are a variety of measurement system available to you.

Time management system. Time management is especially important in an organization where you are working on what could be called billable hours. This system has been used exclusively in the legal field. Lawyers and their associates bill by the client. This billing is also used by numerous consulting companies. It also allows for billing for various sub-activities. These can be to sort out different types of activities that discriminate between what the lead charges versus what a sub-ordinate like an administrative assistant charge. It also allows for material and services costs like printer paper versus travel and lodging costs.

In government agencies, the cost categories may be used to identify the type of regulatory process, level of person doing certain activities, and even the varying steps in the process. The latter is especially important in helping in identifying choke points that may need to be reviewed for changes. A "choke point" could be either a person or a process. The former comes in the form of comparing the performance of individuals on a process increment basis. The latter could mean the one segment of the process needs reengineering to cut the cost involved in time or materials.

Time management systems measure activities by the activity and duration of time involved. One major caveat about using such systems. Don't make the employee spend more time managing their entering such data into the system than it merits. For example, measuring time in 15-minute intervals is micromanagement and will be met by employees with more resentment than not. It is better to measure time in hourly increments with the understanding that it is fair to round and activity up to one hour is its over ½ hour and round down to zero if its less than ½ hour. The process of validating time utilization is done through the earlier exercises in chapter 7 of process mapping and business process reengineering (BPR).

Performance Reward/Penalty Systems. Some organizations utilize systems that provide some form of reward to top producers in terms of some measurement of high productivity. The measurement could be in revenue produced or time process that is cost-effective. In real estate some firms have taken to increasing the commission rates to top performers. This provides an incentive to the real estate agent to work harder to earn more than the traditional 50-50 fee split between agent and brokerage house. In sales the rewards maybe different. Instead of increasing the sales commission, there could be numerous high value gifts such as fun vacations or expensive gifts like computer hardware like laptops. In other agencies that aren't commission based, the use of gift cards is often used as a meaningful way to acknowledge an employee's measured contribution.

Measurement increments rewards can be actions that are performance efficient or cost-effective, cost savings, number of sales calls, customer wait times, sales profit per item, and retention bonus. The latter is used by the U.S. military to get people to reenlist. Such retention bonus can be substantial. Many private and public-sector organizations provide rewards for cost savings suggestions. The reward could be to increase the hourly rate to more than the required time and one half. In recent years, there has been a trend towards rewarding contractors, in the private and public-sector, for on time or even better than on time contract work. This helps eliminate the old problem of contracts that need constant contract extensions that reward the contractor for not being on time. Indeed, contracts that are over the allotted time could find substantial penalties for post contract award time increments.

Mixed measurement messages. It is important to evaluate any new measurement goal against the possibility of it conflicting with already established ones. For example, your quality control initiative could very easily collide with a just in time initiative. You could put your employees in a quandary about what initiative in paramount.

10.2 Sustain Change Program

"Some of the earliest writings of mankind center on change. Dating back as early as 3000 BCE, the I Ching conceived the notion of change as inevitable and resistance to change as one of humankind's greatest causes of pain. These early agents of change wrote that to affect change in a positive way, a balance was required between internal and external forces. But it is one thing to produce a momentary change. It is quite another to sustain the change.

"Stakeholders must have an understanding of the change and why it is important. They also need motivation to move in the direction of the change and to embrace the change as necessary for the future of the organization as well as their own future. Performance incentives must be in place, which reinforce the desired behavior required by the future state envisioned as part of the strategic plan. And, lastly, stakeholders must understand the risks and consequences associated with failure and the rewards associated with success.

"Take the recent example of Toyota. Toyota built its brand and its competitive position around its pioneering Total Quality Management (TQM) concepts. As part of new hire training employees were required to watch a production line until they uncovered some type of defect. If a defect was spotted, the trainee was expected to pull a cord and sound an alarm, halting operations. Quality leaders then arrived to inspect the defect, and everyone celebrated if the alleged defect was validated. The trainee then moved off the line to complete the training program. Other trainees had to remain until they, too, identified potential defects. This practice, which became embedded in the company's culture, fueled its global growth. So how did Toyota end up being sued, fined by government authorities and nursing a badly damaged brand image, as the result of a major vehicle defect? Why was the company not able to sustain its TQM change?

"There is a need to make a shift in most organizations' cultures. Too often change management consists of communication of the change at the start of the project and ends with training on the new process, tool or product, all with a hope for the best. To break with this pattern and embrace the model for sustainable change, organizational leaders, including project and program managers, must go beyond just communicating with and enrolling all stakeholders. They must actively engage their teams in designing, implementing and making ongoing improvements in strategic organizational changes.

Sustaining Change

"Change management constitutes the proactive steps taken to enable transition from the current state to the future state with the goal of improvement that is sustained over time. This whitepaper proposes a path forward for achieving sustainable change.

"PMI's Pulse of the Profession* In-Depth Report: Enabling Organizational Change Through Strategic Initiatives (PMI, 2014) noted that 48% of strategic initiatives are unsuccessful and, as a result, "nearly 15 percent of every dollar spent on strategic initiatives is lost" (p. 4). The good news is that success rates are significantly higher in organizations that report being highly effective at organizational change management. The other good news is that organizational teams can embrace and progress projects requiring significant change if they are effectively engaged in its implementation and improvement. Hornstein (2008) summarized the issue as it relates to IT programs when he stated,

"One of the most important and significant outcomes of organizational change efforts that are coupled with IT implementations is the demonstration of the power of community and community action. That is, the creation of change agent roles, which are populated by organizational members, bringing all staff together to engage one another and the leadership in dialogue about the vision going forward, all bring out the pride and commitment of employees. Furthermore, it then becomes clear that everyone in the organization has great ideas about how the organization can improve itself. Employees often are just waiting for the opportunity to be invited to contribute.

"A Model for Sustainable Change

The foregoing research demonstrates that organizations can move from mere installation to strategic alignment, benefits realization and change agility by following a model for sustainable change. The model in Figure 1 [10.1] is not intended to represent a series of actions, or a stepwise approach. Rather, the intent is that all elements of the model receive ongoing attention, and, in fact, the elements are highly interrelated and are adjusted as the projects and programs of a portfolio are executed" (Harrington, 2015).

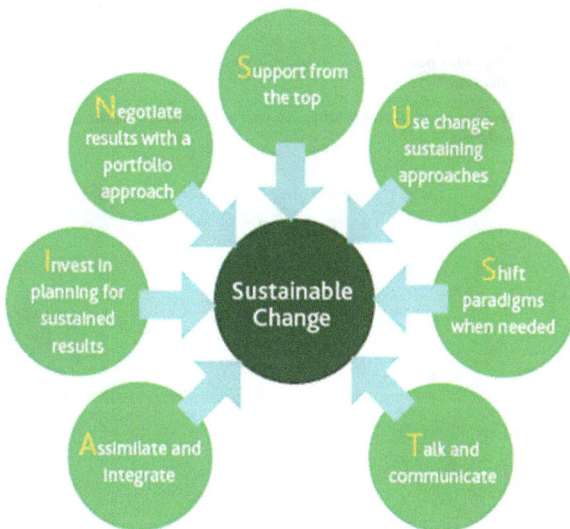

Support from the top	If behaviors within the organization are to change, accountability needs to begin with the executive sponsor and executive leadership. Establishing a crystal clear change agenda sets the foundation for a successful project. Executive leaders also need to support continuing improvement efforts aimed at ensuring that the desired changes become deeply embedded in the culture and actions of staff.
Utilize change-sustaining approaches	At the close of a project and throughout the lifecycle of a program, efforts to sustain important changes should be built into transition plans and/or the next phase of the lifecycle.
Shift paradigms when needed	Shifting mindsets from how business is done now to how it will be done in the future may take minutes or decades. Thus, organizations may need to plan for continuous efforts to communicate the benefits of change to help individuals continue to adjust to a new reality.
Talk and communicate	Change sustainment requires ongoing dialogue and communication so that individuals understand why certain actions, processes, and behaviors are expected of them.
Assimilate and integrate	Utilize change agents for change sustainment.
Invest in planning for sustained results	Through practice and iterations of change, the investment in change will be realized as true project ROI is attained. As additional capacities become available and the organization becomes accustomed to adapting to change, that experience yields a well of resources that can be converted into sustaining prior gains, investment in innovation, and new capacities, product and service lines. This leads to competitive market advantage, building further capacity for additional iterations of change and innovation.
Negotiate results with a portfolio approach	Assess readiness for change before implementing strategies and then adapt to new conditions as warranted.

Table 10.1

10.3 CONTINUOUS IMPROVEMENT

"Continuous improvement; also known as continuous quality improvement (CQI), continuous improvement process (CIP), or Kaizen; is "A philosophy of designing and managing all aspects of an organization in a never-ending quest for quality. The notion is that no matter how well things are going, there are always opportunities to make them better, and hundreds of small improvements can make a big difference in the overall functioning" (Cummings, 2005).

"If you google the words "continuous improvement," then you will get "463,000,000 results (0.53 seconds)" There are also several hundred books on the subject, so I am only going to summarize the concept here. The genesis came from Japanese theorist Masaaki Imai's book *Kaizen: The Key to Japan's Competitive Success* (1986). The process was later implemented through the work of W. Edwards Deming with Japanese automobile manufacturers. It literally revolutionized manufacturing globally as the new gold standard for was the consumer public demanded.

"What Is Continuous Improvement? Definition & Tools

Continuous improvement helps you identify opportunities for work process enhancements and reduce waste. Learn more about Continuous improvement and its advantages. In Lean, continuous improvement is like a religion. Although it seems like a simple thing to achieve, leaders and teams who are not familiar with process improvement techniques have a hard time sustaining it.

To implement this mindset, you need to have a clear understanding of what exactly is continuous improvement, what principles you need to follow and check some of the best practices.

"The Continuous Improvement Model

The term continuous improvement can be very abstract if not placed in a specific context. Explained shortly, it is a never-ending strive for perfection in everything you do. In Lean management, continuous improvement is also known as Kaizen.

Kaizen originated in Japan shortly after the end of the Second World War. It gained massive popularity in manufacturing and became one of the foundations of Toyota's rise from a small carmaker to the largest automobile manufacturer on the planet.

"In the context of the Lean methodology, continuous improvement seeks to improve every process in your company by focusing on enhancing the activities that generate the most value for your customer while removing as many waste activities as possible.

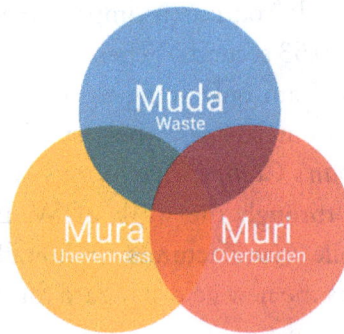

Figure 10.2

There are three types of waste in Lean (Figure 10.2):

+ Muda – The seven wastes

+ Mura – The waste of unevenness

+ Muri – The waste of overburden

Muda consists of 7 major process wastes: transport, inventory, motion, waiting, overproduction, over-processing, defects.

"Removing all of them completely is nearly impossible but focusing on minimizing their negative effects on your work is crucial for successfully implementing continuous improvement.

Mura is caused by unevenness or inconsistency in your process. It is responsible for many of the 7 wastes of Muda. Mura stops your tasks from flowing smoothly across your work process and therefore gets in your way of reaching continuous flow.

"Muri is a major problem for companies that apply push systems. When you assign too much work to your team, you place unnecessary stress on both your team and process.

"Muri is usually a result of Mura, and if you want continuous improvement to become part of your culture, you need to focus on getting rid of those wastes.

"Adopting Continuous Improvement – Tools and Techniques

Understanding the theory behind it is the first step in applying continuous improvement to your management culture. To set yourself up for continuous improvement, you need to create a suitable environment within your company.

"In Lean management, there are three major approaches for achieving continuous improvement:

Plan-Do-Check-Act (PDCA)

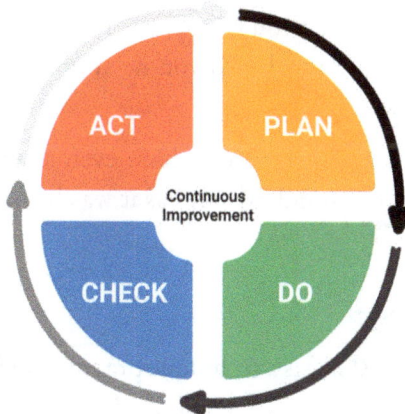

Figure 10.3

"The model Plan-Do-Check-Act is the most popular approach for achieving continuous improvement (Figure 10.3).

"Also known as the Deming circle (named after its founder, the

American engineer William Edwards Deming), it is a never-ending cycle that aims to help you improve further based on achieved results.

"It was first developed for quality control but, in time, became an instrument for achieving continuous improvement.

"In the planning phase, you need to establish the objectives and processes necessary to deliver results per the expected output (the target or goals).

"Setting output expectations is a key to achieving continuous improvement because the accuracy of the goals and their completeness is a major part of the process of improving.

It is recommended to start on a small scale so you can test the effects of the approach.

The second phase is "Do". It is straightforward as you need to execute what you've laid down during the process's planning step.

"After you've completed your objectives, you need to check what you've achieved and compare it to what you've expected. Gather as much data as possible and consider what you can improve in your process to achieve greater results next time.

"If the analysis shows that you've improved compared to your previous project, the standard is updated, and you need to aim for an even better performance next time.

In case you've failed to improve or have even achieved worse results compared to the past, the standard stays as it was before you started your last project.

"Root Cause Analysis

"Root Cause Analysis (RCA) is a technique practiced in Lean management that allows you to achieve   "Kaizen by showing you the root causes of your process's problems.

"It is an iterative practice that drills down into a problem by analyzing what caused it until you reach the root of the negative effect. It can be considered root only if the final negative effect is prevented for good after the cause is removed.

"To apply RCA for continuous improvement, you need to perform a thorough analysis of the problem (Figure 10.4).

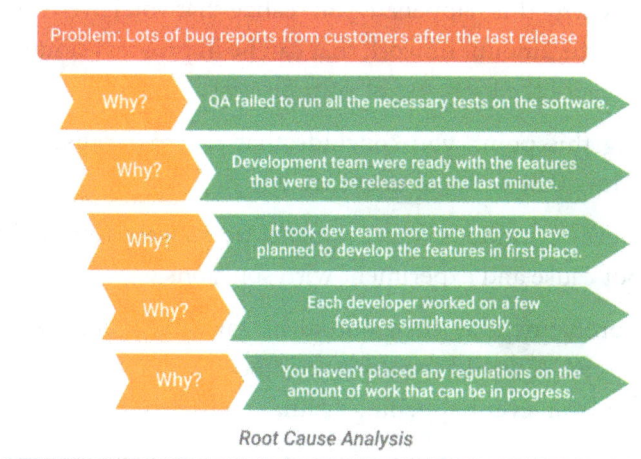

Figure 10.4

"For example, let's say that you are leading a software development team. When you released the latest update of your product, your support team was bombarded with bug reports from customers.

"You begin to look for the root cause starting from the top of the problem.

"You investigate how your QA team allowed for this to happen and discover that they failed to run all the necessary tests on the software.

"Afterward, you look into what caused that and learn that the development team provided them with the features that were to be released at the last possible minute.

"Looking into the cause of that, you find out that the developers finished the majority of features right before they submitted them for quality assurance.

"Digging into the cause of that, you find out that your development team took more time than you have planned to develop the features in the first place.

"Investigating the reason behind that, you discover that your team was inefficient because each developer simultaneously worked on a few features. Therefore, instead of giving features one by one to QA, they submitted a batch that was too large to process on short notice.

"Analyzing why this happened, you realize that you haven't placed any regulations on the amount of work that can be in progress simultaneously and did not ensure the evenness of your process.

"Reaching this point, you conclude that the root cause of the bug problem is Mura (the waste of unevenness).

"To achieve continuous improvement, we suggest you analyze each problem's root cause and experiment with solutions.

"Often, problems may turn out to be far more complex than you think, and the RCA would require a few iterations before preventing the negative effect from ever happening again.

If you are not sure how to perform a root cause analysis, we suggest looking into the 5 Whys for determining root causes.

"Applying Lean Kanban

To continuously improve your process, you need to visualize what needs to be improved clearly.

If you lack visibility, you'll be able to improve from time to time but won't be able to spot symptoms of a problem before it is too late.

"When Toyota was looking for a way to do that, they developed Kanban as a system for improving the workflow efficiency of the production process.

Eventually, Kanban was adapted for knowledge work and managed to help thousands of teams to achieve continuous improvement. The method relies on six core practices for minimizing the wastes in your process (Figure 10.5):

+ Visualize your workflow

+ Eliminate interruptions

+ Manage flow

+ Make process policies explicit

+ Create feedback loops

+ Improve collaboratively

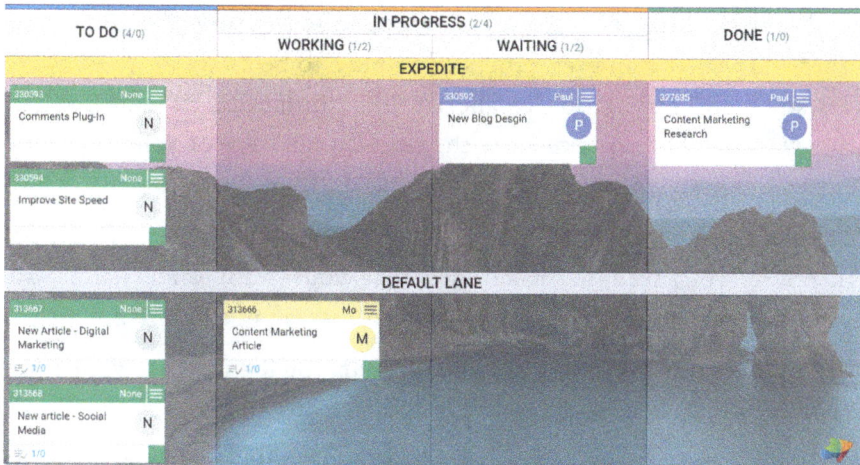

Figure 10.5

"**To visualize your workflow**, the method relies on whiteboards for mapping every step of your process. The board is divided by vertical lines forming columns for the different stages.

A basic Kanban board consists of three columns: Requested, In Progress, Done.

"Each task that your team is working on is hosted on a Kanban card (originally in the form of a post-it-note) and needs to pass through all the stages of your workflow in order to be considered complete.

"Kanban boards allow you to monitor your process's evenness and can be a serious weapon for minimizing Mura.

"Besides, they show you the amount of work that every person on your team has and can help you prevent overburden (Muri) by allowing you to delegate tasks according to your team's capacity.

"Finally, you can monitor the pace at which work is progressing across your workflow and achieve continuous improvement of your workflow efficiency.

"For the sake of **eliminating interruptions**, Kanban relies on limiting the work that can be in progress simultaneously. The goal is to eliminate multitasking, which is nothing more than a constant context switch between assignments and only harms productivity.

"With the help of Kanban, you can **manage the flow** of work in your process. To ensure an even process, you need to be aware of where work gets stuck and take action to alleviate the bottlenecks in your process. This way, you can experiment with the different steps of your workflow and keep improving continuously.

"In Lean management, continuous improvement is a group activity. Therefore, you need to make sure that your team understands the common goal and why their part of the process is important.

"By **making process policies explicit**, you'll encourage your team members to take more responsibility and take ownership of their process.

For positive change to happen, there needs to be a constant flow of knowledge between you and your team.

"The Kanban board itself is a great **feedback loop generator** because it makes it visible who is doing what at any time.

In combination with the widely adopted practice of holding daily stand-up meetings between the team, you can continuously improve information sharing between individuals.

"**Other techniques** that are part of the continuous improvement arsenal are the Gemba walk and the A3 report. The A3 report is a structured approach that helps you deal with problem-solving issues, while the Gemba walk encourages you to go and see where the real work happens. Both are extremely useful, and they can help you discover problematic parts in your workflow.

"Bottom Line

Kaizen is a never-ending quest for perfection, but you'll start feeling the benefits of continuous improvement on your business when your whole team takes it by heart.

Kanban and the other continuous improvement tools can help you with that because your team will obtain lots of knowledge about process improvement and workflow management. As a result, each individual will understand how your process works and how it can be improved.

"In Summary

There are many ways to achieve continuous improvement. All of them have one thing in common - analyzing what can be done better compared to the past. You can sustain continuous improvement by:

+ Minimizing the wastes in your process

+ Creating a suitable environment for your team to improve

+ Implementing the PDCA cycle

+ Always looking for the root cause of existing and potential problems

+ Apply the Kanban method for workflow management" (Kanbanzie, 2021).

10.4 SUCCESSION PLANNING AND ORGANIZATIONAL CONTINUITY

This is a least favorite activity. It is like buying life insurance to provide for your spouse and kids in case you die. The fact is that employees will leave your organization. They may take another job, retire, or die. In any case, there will be a void in your human resource base that you must fill. So, you need to plan for this. Given the criticality of their job, somebody needs to step in, up or down to either temporarily or permanently do the job. Hopefully, you have temporarily covered this because you have contemplated this person leaving (Activity 9.4 Cross Functional Training) or can assign some or all of their work to someone who has done this job in the past.

Today, succession planning is more important than in past years. We are enduring a generational shift that is unprecedented. The post-World War II "Baby Boomers" are retiring in unprecedented numbers. And the generational shift is a difficult one. The replacements have an entirely different mindset. I noticed just how difficult this was in one organization. It was a state forestry department. The outgoing foresters were predominantly older, white males who believed in the concept of forest management and considered themselves "conservationists." This included such practices as clear-cutting entire sections of the forest to create jobs in the wood products industry. The clear cuts would be replanted, and the theory was that after several decades the forest would be reestablished. However, the incoming foresters were increasingly young females. Both the newly minted men and women were staunch "environmentalists." Who believed that clear cutting was an abomination and that the natural cycle of forest fires was nature's version of clear-cutting? The younger generation who had public-sector environmentalist counterparts were even more rabid and used the court system and the Environmental Protection Agency laws to lock down huge sections of forest areas to protect the spotted owl and salmonid habitats. They also embraced the new concept of sustainability.

There are similar stories in the private sector as the generation X

(1965 – 1976), Y (1977 – 1995), and Z (1996-Now) groups started to backfill the Baby Boomer ranks. The culture of any organization faced significant changes. The new Internet world of social media like Facebook and Google transformed the global and national cultures, which in turn forced change in all organizations. A new high-tech lexicon was created to explain the new cultural machinations. Words like scrum, agile, and product owner found their way into the organizational change management process. Indeed, there is a sub-genre of OCM dedicated solely to technological change where people can address complex adaptive problems, while productively and creatively delivering products of the highest possible value.

So, the challenge to the organizational leadership and to their human resource people was the difficult task of deciding if the organization was going to indoctrinate the incoming new generational groups to integrate them into the existing organizational culture or if the organizational culture would be transformed by them and market forces. A good example of this is the Nike company. Nike was founded in 1964 by its founder Philip Knight. Knight writes about this cultural change challenge in his autobiography *Shoe Dog* (Knight, 2016). A firm that was culturally born in the radical cultural changes of the 1960s, was forced to address the evolving new worlds of the alphabet generations X, Y, and Z. In Nike's case, the greater market forces were important because they sold predominantly to a younger crown.

Succession planning is "the ongoing of identifying successors to the critical roles of an organization and developing them so they're ready to move into leadership roles." The "basic steps of the succession planning process:

+ Assess the operation.

+ Determine key positions.

+ Identify and assess candidates.

+ Create development plans.

+ Measure, monitor, report, and revise" (Atwood, 2020).

The purpose of succession planning is more than an exercise geared to developing future leaders. It is also important for backfilling any critical job. As noted in the state forestry example, succession planning involved literally all of your middle management and technical positions. When faced with a generational sea change, your entire organization is at risk. This generational shift can result in the redefinition of the organization's actual mission. In the case of the state forestry agency, the agency's mission was changed by a new generation of younger politicians who embraced such concepts as *sustainability* and *climate change*. In the case of Nike, the mission remained the same, but the target audience preferences changed and therefore its new generation of salespeople and product development people came into play.

Succession planning is about consideration of retirements, having key people who are the only ones who have specific knowledge, and the case where someone exits "without giving notice" (Atwood, 2020). A good example of the latter was the death of Apple's founder Steve Jobs. Unlike its rival Microsoft, Apple was totally invested in the founder's vision, leadership and day-to-day management. Microsoft had successfully and painlessly ushered its founders, Bill Gates and Paul Allen, out the door. Apple did not. Steve Jobs' departure occurred twice in a manner that was detrimental to the organization's continuity. He was forced out of his own organization through a coup in 1985. After successfully regaining this leadership role in 1997 and saving the company from bankruptcy, he then contracted pancreatic cancer in 2003 which he battled for several years. He finally succumbed in 2011. The problem was that charismatic Steve Jobs was Apple. At the time of transition, uncharismatic Bill Gates was not Microsoft.

CHAPTER 6

CONCLUSION

Those who cannot change their minds cannot change everything. –
George Bernard Shaw

So, there you have it. I have presented you with: (1) PSOCM˚ is a 3-Phase, 10-Step, 39-Action comprehensive, life-cycle series, change management model based on a systematic literature review and meta-analysis of the top 22 change management processes. (2) The diagnostic tool using the PORTEF/STEPPE methodology. (3) You also have Carson's Theorem the puts us near the rapidly approaching paradigm shift – the *transmogrification*.

The latter may merely be the penultimate or next to the last change. Because the ultimate would be the complete obliteration of humanity. The last neurotransmission. When and how will that occur? That is the stuff of science fiction, of Asimov, Bradbury and Heinlein. I have no idea. It would be as pointless as predicting the Rapture. If you are to believe the science fiction writers, then we may elude extinction by fulfilling the Biblical allegory by literally living planet Earth.

I want to end my book with a bit of confirmation bias on my part. As I write this, I am 75 years old. I am on the cusp, near the *tipping point*. Will I live long enough to get my spiffy new body? Or will I die, in the medical sense, and cryogenically freeze my brain for a future download? Or will science find the key to stopping the aging process? I have to tell you that my concern for the future makes me wary of living in it. It looms in my mind like a scene from Blade Runner where humankind has lost control of technology. We shall see. So, let me close with a snippet from Sir William Shakespeare's play *Hamlet*:

"To be, or not to be, that is the question:
Whether 'tis nobler in the mind to suffer
The slings and arrows of outrageous fortune,
Or to take Arms against a Sea of troubles,
And by opposing end them: to die, to sleep;
No more; and by a sleep, to say we end
The heart-ache, and the thousand natural shocks
That Flesh is heir to? 'Tis a consummation
Devoutly to be wished. To die, to sleep,
To sleep, perchance to Dream; aye, there's the rub,
For in that sleep of death, what dreams may come,
When we have shuffled off this mortal coil,
Must give us pause."

Indeed. The final change.

Quotes

- A -

Growth for the sake of growth is the ideology of the cancer cell.
- **Edward Abbey,** writer, essayist, novelist (1927-1989).

There is a theory which states that if anyone discovers exactly what the universe is for and why it is here, it will instantly disappear and be replaced by something even more bizarrely inexplicable. There is another theory which states this has already happened.
- **Douglas Adams**, author, *The Hitchhikers Guide to the Galaxy* (1952-2001).

More than any other time in history, mankind faces a crossroads. One path leads to despair and utter hopelessness. The other, to total extinction. Let us pray we have the wisdom to choose correctly.
- **Woody Allen,** comedian and writer.

The universe is change; our life is what our thoughts make it.

Observe always that everything is the result of change, and get used to thinking that there is nothing Nature loves so well as to change existing forms and make new ones of them.
- **Marcus Aurelius**, Emperor of Rome (121-180 AD).

- B -

Not everything that is faced can be changed. But nothing can be changed until it is faced.

Most of us are about as eager to change as we were to be born, and go through our changes in a similar state of shock.
- **James Baldwin**, *As Much Truth As One Can Bear* (1962).

You got to be careful if you don't know where you're going, because you might not get there.
- **Yogi Berra**, baseball catcher (1925-2015).

So do not worry about tomorrow, for tomorrow will bring worries of its own. Today's trouble is enough for today.
- **Bible**, Matthew (6:34).

For everything there is a season, and a time for every matter under heaven.
- **Bible**, Ecclesiastes (3:1).

Destiny is not a matter of chance, but a matter of choice. It is not a thing to be waited for, It is a thing to be achieved.
- **Williams Jennings Bryan,** lawyer, orator, three-time candidate for president (1860-1925).

As a net is made up of a series of ties, so everything in this world is connected by a series of ties. If anyone thinks that the mesh of a net is an independent, isolated thing, he is mistaken. It is called a net because it is made up of a series of interconnected meshes, and each mesh has its place and responsibility in relation to other meshes.
- **Gautama Buddha**, Indian an ascetic and sage (5th-4th Century, B.C.).

Nothing in the world lasts. Save eternal change.
- **Honorat de Bueil** (1580-1670). French aristocrat, soldier, poet, dramatist.

You can never plan for the future by the past.
- **Edmund Burke**, Irish statesman, writer (1729–1797).

Make not little plans; they have no magic to stir men's blood and probably themselves will not be realized. Make big plans; aim high in hope and work, remembering that a noble, logical diagram once recorded will never die, but long after we are gone will a living thing, asserting itself with ever-growing insistency.
- **Daniel H. Burnham**, architect (1846-1912).

A change came o'er the spirit of my dream.
- **Lord Byron**, *(1788-1829)* English poet, novelist.

- C -

Change, indeed, is painful; yet ever needful; and if Memory have its force and worth, so also has Hope.
- **Thomas Carlyle**, (1795-1881) British historian, writer.

I wonder if I've been changed in the night. Let me think.
Was I the same when I got up this morning?
I almost think I can remember feeling a little different.
But if I'm not the same, the next question is 'Who in the world am I?' Ah, that's the great puzzle!"
- **Lewis Carroll**, English novelist and poet, *Alice's Adventures in Wonderland* (1832-1898).

"Would you tell me which way I ought to go from here?" asked Alice.
"That depends a good deal on where you want to get," said the Cat.
"I really don't care where" replied Alice.
"Then it doesn't much matter which way you go," said the Cat.
- **Lewis Carroll**, English novelist and poet, *Alice's Adventures in Wonderland* (1832-1898).

Either you manage change or change manages you.
- **Richard Carson**, (1925-2015) Pacific Northwest planner and writer.

Forewarned, forearmed; to be prepared is half the victory.
- **Miguel de Cervantes Saavedra**, Spanish writer, Don Quixote (1547-1616).

Planning lies with men; success lies with heaven.

If you are planning for a year, sow rice; if you are planning for a decade, plant trees; if you are planning for a lifetime, educate people.

He, who could foresee affairs three days in advance would be rich for thousands of years.
- **Chinese** proverb.

Those who plan do better than those who do not plan even thou they rarely stick to their plan.

Those who fail to learn from the past are doomed to repeat it.
- **Winston Churchill**, British Prime Minister (1874-1965).

Longing not so much to change things as to overturn them.

Before beginning, plan carefully.
- **Marcus Tulius Cicero**, Roman statesman and orator (106-43 BC).

A man who does not plan long ahead will find trouble at his door.
- **Confucius**, Chinese philosopher and religious leader (551-479 BC).

Every public action which is not customary, either is wrong or, if it is right, is a dangerous precedent. It follows that nothing should ever be done for the first time.

Nothing is ever done until everyone is convinced that ought to be done, and has been convinced for so long that it is now time to do something else.
- **F.M. Cornford**, British author, poet, translator (1874-1943).

Always plan ahead. It wasn't raining when Noah built the ark.
- **Richard Cushing**, novelist (1895-1970).

- D -

It is not the strongest of the species that survive, not the most intelligent, but the one most responsive to change.
- **Charles Darwin** (1809-1882), scientist.

Change begets change. Nothing propagates so fast.
- **Charles Dickens**, *(1812-1870)*, English novelist.

If you can dream it, you can do it.
- **Walt Disney** (1901-66), American animator, showman, film producer.

Plans are only good intentions unless they immediately degenerate into hard work.
What gets measured gets done.
- **Peter Drucker**, writer (1959-Present).

- **E** -

I have not failed. I've just found 10,000 ways that won't work.
- **Thomas Edison**, inventor (1847-1931).

It's not the plan that's important, it's the planning.
- **Dr. Graeme** (1965-Present).

The world will not evolve past its current state of crisis by using the same thinking that created the situation.

The significant problems we face cannot be solved at the same level of thinking we were at when we created them.

God does not play dice with the universe.

I do not believe in a personal God and I have never denied this but have expressed it clearly. If something is in me which can be called religious then it is the unbounded admiration for the structure of the world so far as our science can reveal it.
- **Albert Einstein**, scientist (1879-1955).

Plans are worthless. Planning is essential.

In preparing for battle I have always found that plans are useless, but planning is indispensable.

In the councils of government, we must guard against the acquisition of unwarranted influence, whether sought or unsought, by the military-industrial complex. The potential for the disastrous rise of misplaced power exists and will persist.
- **Dwight D. Eisenhower**, general and president (1890 - 1969).

It is never too late to be what you might have been.
- **George Eliot** (1819-1880).

A thousand policemen directing traffic cannot tell you why you come or where you go.
- **T.S. Elliott.**

Few people have any next, they live from hand to mouth without a plan, and are always at the end of their line.
- **Ralph Waldo Emerson**, poet (1803-1882).

If you don't like something, change it. If you can't change it, change the way you think about it.
- **Mary Engelbreit**, Artist.

This primitive, naive but intrinsically correct conception of the world is that of ancient Greek philosophy, and was first clearly formulated by Heraclitus: everything is and is not, for everything is fluid, is constantly changing, constantly coming into being and passing away.

- **Friedrich Engels** (1820–1895). German social
scientist, author, journalist, businessman, political theorist, philosopher, and co-author of Marxist theory.

What I have done here no one has done before.

- **Enheduanna** (2285 - 2250 BC). Sumerian priestess. First author in world history of literature.

Long-range planning works best in the short term.
- **Euripides,** poet (480-406 AD).

There are some people who live in a dream world, and there are some who face reality; and then there are those who turn one into the other.
- **Douglas H. Everett.**

As for the future, your task is not to foresee it, but to enable it.

In anything at all, perfection is finally attained not when there is no longer anything to add, but when there is no longer anything to take away. Perfection is achieved, not when there is nothing more to add, but when there is nothing left to take away.
- **Antoine de Saint Exupery,** poet and pilot (1900-1944).

- F –

The past is never dead. It's not even past.
- **William Faulkner,** *National Geographic* (1897-1962).

To accomplish great things, we must not only act but also dream. Not only plan but also believe.
- **Anatole France** (1844-1924), French critic, writer, *Penguin Island.*

The Constitution only gives people the right to pursue happiness. You have to catch it yourself.

By failing to prepare, you are preparing to fail.
- **Benjamin Franklin.**

Change the environment: do not change the man.

When I'm working on a problem, I never think about beauty. I think only

how to solve the problem. But when I have finished, if the solution is not beautiful, I know it is wrong.
- **Richard (Bucky) Buckminster Fuller,** (1895-1983).

- G -

Be the change that you wish to see in the world.
- **Mahatma Gandhi**, Indian activist.

Yet, the timeless in you is aware of life's timelessness, and knows that yesterday is but today's memory and tomorrow is today's dream.
- **Kahlil Gibran**, Lebanese writer (The Prophet, 1923).

- H -

Men often oppose a thing merely because they have had no agency in planning it, or because it may have been planned by those whom they dislike.
- **Alexander Hamilton** (1755 - 1804).

If a builder builds a house for someone, and does not construct it properly, and the house which he built fall in and kill its owner, then that builder shall be put to death.
- **Hammurabi,** King of Babylon, Code of Laws section 229 (1780 BC).

Intelligence is the ability to adapt to change.
- **Stephen Hawking**, physicist.

All is flux, nothing stays still.

Nothing endures but change.

You could not step twice into the same river for other waters are ever flowing on to you.
- **Heraclitus of Ephesus**, pre-Socratic Greek philosopher (500-480 B.C.)

An evil plan does mischief to the planner.

- **Hesiod**, Greek poet and author of *Theogony* (circa 800 BC).

Reduce your plan to writing. The moment you complete this, you will have definitely given concrete form to the intangible desire.
- **Napoleon Hill.**

Zeus does not bring all men's plans to fulfillment.
- **Homer**, poet and author of *The Iliad* (800 BC - 700 BC).

Change is not made without inconvenience, even from worse to better.
- **Richard Hooker**, as quoted in the preface of Samuel Johnson's Dictionary of the English Language (1755).

The only people, scientific or other, who never make mistakes are those who do nothing.
- **Thomas Huxley.**

- I -

A community is like a ship: everyone ought to be prepared to take the helm.
- **Henrik Ibsen**, writer.

There is a certain relief in change, even though it be from bad to worse!
- **Washington Irving,** *Tales of a Traveler* (1824).

- J -

While real trolleys in Newark, Philadelphia, Pittsburgh, and Boston languish for lack of patronage and government support, millions of people flock to Disneyland to ride fake trains that don't go anywhere.
- **Kenneth J. Jackson.**

Change is not made without inconvenience, even from worse to better.
– **Samuel Johnson**, English poet, playwright, essayist, moralist, biographer, editor (1709-1784).

Mistakes are the portals of discovery.
- **James Joyce**, writer.

A good plan is like a road map: it shows the final destination and usually the best way to get there.
- **H. Stanely Judd.**

If there is anything we wish to change in the child, we should first examine it and see whether it is not something that could not be better changed in ourselves.
- **Carl Gustav Jung**, Swiss psychiatrist (1875-1961).

- K –

The more things change, the more they stay the same.
- **Alphonse Karr,** *Les Guêpes* (1849).

Plus ça change, plus c'est la même chose. What goes around comes around.
- **Jean-Baptiste Alphonse Karr**, French novelist.

The best way to predict the future is to invent it.
- **Alan Kay.**

Once it was necessary that the people should multiply and be fruitful if the race was to survive. But now to preserve the race it is necessary that people hold back the power of propagation.
- **Helen Keller.**

But Goethe tells us in his greatest poem that Faust lost the liberty of his soul when he said to the passing moment: "Stay, thou art so fair." And our liberty, too, is endangered if we pause for the passing moment, if we rest on our achievements, if we resist the pace of progress. For time and the world do not stand still. Change is the law of life. And those who look only to the past or the present are certain to miss the future.
- **John F. Kennedy**, 35th President of the United States. Address in the

Assembly Hall at the Paulskirche in Frankfurt (June 25, 1963). Note: He was assassinated 5 months later in Dallas, Texas.

There are going to be times when we can't wait for somebody. Now, you're either on the bus or off the bus. If you're on the bus, and you get left behind, then you'll find it again. If you're off the bus in the first place — then it won't make a damn.
- **Ken Kesey**, *The Electric Kool-Aid Acid Test* (1968).

But the 'long run' is a misleading guide to current affairs. 'In the long run' we are all dead.
- **John Maynard Keyes** (1923).

Always have a plan, and believe in it. Nothing happens by accident.
- **Chuck Knox.**

God changes not what is in people, until they change what is in themselves.
- **The Koran 13:11.**

- L -

Planning is bringing the future into the present so that you can do something about it now.
- **Alan Lakein,** writer.

A great change in life is like a cold bath in winter — we all hesitate at the first plunge.
- **Letitia Elizabeth Landon,** *Romance and Reality* (1831).

Life is what happens to us while we're too busy making other plans.
- **John Lennon,** The Beatles (1940 - 1980), "Beautiful Boy".

The possibility that we may fail in the struggle ought not to deter us from the support of a cause we believe to be just.

If we could first know where we are, and whither we are tending, we could better judge what to do, and how to do it.
- **Abraham Lincoln**, U.S. president.

All things must change. To something new, to something strange.
- **Henry Wadsworth Longfellow,** *Kéramos* (1878).

Good judgment is the result of experience. And experience is frequently the result of bad judgment.
- **Robert Lovett**, wall street banker, advising attorney general Robert F. Kennedy during the Cuban Missile Crisis (1969).

- M -

It must be considered that there is nothing more difficult to carry out, nor more doubtful of success, nor more dangerous to handle, than to initiate a new order of things.
- **Niccolò Machiavelli**, The Prince (1532).

To under manage reality is not to keep free. It is simply to let some force other than reason shape reality.
- **Robert S. McNamara**, Secretary of Defense for Presidents Kennedy and Johnson, The Essence of Security (1968).

Growth is inevitable and desirable, but destruction of community character is not. The question is not whether your part of the world is going to change. The question is how.
- **Edward T. McMahon**, The Conservation Fund.

For every complex and difficult problem, there is an answer that is simple, easy, and wrong.
- **H. L. Mencken**, journalist.

No plan survives contact with the enemy.
- **Field Marshal Helmuth von Moltke.**

Trend is not destiny.
- **Lewis Mumford**, writer.

- N -

God, give us grace to accept with serenity the things that cannot be changed, courage to change the things which should be changed, and the wisdom to distinguish the one from the other.
- **Reinhold Neibuhr** (1892-1971). *Serenity Prayer* (1934).

The snake which cannot cast its skin has to die. As well the minds which are prevented from changing their opinions; they cease to be mind.

The snake which cannot cast its skin has to die. As well the minds which are prevented from changing their opinions; they cease to be mind.
- **Friedrich Nietzsche,** German philosopher (1844-1900).

There came a time when the risk to remain tight in the bud was more painful that the risk it took to blossom.
- **Anais Nin,** writer.

-- O -

Change will not come if we wait for some other person or some other time. We are the ones we've been waiting for. We are the change that we seek.
- **Barak Obama**, U.S. President.

-- P -

When we are planning for posterity, we ought to remember that virtue is not hereditary.
- **Thomas Paine**, *Common Sense* (1776).

In the space of two days I had evolved two plans, wholly distinct, both of which were equally feasible. The point I am trying to bring out is that one does not plan and then try to make circumstances fit those plans. One tries to make plans fit the circumstances.
- **George S. Patton**, general (1947).

A good plan today is better that a perfect plan tomorrow.
- **Geoge S. Patton**, general.

Plan your work for today and every day, then work your plan.
- **Norman Vincent Peale,** (May 31, 1898 – December 24, 1993.

American minister and author.

The real voyage of discovery and change does not consist in seeking new landscapes, but in having new eyes.

We do not succeed in changing things according to our desires, but gradually our desire changes.
- **Marcel Proust**, French novelist (1871–1922).

- Q -

But if you build your life on dreams it's prudent to recall; A man with moonlight in his hand has nothing there at all.
-- **Don Quixote** from Cervantes Saavedra›s novel *Don Quixote de la Mancha.*

- R -

If you want to change the world, change yourself.
- **Tom Robbins**, *Even Cowgirls Get the Blues* (1976).

It takes as much energy to wish as it does to plan.
- **Eleanor Roosevelt**, U.S. First Lady.

The only limit to our realization of tomorrow will be our doubts of today.

Let us move forward with strong and active faith.
- **Franklin Delano Roosevelt**. U.S. President [He never gave this speech. He died on the day before it was to be delivered].

Yesterday I was so clever, so I wanted to change the world. Today I am so wise, so I am changing myself.
- **Rumi**, Persian poet, mystic.

- **S** -

If you want to make an apple pie from scratch, you must first create the universe.
- **Carl Sagan**, scientist and writer.

True change is evolutionary, not revolutionary.
- **L.K. Samuels**, *In Defense of Chaos: The Chaology of Politics, Economics and Human Action* (2013).

Those who cannot remember the past are condemned to repeat it.
- **George Santayana**, poet.

Our plans miscarry because they have no aim.
- **Lucius Annaeus Seneca**, Roman philosopher and stateman (4 BC-65 AD).

We know what we are, but know not what we may be.

There are more things in heaven and earth, Horatio, Then are dreamt of in your philosophy.
- **William Shakespeare** (1564-1616), English playwright.

Those who cannot change their minds cannot change everything.

You see things and say "Why?" But I dream things that never were; and I say "Why not?"
- **George Bernard Shaw**, Irish playwright.

Nothing is so painful to the human mind as a great and sudden change.
- **Mary Wollstonecraft Shelley**, English writer (Frankenstein).

Planning ahead is a measure of class. The rich and even the middle-class plan for generations, but the poor can plan ahead only a few weeks or days.
- **Gloria Steinam**, *The Time Factor* (1980).

A plan once made and visualized becomes a reality along with other realities-never to be destroyed but easily to be attacked.
- **John Steinbeck**, *The Pearl*.

We're told every day, "You can't change the world." But the world is changing every day. Only question is...who's doing it? You or somebody else?
- **J. Michael Straczynski**, *At The Midpoint - Spoilers for everything* (1995).

Form ever follows function.
- **Louis Sullivan** (1886).

It's a bad plan that admits of no modification.
- **Publilius Syrus**, Roman slave and poet (circa 100 BC).

- T -

Change your anchor to what did not happen rather than what did happen.

In the medical and social domains, treatment should never be equivalent to silencing symptoms.

Just as statisticians understand the risks of roulette sequences better than carpenters, probabilists understand systemic ecological risks better than biologists.

Let us find what risks we can measure and these are the risks we should be taking.

Most mistakes get worse when you try to correct them.

Never rid anyone of an illusion unless you can replace it in his mind with another illusion.

Probability is the intersection of the most rigorous mathematics and the messiest of life.

The problem with the idea of "learning from one's mistakes" is that most of what people call mistakes aren't mistakes.

To understand how something works, figure out how to break it.
- **Nassim Nicholas Taleb** (2010). *The Bed of Procrustes: Philosophical and Practical Aphorisms.*

If you have built castles in the air, your work need not be lost; that is where they should be. Now put the foundations under them.

I am amused to see from my window here how busily man has divided and staked off his domain. God must smile at the puny fences running hither and tither everywhere over the land.

In the long run, men only hit what they aim at. Therefore, though they should fail immediately, they had better aim at something high.

Go confidently in the direction of your dreams. Live the life you have imagined.
- **Henry David Thoreau** (1817-62), American writer.

Change is not merely necessary to life - it is life.
- **Alvin Toffler**, *Future Shock* (1970).

True life is lived when tiny changes occur.
- **Leo Tolstoy.**

If we want things to stay as they are, things will have to change.
- **Giuseppe Tomasi di Lampedusa**, *Il Gattopardo* (1958).

Life is a series of natural and spontaneous changes. Don't resist them; that only creates sorrow. Let reality be reality. Let things flow naturally forward in whatever way they like.
- **Lao Tzu**, Chinese philosopher.

Plan for what is difficult while it is easy, do what is great while it is small. The difficult things in this world must be done while they are easy, the greatest things in the world must be done while they are still small. For this reason sages never do what is great, and this is why they achieve greatness.

In the practical art of war, the best thing of all is to take the enemy's country whole and intact; to shatter and destroy is not so good. So, too, is better to recapture an army entire than to destroy it, to capture a regiment; a detachment or a company than to destroy them.
- **Sun Tzu**, Chinese General, (*The Art of War*, 400 BC).

- **U** –

Dreams come true; without that possibility, nature would not incite us to have them.
- **John Updike**, writer.

- **V** -

Iron rusts from disuse; water loses its purity from stagnation ... even so does inaction sap the vigor of the mind.
- **Leonardo da Vinci**, artist and inventor.

Change everything, except your loves.

Illusion is the first of all pleasures.
- **Voltaire** (1694 - 1778), François-Marie Arouet, known by his *nom de plume* Voltaire was a French writer, historian and philosopher).

- W -

They always say time changes things, but you actually have to change them yourself.
- **Andy Warhol**, American artist, *The Philosophy of Andy Warhol* (1977).

It is too probable that no plan we propose will be adopted. Perhaps another dreadful conflict is to be sustained. If to please the people, we offer what we ourselves disapprove, how can we afterwards defend our work? Let us raise a standard to which the wise and the honest can repair.
- **George Washington**, presiding officer, first Continental Congress (1787).

Mistakes are lessons of wisdom. The past cannot be changed. The future is yet in your power.
- **Hugh White**, politician.

The art of progress is to reserve order amid change, and to preserve change amid order.

"One and one make two" assumes that the changes in the shift of circumstance are unimportant. But it is impossible for us to analyze this notion of unimportant change.

Mere conservation without change cannot conserve. For after all, there is a flux of circumstance, and the freshness of being evaporates under mere repetition.
Alfred North Whitehead, philosopher.

The only thing that one really knows about human nature is that it changes. Change is the one quality we can predicate on it.
- **Oscar Wilde** (1854-1900), *Aphorisms*.

He who rejects change is the architect of decay. The only human institution which rejects progress is the cemetery.

- **Harold Wilson**, Prime Minister of the United Kingdom. Speech to the Consultative Assembly of the Council of Europe, Strasbourg, France (1967).

For we must assume that we shall be a city upon a hill. The eyes of all people are upon us.
- **John Winthrop**, *A Model of Christian Clarity* (1630).

Planning is a process of choosing among those many options. If we do not choose to plan, then we choose to have others plan for us.
- **Richard I. Winwood**, author, religious leader, and business executive.

- Z -

When the rate of change increases to the point that real time required to assimilate change exceeds the time in with change must be manifest, the enterprise is going to find itself in deep yogurt.
- **John Zachman**, *Principles of the Business Rule Approach* (2003).

GLOSSARY

Action Research (AR): A method of collaboration between a change agent and members of an organizational system. Key aspects of the model are diagnosis, data gathering, and feedback to the client group, data discussion and work by the client group, action planning and action. The sequence tends to be cyclical, with the focus on new or advanced problems as the client group learns to work more effectively together.

As-is state: This is the current situation in the organization, i.e., the pre-change people, processes, technology, structure, strategy, culture, etc.

Balanced Scorecard: An integrated set of measures built around the mission, vision, and strategy. Measures address the financial perspective, customer perspective, internal business process perspective, and learning and growth perspective.

Baseline: The level of performance which is used for comparison after the change. This may just be past performance, but where other changes are going on this needs to be adjusted to take account of their impact.

Benefit: A measurable improvement, resulting from change, which is considered advantageous by at least one stakeholder, and contributes to the overall organizational objectives.

Best Practices/Best Management Practices (BMP): A method or technique that consistently achieves superior results as compared to other means.

Boundary spanners. People who connect the formal and /or informal network to other part of the organization.

Boundary systems. The systems that set the limits of authority and action and determine acceptable and unacceptable behavior, for example, limits to spending authority placed on managerial levels.

Business process reengineering (BPR): It is a business management strategy, originally pioneered in the early 1990s, focusing on the analysis and design of workflows and business processes within an organization. BPR aimed to help organizations fundamentally rethink how they do their work in order to improve customer service, cut operational costs, and become world-class competitors.

Change capable: The ability to adapt and evolve successfully again and again, even though specific change initiatives may vary dramatically in terms of scope, depth, and complexity.

Change culture: When the rewards for risk are taking are high, when senior executives resist hearing bad news, and when there is internal competition between units, risk is increased.

Change curve: is a way of understanding and visually representing the level of an individual's confidence, morale and roll competence through a period of change. From its starting level, for most people it rises slightly, dips, rises again and levels out. Effective change management involves ensuring that the dip is as shallow and narrow as possible and that the curb levels out higher than it started.

Change initiative: An organized, concerted effort to alter part of or all of an organization.

Change fatigue: is neither an acceptance nor rejection of change but is the state of being overwhelmed and exhausted by the amount of change going on and unable to absorb any more.

Change management: is an approach to moving organizations and their stakeholders, in an organized manner, from their current state to a desired future state. Effective change management tries to do so in a manner which causes the least anxiety and resistance and therefore is the most likely to succeed.

Coaching: and mentoring tend to be used interchangeably, although there are subtle differences. Both involve helping the subject, for example through questioning, challenging or educating them. Mentoring tends to primarily relate to identifying and nurturing their potential to improve their prospects or position, whereas coaching is usually focused more on a particular circumstance or issue and is often more educative. Mentors often use their own personal networks to assist the progression of their mentee, coaching can be less personal than this.

Coalition building: The forming of partnerships to increase pressures for or against change.

Communication channels: are the routes used to pass messages, such as social media, email, verbal presentations, reports, etc.

Communications strategy: usually outlines the

- Background for the change – outlining what is going on in the organization as the change unfolds, the overall demands in communications
- Communication Principles
- Target audience or audiences
- Objectives for each audience
- Plan for where the communications efforts are to be coordinated
- Roles & Responsibilities
- Budget and other resources
- Relevant standards & measurements – to ensure there are feedback loops which tell change management leaders if the communication efforts are having the desired effect

Continuous improvement: Also known as continuous quality improvement (CQI) or Kaizen, is "A philosophy of designing and managing all aspects of an organization in a never-ending quest for quality. The notion is that no matter how well things are going, there are always opportunities to make them better, and hundreds of small improvements can make a big difference in the overall functioning" (Cummings, 2005).

Deliverables: A term used in project management to describe a tangible or intangible object produced as a result of the project. It can be a report, document, server upgrade or any other building block of an overall project. Deliverables are laid out on a timeline and may delay overall completion if not performed/produced as scheduled.

Diagnostic/steering controls: The traditional managerial control systems that focus on key performance variables, for example, sales data responding to changed selling efforts.

DICE Framework: A process-oriented approach to assessing and managing the risks associated with risk projects.

Duration: Measures how frequently the change project is formally reviewed. As duration increases, risk increases.

Dynamism: Continuous change in the organization.

Endothermic: Describe a change program that consumers energy and creates opposition, which then requires more energy from the change agent.

Exothermic: Describes a change situation when energy is liberated by actions.

External Change Impacts: There are six types of external change impacts on the individual, the organization, and on humanity. They are socio-cultural, technology, economic, political, pandemic, and environment. I have created the acronym for them.

Force field analysis: involves listing the factors (forces) which are in favor of a particular action/change and those which are against. Each factor is then given a score and the total of those scores determine whether the analysis is favorable or not. Organizations which do use force field analysis need to decide what will be considered in order to allocate a score of what the range of scores will be. This can therefore be quite a subjective approach, despite its seeming use of statistics.

Gap analysis: is a technique that can help organizations understand where they are, where they want to go and what actions are needed in order to get there. It is the process of assessing the current, as-is state and the future, to-be state in order to assess how to make the transition from one state to another.

GROW process: A popular structure for coaching is the GROW process, whereby the coach guides the conversation with the person being coached to talk about the

- Goal – what they want to achieve
- Reality – where is that person now, what things are getting in their way
- Options – what can be done in order to help them reach their goal
- Will and wrap-up – create a plan of action and the motivation to carry out that plan

Incremental change: Continuous improvements made to the organization in an ongoing, adaptive manner. These are gradual changes to the current state. Incremental change does not usually challenge the existing culture of an organization.

Internal Change Impacts: There are six types of internal change impacts on the individual and the organization. They are the physical layout/ assets, organizational culture, rules/procedures/processes, technology and tools, employee resources, and financial resources.

Intervention: Any action on the part of the change agent. Intervention carries the implication that the action is planned and deliberate and presumably functional. Requires valid information, free choice, and a high degree of ownership by the client system of the course of action.

Informal organization: Represented by those structures, systems, and processes that emerge spontaneously from the interaction of people within the formal systems and structures that define the organizational context.

Lagging indicator: These are metrics which demonstrate the performance levels in the future state, once achieved. Examples would include post-change initiative profit levels or customer satisfaction.

Leading indicator: These are metrics which give an indication of the progress of the change initiative towards the future state performance levels. Examples would include the number of enquiries about a product due to be released or the occupancy levels of a building which, once empty, can be closed and sold.

Management System Processes:

1. Setting objectives
2. Planning strategy
3. Establishing goals
4. Developing company [organizational] philosophy
5. Establishing policies
6. Planning the organization structure
7. Providing personnel
8. Establishing procedures
9. Providing facilities
10. Providing capital
11. Setting standards
12. Establishing management programs and operational plans
13. Providing information control
14. Activating people

Measurement and control systems: Developed to focus, monitor, and manage what is going on in the organization.

Mechanistic organizations: Exhibit machine like qualities. They rely on formal hierarchies with centralized decision making and a clear division of labor. Rules and procedures are more clearly defined, and employees are expected to follow them. Work is specialized and routine.

Metrics/measures: These are specific statistics which demonstrate the progress or success of the change. Individual lagging or leading indicators are metrics.

Network Influencers:

1. Central connectors – informal go-to people who have influence with people in the organization.
2. Information brokers – provide information.
3. Boundary spanners – have far reaching links across groups.

Objective: The key aim of the organization which the benefits contribute to, and the dis-benefits detract from. For example, improving market share, expanding services, or minimizing risk.

Organic organization: Exhibit organism qualities as they are more flexible. They have fewer rules and procedures, and there is less reliance on the hierarchy of authority for centralized decision making. The structure is flexible and not as well defined. Jobs are less specialized. Communications is more informal and lateral communications more accepted.

Organizational culture: Is the shared story of the individuals within it. It is the deeply ingrained social fabric of the organization that drives people's behavior. It is made up of the values, belief systems, dominant leadership styles, collective unspoken assumptions, stories, myths, legends and rituals as well as its character and orientation.

Organizational development: Organizational development is a long-term effort led and supported by top management, to improve an organization's visioning, empowerment, learning, and problem-solving processes, through an ongoing, collaborative management of organizational culture-with special emphasis on the consultant-facilitator role and the theory and technology of applied behavioral science, including participant action research.

Organizational structure and systems: How the organization formally organizes itself to accomplish its mission. Structure is how the organization's tasks are formally divided, grouped, and coordinated. The structures would include the organizational hierarchy, the structure of any manufacturing operation, as well as other structures. Systems are the formal processes of coordination within the organization.

Outcome: A change of state (from as-is to to-be, or a stage along the way). This may be as the results of a product being made available or a transformational change being completed. Examples include revised team structures, revised working practices, ability to access IT systems on the move, or a production line going operational.

Performance audit (1) - Audit methodology (ICMA): This audit required an immense amount of fieldwork, as each HR element (e.g., labor negotiations, classification/compensation, and employee benefits) is multi-faceted and full of nuance. As such, the audit team covered extensive territory in its efforts to research and examine as much key data and information as possible. During our review, the Office performed the following activities:

+ Conducted a historical examination of key events and audits/studies of the County's HR function

+ Evaluated human resource department's policies and procedures against the State's Local Agency Personnel Standards (LAPS)

+ Performed financial research and analysis of historical HRD expenditures, numbers and costs of positions, costing of salary and benefits mechanisms, and evaluation of potential cost savings areas

- Interviewed nearly all HRD staff, executive and HR professional staff from most of the County's agencies/departments, representatives from some employee labor organizations, representatives from the Retired Employees' Association of Orange County, some former HRD executives, and representatives from some Board Offices

- Reviewed all major employee benefits areas, including, but not limited to significant employee benefits programs, including health plans, defined contribution plans, and employee assistance programs; performance guarantees with vendors; and policies and procedures

- Reviewed County Classification and Compensation Plans and associated policies and procedures

- Reviewed Labor Relations information such as Memoranda of Understanding and examined labor negotiations working papers

- Benchmarked HR organizations and HR issues in comparable public jurisdictions

- Examined HRD-related databases and programs such as: OnBase document management system, CAPS Data Warehouse, CAPS+/AHRS, and the NEOGOV automated recruiting system

- Examined HRD contracts with outside vendors for a variety of HR services

- Developed a survey to ascertain stakeholder feedback on both HRD and the Countywide HR system

This performance audit was conducted in accordance with generally accepted government auditing standards. Those standards require that the audit team plan and perform the audit to obtain sufficient, appropriate evidence to provide a reasonable basis for our findings and conclusions based on audit objectives. The audit team believes that the evidence obtained in this audit provides a reasonable basis for its findings and conclusions based on audit objectives.

Performance audit (2) - Audit methodology

PORTEF: Acronym for Internal Change Impacts. There are six types of internal change impacts on the individual and the organization. They are the Physical layout/assets, Organizational culture, Rules/procedures/processes, Technology and tools, Employee resources, and Financial resources.

Power tactics: Strategies and tactics deployed to influence others to accept one's ideas of plans.

Problem Statement: A problem statement is a concise description of an issue to be addressed or a condition to be improved upon. It identifies the gap between the current (problem) state and desired (goal) state of a process or product. Focusing on the facts, the problem statement should be designed to address the Stakeholder Analysis. The first condition of solving a problem is understanding the problem, which can be done by way of a problem statement.

Product: A tangible item which the organization requires in order to make a change and realize a benefit. Examples include IT systems, new teams, buildings, machinery or research results.

Psychological contract: Represents the sum of the implicit and explicit agreements believed to have been reached with key individuals and the organization concerning our employment relationship.

Qualitative: Measures which indicate a level of performance, but which cannot be given a specific value. For example, customer satisfaction can be measured through satisfaction scores, but the degree of value of the increase in these scores cannot be quantified.

Quantitative: Measures which indicate a level of performance and where the increase or decrease in these measures can be valued. For example, staff turnover is a measure whose variation can be given a fixed value (value does not have to be financial).

Resistance Management Plan: The resistance management plan is the identification of what resistance might look like, where it might come from and what steps will be taken to mitigate or prevent the resistance. This is a proactive effort to address concerns and build support early in the project, rather than waiting until implementation.

Return on investment (ROI): specific quantitative measure, the ratio between the amount of money spent on achieving the change (known as cost of change) and the financial value of the improvement (the return). The return needs to take into account both the positive value of any improvements (known as benefits) and the negative value of any disadvantageous results of the change (known as dis-benefits). Using this method requires organizations to attempt to put a financial value on benefits which may not be financial, such as improved staff morale, customer satisfaction or increase reputation, hence the move in many organizations towards a portfolio of financial and non-financial measures which give a rich picture of the value of the change.

Resources: financial, human, knowledge, technology.

Sponsors/Sponsorship: Roles in project management.

+ **Executive Sponsorship (or Project Sponsor):** A term that applies to different business areas, including change management. This concept is important in change management because it can make or break a program. With executive support, change programs are much more likely to succeed. Without it, obstacles will be harder to overcome. And change managers won't have the credibility they need when that need arises.

+ **Mediator sponsor:** A leader who is able to help resolve any conflicts between individuals or teams affected by changes.

+ **Planner sponsor:** A highly process-oriented senior manager who is able to assist in the planning and implementation of change activities.

+ **Primary sponsor:** The leader who authorizes and is responsible for the change initiative. Typically, they lead the change management leadership team and provide the funds for the project.

- **Speech-maker sponsor:** A leader with the undesirable trait of assuming that merely making a presentation on the need to change constitutes sufficient personal involvement in the change effort.

- **Sponsor:** A senior leader inside an organization who supports the change management leadership team.

- **Sponsorship Roadmap:** The sponsorship roadmap provides specific details about what the executives and senior leaders need to do to make the change successful. In all four of the Prosci° change management benchmarking studies, effective sponsorship was identified as the number one contributor to success. The three high-level responsibilities of the sponsor are active and visible participation, building coalitions and communication of business messages about change. The sponsorship roadmap is the document that puts real actions to the role of the sponsor.

- **Unblocker Sponsor:** A senior leader with sufficient authority whose intervention may be sought in removing difficult organizational obstacles which hamper progress during the change.

Stakeholder: A person or group which has an interest in the process or result of a change initiative. They do not necessarily have to be directly or indirectly affected by a change initiative to be a stakeholder; some stakeholders are unaffected but can wield direct or indirect influence, such as damaging an organization's reputation or encouraging public support. Examples of stakeholder groups include customers, groups of employees, people with specific roles within the organization, the media, government, society, competitors, trades unions, campaign groups, etc.

Stakeholder analysis: is about identifying who has an interest in or influence over a change initiative and what their characteristics are.

Stakeholder analysis: involves thinking about the 5Ws:

- Who the stakeholder or stakeholder group is?

- What might be their needs and expectations from the potential change?

- What that stakeholder or stakeholder group's level of influence (or power) within the organization is?
- What their likely attitude towards the potential change?
- What barriers or potential sources of resistance could prevent the individual or group moving towards the change?

Stakeholder mapping: involves representing stakeholders on a grid that displays their level of power (or influence) on one axis from low to high, and their likely attitude toward the change on the other from positive to negative.

STEPPE: Acronym for External Change impacts. There are six types of external change impacts on the individual, the organization, and on humanity. They are Socio-cultural, Technology, Economic, Political, Pandemic, and Environment.

Strategic organizational change (SOC): Leverages opportunities in the external business environment through changes in the internal workings of the organization. By considering multiple dimensions of the change process, change leaders become adept at understanding where they are now, what changes need to be made, and how they can implement those changes and build in ongoing adaptation and evolution.

Strategic planning process:
Step 1. Initiating and agreeing on strategic planning process.
Step 2. Identifying organizational mandates.
Step 3. Clarifying organizational mission and values.
Step 4. Assessing the external environment; opportunities and threats.
Step 5. Assessing the internal environment; strengths and weaknesses.
Step 6. Identifying the strategic issues facing the organization.
Step 7. Formulating strategies to manage the issues.
Step 8. Establishing an effective organizational vision for the future.

Strategic principles:

1. Who – strategic leader makes a commitment

2. Why – articulate aims and purposes

3. Where – determine context to be managed

4. When – make choices about duration.

5. What – select content of strategy.

6. How – make decisions about process.

Strategy Map: The visualization of how the vision and strategy can be systematically brought to fruition.

Survivor syndrome: Refers to the reaction of employees who survive a poorly handled, traumatic change such as downsizing and layoffs.

Sustainable change helps an organization move from making conscious efforts to change to establishing a new, accepted way of doing business and can feed on itself thus creating the continuous improvements most have given up on as unobtainable.

SWOT analysis is a strategic planning technique used to help a person or organization identify strengths, weaknesses, opportunities, and threats related to business competition or project planning. SWOT stands for:

1. Strengths. One or more skills, distinctive competencies, capabilities, competitive advantages, or resources that the organization can draw on in selecting a strategy.

2. Weaknesses. The lack of one or more skills, distinctive competencies, capabilities, competitive advantages, or resources.

3. Opportunities. Situations in which benefits are clear and can be realized if certain actions are taken.

4. Threats. Situations that give rise to potentially harmful events and outcomes if action is not taken in the immediate future. They must be actively confronted to prevent trouble.

T-Groups: Trainers and participants joined in the common task of working in a group and learning from the work at the same time.

To-be state: this is the desired future situation in the organization, i.e., the pre-change people, processes, technology, structure, strategy, culture, etc.

Training needs analysis is the process of identifying the knowledge and skills gaps of individuals, teams, functional units or organizations in order to develop a learning program to address those gaps. Training needs analyses often form the basis of long-term, business as usual learning programs, ensuring that the training remains relevant and aligned with organizational need. For this reason, the impact of the change initiative's TNA on the organization's ongoing learning program needs to be considered.

Transformational change: Change, which is not merely an extension of improvement or modification of the current state of an organization, but one which involves a complete and fundamental change to the organization, involving changes to processes and systems, people, structure and/or culture.

Unblocker sponsor: A senior leader with sufficient authority whose intervention may be sought in removing difficult organizational obstacles which hamper progress during the change.

VIRO Framework analysis: The VIRO framework is a scalable set of four questions which can be used to focus down onto an individual resource or capability or up to an entire organizational market. It is based on four questions asked about: value, rarity, inimitability, and organization.

Value: concerns the value of the item in question to the organization - does it enable the organization to achieve something new or reduce/avoid a threat or risk?

Vision statement: The change vision statement is an inspiring description of what the changed organization will look like. It should be short, punchy, easily understood, appeal to all communication styles and be memorable. If leaders cannot easily, quickly, and convincingly encapsulate a change, it is unlikely they will persuade others to buy into it. The vision should be what the organization returns to when confusion develops about the change and what it uses to enthuse stakeholders to support the change.

Bibliography

Ahmed, Anan (August 09, 2019). *The Definition of a Procedures Manual.* Bizfluent. Retrieved February 1, 2023 from: https://bizfluent. com/list-6499662-general-office-practices-procedures.html

American Museum of Natural History (2023). Retrieved January 17, 2023 from: https://www.amnh.org/exhibitions/butterflies/ metamorphosis

ASQ. *What is Total Quality Management *(TQM)?* Retrieved November 1, 2021 from: https://asq.org/quality-resources/total-quality-management

Atwood, C.G. (2020). *Succession Planning Basics.* 2nd Ed. Atd Press, Alexandria, VA. 2, 6.

Balanced Scorecard Institute. Strategic Planning Basics. Retrieved November 1, 2021 from: https://balancedscorecard.org/ strategic-planning-basics/.

Balough, E.; Miller, B; Ball, J. (2015). *Improving Diagnosis in Healthcare,* National Academy Press, Washington, D.C., 31-69. Retrieved February 1, 2023 from: https://www.ncbi.nlm.nih.gov/books/ NBK338596/

Bandura, A. (1986). *Social foundations of thought and action: a social cognitive theory.* Englewood Cliffs, N.J.: Prentice-Hall.

Baynes, Wilhelm (1950). *The I Ching or Book of Changes.* New York, N.Y.: Bollinger Series XIX, Princeton University Press. *lviii-lxii,* 289, 322-323.

Billy, I. A. (2014). *Change Management for the 21st century and Beyond: Change Management,* CreateSpace Independent Publishing Platform.

BPIR.com (Nov. 1, 2021). What is Performance Measurement? Retrieved February 1, 2023 from: https://www.bpir.com/what-is-performance-measurement/

Bunker, K. (June 24, 2009). Nowadays, Leadership Means Being More Human. *Forbes Magazine.* Retrieved February 1, 2023 from: https://www.forbes.com/2009/06/24/human-change-management-leadership-managing-ccl.html#7718763d60cf

Buler, E.R. (2018). *Leading Exponential Change.* Jewett City: CT, Innovast Publishing, 18.

Burke, W.W. (2005). *Organization Change: Theory and Practice.* Sage Publications, Thousand Oaks, CA. 198-199.

Cameron, K S. & Quinn, R.E. (1999). *Diagnosing and Changing Organizational Culture Based on the Competing Values Framework,* Reading: MA, Addison-Wesley Publishing Company, _.

Caredda, S. (April 7, 2020). *Models: Satir Change Model.* Retrieved from: https://sergiocaredda.eu/organisation/tools/models-satir-change-model.

Carter, L.; Giber, D.; Goldsmith, M. (2001). *Best Practices in Organization Development and Change.* Jossey-Bass/Pfeiffer, San Francisco, CA. 137, 168.

Cawsey, T.F., Deszca, G., Ingols, C. (2016). *Organizational Change: An Action-Oriented Toolkit,* Sage Publications, Los Angeles, CA. 51, 55,375.

Center for Disease Control (2021). Problem Identification. Retrieved February 1, 2023 from: https://www.cdc.gov/policy/polaris/policyprocess/problem-identification/index.html

Ciampa, Dan (1992). <u>Total Quality: A User's Guide for Implementation</u>. Reading, MA, Addison-Wesley. *p. xxii*

Colquitt, J.A.; LePine, J.A.; Wesson, M.J. (2013). *Organizational Behavior: Improving Performance and Commitment in the Workplace*. 4th ed. New York: NY, McGraw-Hill Education, 6.

Community Tool Box. *Developing A Plan*. Retrieved November 1, 2021 from: <u>https://ctb.ku.edu/en/table-of-contents/participation/promoting-interest/communication-plan/main</u>

Cummings, T.G.; Worley, C.G. (2005). *Organization Development and Change*. Thomson South-Western, Australia. 119

Davis, James (April 14, 2020). *The Complete Guide to Customer Service Training (incl. Ideas, Games, Videos and Programs)*. Retrieved February 1, 2023 from: <u>https://www.messagely.com/customer-service-training/</u> .

Deshler, R. (February 9, 2021). *The Role of Leadership in Change Management*. AlignOrgSolutions. Retrieved February 1, 2023 from: <u>https://alignorg.com/the-role-of-leadership-in-change-management/</u>

Doka KJ (2016). *Grief Is a Journey: Finding Your Path Through Loss*. New York, NY. Simon and Schuster, 6.

Dury, Ian (1977). *Sex & Drugs & Rock & Roll*, Still Records.

Eby, Kate (Feb 24, 2017). Essential Guide to Business Process Mapping. SMARTSHEET. Retrieved February 1, 2023 from: <u>https://www.smartsheet.com/essential-guide-business-process-mapping</u>

Eckes, George (2003). *Six Sigma for Everyone*. Hoboken, NJ: John Wiley & Sons, 37

Gleason, B. (Jun 4, 2018). The Critical Role of Leadership Development During Organizational Change. *Forbes*. Retrieved from: https://www.forbes.com/sites/brentgleeson/2018/06/04/leadership-developments-role-in-successful-organizational-change/#23bf96f9fdd6

Government Auditing Standards (2018 Revision). United State Government Accountability Office, Washington, D.C., By the Comptroller General of the United States, 125.

Grosman, D. (February 17, 2020) *Change Management Communication: 5 Step Planning Guide*, Retrieved February 1, 2023 from: https://www.yourthoughtpartner.com/blog/change-management-communication

Handel, M.J. (2003). *The Sociology of Organizations*. Thousand Oaks: CA, Sage Publications, 11.

Harrington, H.J.; Voehl, F.; Voehl, C.F. (2015). *Model for Sustainable Change*. PMI White Papers. Retrieved February 1, 2023 from: https://www.pmi.org/learning/library/model-sustainable-change-11122

Implementation Management Associates (Nov. 1, 2021), The AIM Change Management Methodology. Retrieved February 1, 2023 from: https://www.imaworldwide.com/aim-change-management-methodology

INC. (Feb. 6, 2020). Training and Development. Retrieved February 1, 2023 from: https://www.inc.com/encyclopedia/training-and-development.html#:~:text=Training%20and%20development%20describes%20the,of%20educational%20methods%20and%20programs.&text=%22Employees%20today%20must%20have%20access,just%20to%20keep%20up'%C2%A6.

Indeed: Career Guide (December 17, 2020). *Carrot and Stick Motivation:*

Definition and Examples in the Workplace. Retrieved February 1, 2023 from: https://www.indeed.com/career-advice/career-development/carrot-and-stick-motivation

Indeed: Career Guide (November 23, 2020). *How to write a problem statement step by step.* Retrieve February 1, 2023 from: https://www.indeed.com/career-advice/career-development/how-to-write-a-problem-statement

Inteqgroup (October 16, 2021). *Business Process Reengineering: 6 Key Steps + Some Secret Sauce.* Retrieved February 1, 2023 from: https://www.inteqgroup.com/blog/6-key-business-process-reengineering-steps

Kanbanzie (March 10, 2021). Retrieved February 1, 2023 from: https://kanbanize.com/lean-management/improvement/what-is-continuous-improvement

Kantar (June 11, 2019). *Accelerated Growth Sees Amazon Crowned 2019's BrandZ Top 100 Most Valuable Global Brand.* www.prnewswire.com. Retrieved October 11, 2020. https://theairlinewebsite.com/topic/495958-accelerated-growth-sees-amazon-crowned-2019s-brandz%E2%84%A2-top-100-most-valuable-global-brand/

Knight, P. (2016). *Shoe Dog: A Memoir by the Creator of Nike.* Scribner, New York, NY.

Koberg, D. and Bagnall, J. (January 1, 1974). *The Universal Traveler: A Soft-Systems Guide to Creativity, Problem-Solving, & the Process of Reaching Goals.* Crisp Publications. Menlo Park, CA. 10, 24.

Kotter, J.P. (1996). *Leading Change.* Boston: MA, Harvard Business School Press, Retrieved February 1, 2023 from: https://www.accipio.com/eleadership/mod/wiki/view.php?id=1874

Kritsonis, A. Comparison of Change Theories. *International Journal of Scholarly Academic Intellectual Diversity*, 2004-2005, 8(1), 2-3, 5.

Kurzweil, R. (March 7, 2001). *The Law of Accelerating Returns.*, Oxford Languages. Retrieved February 1, 2023 from: https://languages.oup.com/google-dictionary-en/

Laidlaw Scholars (April 19, 2021). *Leadership Quote of the Week.* Retrieved February 1, 2023 from: https://laidlawscholars.network/posts/the-one-most-adaptable-to-change-is-the-one-that-survives#:~:text=Charles%20Darwin%3A%20It%20is%20not,in%20which%20it%20finds%20itself

Lessonly (2021). *Leadership Training Topics.* Retrieved February 1, 2023 from: https://www.lessonly.com/leadership- training-topics/

Lupton, Ellen (December 22, 2009). Before Design Thinking. PRINT, Retrieved February 1, 2023 from: https://www.printmag.com/post/before-design-thinking

Mack, N.; Woodsong, C.; MacQueen, K.M.; Guest, G.; Namey, E. (2011). *Qualitative Research Methods: A Data Collector's Field Guide.* Family Health International (FHI) and U.S. Agency for International Development (USAID). Research Triangle Park, NC.

Management Study Guide. Performance Appraisal. Retrieved November 1, 2021 from: https://www.managementstudyguide.com/performance-appraisal.htm

McNamara, C. *How to Build Highly Effective Teams.* Retrieved November 1, 2021from: https://managementhelp.org/groups/team-building.htm#build

Morgan, D.L. (1997). Focus Groups As Qualitative Research. Qualitative Research Methods Series 16, 2nd Edition, A Sage

University Paper. Thousand Oaks: CA.

Morgan, R. *How to Write an Effective Problem Statement*, ISIXSIGMA, Retrieved November 1, 2021 from: https://www.isixsigma.com/new-to-six-sigma/getting-started/how-to-write-an-effective-problem-statement/

Nancy Harris and Associates. Retrieved November 1, 2021 from https://www.nancyharrisonandassociates.com/about-2

Newman, Emily (June 24, 2015). *Cross-Functional Training Important for Business.* Yonyx. Retrieved February 1, 2023 from: https://corp.yonyx.com/customer-service/cross-functional-training-important-for-business/

Nietzsche, Friedrich. *Twilight of the Idols; and the Anti-Christ.* Trans. R. J. Hollingdale. Harmondsworth: Penguin, 1977

NNDB. *Parmenides.* Retrieved April 19, 2022 from: https://www.nndb.com/people/777/000087516/

Norcross, J.C.; Goldfried, Marvin R. (1993). *Handbook of psychotherapy integration.* Oxford series in clinical psychology (2nd ed.).

Office of Associate Director for Policy and Strategy, *What is Problem Identification?* Center for Disease Control. Retrieved November 1, 2021 from: https://www.cdc.gov/policy/polaris/policyprocess/problem_identification.html#:~:text=Problem%20Identification%20consists%20of%3A,effect%20on%20a%20population's%20health

Parade|Life (2022). *101 Uplifting Quotes About Change for When You Need a Little Push Before Taking a Big Leap.* Retrieved February 1, 2023 from: https://parade.com/975999/marynliles/quotes-about-change/

Peterdy, Kyle (January 17, 2023). *What is ESG (Environmental, Social, and Governance)?* CFI. Retrieved February 3, 2023 from: https://corporatefinanceinstitute.com/resources/esg/esg-environmental-social-governance/#:~:text=Key%20Highlights-,ESG%20is%20a%20framework%20that%20helps%20stakeholders%20understand%20how%20an,pollution%20reduction%2C%20and%20corporate%20philanthropy .

Powell, Dr. Jevon (March 18, 2011). *Employee Involvement.* Scontrino-Powell. Retrieved February 1, 2023 from: http://www.scontrino-powell.com/2011/employee-involvement/

ProjectManager (March 10, 2021). Retrieved February 1, 2023 from: https://www.projectmanager.com/critical-path-method

Prosci. *What is the ADKAR*, Retrieved November 1, 2021 from: https://www.prosci.com/adkar/adkar-model

Rea, L.M. and Parker, R.A. (2014). *Designing and Conducting Survey Research: A Comprehensive Guide.* Jossey-Bass, San Francisco, CA. 11, 14-15, 31-33, 42-43, 46, 49, 51, 54.

Rébé, N. (2021) *Artificial intelligence: robot law, policy and ethics.* Koninlijke Brill, The Netherlands. 48.

Rothwell, W.J.; Roland, S.; McLean, G.N. (1995). *Practicing Organizational Development: A Guide for Consultants.* Pfeiffer & Company. Amsterdam. 149-150.

RPC Leadership Associates (October 11, 2022). Retrieved February 1, 2023 from: https://www.rpcleadershipassociates.com/index.php/blog/the-art-of-progress-is-the-preserve-order-amid-change-and-preserve-change-amid-order

Sauro, J. (October 20, 2015). *4 Types of Observational Research.* MeasuringU. Retrieved February 1, 2023 from: https://measuringu.com/observation-role/

Scott, W.R. (1992). *Organizations: Rational, Natural, and Open Systems.* Engelwood Cliffs: NJ, Prentice Hall, 21-26, 27.

Schein, E.H. (2004). *Organizational Culture and Leadership.* San Francisco: CA, John Wiley & Songs. 340-348.

Schwarz, Roger (June 15, 2016). *8 Ground Rules for Great Meetings.* Harvard Business Review. Retrieved February 1, 2023 from: https://hbr.org/2016/06/8-ground-rules-for-great-meetings

Shedd, D. (July 5, 2011). *Nine Keys to Driving Cultural Change.* Wharton Magazine.

Shelley, Mary *Frankenstein: 1818 text* (Oxford University Press, 2009). Edited with an introduction and notes by Marilyn Butler.

Sinitsyn, Nikolai and Yan, Bin (September 21, 2020). *Scientific American.* Retrieved February 1, 2023 from: https://www.scientificamerican.com/article/the-quantum-butterfly-noneffect/

Sirkin, H., Keenan, P., Jackson, A. (October 2005). *HBR's 10 Must Reads.* Boston, MA. Harvard Business Review, 155.

Smartsheet. *Everything You Need to Know About Business Process Reengineering.* Retrieved November 1, 2021from: https://www.smartsheet.com/newbies-business-processing-reengineering-guide-experts-insights

Sobierski, T (January 21, 2020). *Organizational change management: What it is & why it's important.* HBS Online.

Slideserve. Research Questions & Hypothesis. Retrieved from: PPT - Research Questions & Hypotheses PowerPoint Presentation, free download - ID:379575 (slideserve.com).

Sparkes, M. (January 13, 2015). Top scientists call for caution over artificial intelligence. *The Telegraph*.

Spradlin, D. (September 2012). Are You Solving the Right Problem? *Harvard Business Review*. Retrieved February 1, 2023 from: https://hbr.org/2012/09/are-you-solving-the-right-problem/html

Survey Anyplace. Retrieved November 1, 2021 from: https://surveyanyplace.com/culture-assessment/html.

Taleb, N., *The Black Swan: The Impact of the Highly Improbable*, New York, NY, Random House, 40-41.

McKinsey 7s Model. Strategic Management Insights. Retrieved November 1, 2021 from: https://strategicmanagementinsight.com/tools/mckinsey-7s-model-framework.html

Takahashi, Dean (April 18, 2005). "Forty years of Moore's law". *Seattle Times*. San Jose, CA

Tamir, U. (January 4, 2020). *What is DICE Framework in Change Management?* Retrieved June 24, 2022 from: https://changemanagementinsight.com/dice-framework/

Technology Networks (December 20, 2016). *4 Scientists That Were Disregarded During Their Time*. Retrieved February 1, 2023 from: https://www.technologynetworks.com/tn/lists/4-scientists-that-were-disregarded-during-their-time-277692.

Tool Hero. *What is the Bridges' Transition Model?* Retrieved November 1, 2021 from: https://www.toolshero.com/change-management/bridges-transition-model/

UpBoard. Retrieved November 1, 2021 from: https://upboard.io/beckhard-harris-change-process-online-tools-templates-web-software/html.

U.S. Bureau of Labor Statistics (April 28, 2016), *Business Employment Dynamics*, Retrieved February 1, 2023 from: https://www.bls.gov/bdm/entrepreneurship/entrepreneurship.htm

Uwah, E.D. *et. al.* (September 19, 2009), *Strategic Interventions in Change Management Process.* Retrieved February 1, 2023 from: https://papers.ssrn.com/sol3/papers.cfm?abstract_id=1475538

Vaill, Peter (2001). *An Annotated Bibliography of Foundational Literature in Organizational Behavior and Development*, University of St. Thomas.

Vinge, V. "The Coming Technological Singularity: How to Survive in the Post-Human Era", in *Vision-21: Interdisciplinary Science and Engineering in the Era of Cyberspace*, G. A. Landis, ed., NASA Publication CP-10129, pp. 11–22, 1993.

Walton, Mary (1986). *The Deming Management Method*, New York, NY, Putnam Publishing 34-36.

Westchester University, Retrieved November 1, 2021 from: https://www.wcupa.edu/coral/tuckmanStagesGroupDelvelopment.aspx

WhatIs.com. *Communication Plan.* Retrieved November 1, 2021 from: https://whatis.techtarget.com/definition/communication-plan

PSOCM® SCHEDULE (TEMPLATE)

A Gantt chart is a type of bar chart that illustrates a project schedule. This chart lists the Actions to be performed on the vertical axis, and monthly time intervals on the horizontal axis. The width of the horizontal bars in the graph shows the duration of each activity. Gantt charts illustrate the start and finish dates of the terminal elements and summary elements of a project. Terminal elements and summary elements constitute the work breakdown structure of the project. Modern Gantt charts also show the dependency (i.e., precedence network) relationships between activities.

The entire length of the PSOCM® process is between 3 and 5 years, depending on the need for organizational change. The time frame is dependent on the type of industry involved and the need to address change. The time frame is shorter for more high technology organizations and longer for more traditional organizations. However, this longer phase (3-5 years) is for the monitoring (10.4). Most of the OCM development activities (1.1-10.4) should occur within an 18-month time frame.

People Sustained Organizational Change Management (PSOCM®) Gantt Chart

Steps	Months	1	2	3	4	5	6	7	8	9	10	11	12	13	14	15	16	17	→ 18
Step 1.1 - Problem Identification																			
Step 1.2 - Starts at the Top																			
Step 1.3 - PSOCM® Schedule																			
Step 1.4 - Human Dynamic																			
Step 1.5 - Communication Plan																			
Step 2.1 - Initial Group Meeting																			
Step 2.2 - Setting Ground Rules																			
Step 2.3 - Employee Involvement																			
Step 3.1 - Existing Vision & Mission																			
Step 3.2 - Document Review																			
Step 3.3 - Performance Measurement																			
Step 3.4 - Cultural Assessment																			
Step 4.1 - Participant Observer																			
Step 4.2 - Structure/Unstructured																			
Step 4.3 - Focus Groups																			
Step 4.4 - Open Houses																			
Step 4.5 - Surveys																			
Step 5.1 - Problem Statement																			
Step 5.2 - Diagnose Problem																			
Step 6.1 - OCM Interventions																			
Step 7.1 - Process Mapping																			
Step 7.2 - Bus. Process Reengineering																			
Step 8.1 - Cultural Change																			
Step 8.2 - Strategic Plan																			
Step 8.3 - Taking Action																			
Step 9.1 - Carrot and Stick																			
Step 9.2 - Executive Leadership Train.																			
Step 9.3 - Employee Training & Dev.																			
Step 9.4 - Cross Functional Training																			
Step 9.5 - Customer Service Training																			
Step 9.6 - Team Building																			
Step 9.7 - Procedure Manual Standard																			
Step 9.8 - Perf. Measures/Expectations																			
Step 9.9 - Perfo.Appraisal/Management																			
Step 9.10 - Total Quality Management																			
Step 10.1- Monitor Performance																			
Step 10.2- Sustain Change Program																			
Step 10.3- Continuous Improvement																			
Step 10.4- Succession Plan																			

Sample Problem Statements

1. We want all of our software releases to go to production seamlessly, without defects, where everyone is aware and informed of the outcomes and status. Today we have too many release failures that result in too many rollback failures. If we ignore this problem; resources will need to increase to handle the cascading problems, and we may miss critical customer deadlines which could result in lost revenue, SLA penalties, lost business, and further damage to our quality reputation.

2. Overfill has been a serious problem facing our city waste facilities for the last decade. By some estimations, our city dumps are, on average, 30% above capacity—an unsanitary, unsafe, and unwise position for our city to be in. Several methods have been proposed in order to combat this. Perhaps the most popular of these is the simplest: building two new landfills on the county outskirts. Others have proposed stronger recycling campaigns and larger per-bag waste disposal costs as a way to lessen the potential damage to our trash situation. The facility is close to drowning in trash. Action is needed if our city is to remain the clean, safe place to live it has always been.

3. The boarding protocols used by ABC Airlines should aim to get each flight's passengers aboard the plane quickly and efficiently so that the plane can take off as soon as possible. The process of boarding should be optimized for time-efficiency but also should be straightforward enough that it can be easily understood by all passengers.

4. At the same time that the United States is becoming more diverse, colleges and universities find they must defend themselves against attacks on affirmative action. In response to lawsuits brought against affirmative action in college admissions, many have argued that diversity is a "compelling interest" in that

it enhances higher education through the benefits it brings to individual students (Astone and Nunez-Wormack, 1990;Duster, 1993; Hurtado et al., 1998; Liu, 1998; Smith and Associates, 1997; Tierney,1993). In a climate where affirmative action is under increased scrutiny, it is important that researchers extend this line of inquiry to all levels of higher education. One avenue that is beginning to emerge is the positive impact that diverse faculty have on student experiences.

5. Previous research has found that racially diverse educational environments are associated with positive intellectual and social outcomes for college students (Astin, 1993; Chang,1999; Gurin, 1999; Smith & Associates, 1997). Racial diversity in the student body is linked to the likelihood that a student will interact with someone of a different race or ethnicity and engage in discussions of racial or ethnic issues. Frequent interaction across racial lines and discussion of racial and ethnic issues positively predicts student retention, intellectual and social self-concept, and overall satisfaction with college (Gurin, 1999; Smith & Associates, 1997). The existing evidence, however, is based largely on quasi-experimental or correlational designs using self-report data. No study to date has randomly assigned students to conditions of racial diversity and directly examined cognitive outcomes.

6. A high magnitude earthquake and a destructive tsunami recently demolished eleven Japanese cities. These tremendous storms caused leaks in three nuclear power plant reactors causing an even larger toxicological danger, referred to by MSNBC respondents as, "the greatest leak of radiation since the1986 Chernobyl disaster." (msnbc.com, 2011) The 20-kilometer exclusion zone around Fukushima has forced the evacuation of 50,000 households, extermination of livestock, and disposal of crops. (Sato,2011) The current devastation leaves the Japanese government burdened with around $309 billion in repairs, making it the world's most expensive natural disaster on record. ACF would like to supply drinking water and sanitation infrastructures to help survivors flush out the toxins from radiation and post-traumatic stressors. Proper hydration

prevents further malnutrition and deterioration in health. ACF International proposes a project called, Hitachi Operation Prosperity Enclosure (HOPE), as a resolution to water scarcity and sanitation solutions through sustainable conservation of recycled resources.

7. Information literacy is a prevalent topic in the literature of library and information science (LIS), and most writings on the topic focus on methods for engaging faculty to work together with librarians to integrate information literacy into the overall curriculum. Attention from the regional accreditation organizations to information literacy, especially as it is defined by ACRL, implies both a responsibility for librarians to participate actively in student learning outcomes through a program of study in information literacy, and serves as an opportunity for librarians to become true partners in student learning. Nevertheless, no study has examined the extent to which discussion of the accreditation organizations, their guidelines, and related documents appear in the scholarly communications of LIS. The purpose of this study is to fill that void by determining the extent to which particular accreditation documents are explicitly addressed, and by identifying any patterns as to the particular documents, or themes within those documents, which comprise the focus of these writings. In particular, this study analyzes the conversation librarians are having about information literacy, and the extent to which these discussions reach outside of the library profession and reference the six regional accreditation organizations' statements on information literacy (Slideserve).